# GUERILLA DAYS IN IRELAND

COMMANDANT GENERAL

TOM BARRY

MERCIER PRESS

MERCIER PRESS
Cork
www.mercierpress.ie

First published by *The Irish Press* in 1949
First paperback edition published in 1962 by Anvil Books Ltd
This edition by Mercier Press, 2013



ISBN: 978 1 78117 171 4

A CIP record for this title is available from the British Library

*To my wife, Leslie Mary*

# CONTENTS

# INTRODUCTION

'IN war,' said Napoleon, 'it is not the men who count, it is the man.' Tom Barry exemplifies this.

His book is not a history of the Anglo-Irish War in West Cork. It is his own personal account of that war. He says in his preface that no one other than his wife and his solicitor read any part of it before it went to the publisher. It is invaluable as an account of what he thought, and of why and how he acted during the single year which established his reputation as the most successful Irish guerilla leader of his time. It is an authentic story. The real Tom Barry speaks throughout; fearless, aggressive, assertive and energetic. There is no false modesty, no straining after effect and, above all, no gloss based on hindsight. Such sweeping statements as there are reflect the man. Kilbrittain was 'the best company in Ireland'; Liam Deasy 'the best brigade adjutant'; Charlie Hurley 'one of the greatest patriot soldiers of Ireland of any generation' and 'there never was the equal of Charlie Hurley'.

It is remarkable also for the fact that, unlike other books on the period, it is uninfluenced by the bitter divisions of the Civil War and free from attempts to belittle or ignore the achievements of men who opposed him in it.

It is a measure of Barry's quality that he so quickly established his pre-eminence among the galaxy of leaders which West Cork had already produced when he arrived on the scene in 1920. These were men who were again to prove themselves outstanding in other times and circumstances.

Although Barry refers to the 'inactive areas' and the 'hard-pressed fighting brigades', many readers of his story seem to have got the impression from other sources that West Cork was typical. This is far from the truth. Barry describes his victories. He suffered no defeat; but what Florrie O'Donoghue described as 'the bitter lessons of Clonmult, Mourne Abbey, Dripsey and Nadd' were paralleled in West Cork at Upton, in Dublin at the Custom House and on a lesser scale in many other places.

Collins exaggerated when, in an emotional outburst after Seán MacEoin's capture, he wrote, 'Cork will now fight alone.' As a County Cork man he took justifiable pride in the lead given by all three Cork brigades in the fight against the British, whose heaviest concentration of troops and police – Dublin district apart – was in Cork. This is manifestly true of his regard for the fighting men of his native West Cork.

In June 1920, when Barry became active, there were about 14,000 all ranks, excluding RIC and Auxiliary Division RIC, in what was later to become the martial law area. By July of the following year this number had risen to about 25,000.

In June 1921 there were fifty-one British infantry battalions in Ireland. Five were guarding internment camps, leaving forty-six, of which twenty were in the martial law area and twelve in Dublin district, which had heavy guard duties for the seat of government. Only fourteen were assigned to the remaining twenty-three counties.

Of the twenty battalions in the martial law area, twelve plus a machine-gun corps and a cavalry regiment were in County Cork, three in County Tipperary (of which two were in Tipperary town and mainly engaged against the East Limerick Brigade), two in County Limerick, one plus a cavalry regiment in Clare, and one in Kerry; one covered the three counties of Waterford, Kilkenny and Wexford.

Of even greater significance is the fact that when seventeen additional battalions and a mounted brigade were sent to Ireland between June 14th and July 17th, 1921, seven of the battalions and the whole mounted brigade were allotted to the martial law area, five to Dublin District and five to the remaining twenty-three counties.

Apart from the ex-ranker General Boyd, who as commander of Dublin District was the most successful, Barry was opposed by the most formidable combination of British officers then in Ireland. Strickland, commander of the Sixth Division that covered the martial law area, if not brilliant, was at least more competent than his peers. Captain Kelley of his intelligence staff earned the respect of the extraordinarily able and successful IRA intelligence officer in Cork, the historian Florrie O'Donoghue. Percival, who looms large in all accounts of the fight in West Cork, was a most energetic intelligence officer (not OC of the Essex as Barry and Deasy believed) and his successes become evident in Barry's account. He was decorated for his services in Cork, and became something of an authority on guerilla warfare on the basis of his experience here. His failure as a general and C-in-C in Singapore should not obscure the menace he was to the West Cork IRA. Montgomery, as Brigade Major of the 17th Brigade, was thought by his superiors and contemporaries to 'have done well in Ireland' and to have given promise of the qualities admired by some when he later became Britain's most famous field marshal. Between them they eventually developed towards the last months of the war the only tactics that seriously menaced the survival of the IRA units. As Florrie O'Donoghue says (in *No Other Law*) they 'could to a large extent immobilise our basic organisation, disrupt communications, and add to our losses in men killed and captured'. One can, however, safely say that Montgomery and Percival met their match in Barry, and in hindsight he had a better idea of how the new British tactics could be frustrated than any other pre-Truce leader with whom one has discussed the topic, bar Mossie Donegan.

The reputation of Percival for permitting, if not instigating, the torture of prisoners steeled the resolution of the people as well as the IRA, and Montgomery's attitude of 'regarding all civilians as Shinners' and 'never having any dealings with them' was conducive to providing the IRA with recruits from people previously neutral or hostile.

It must be evident to any student of the period that Barry was unique in the measure of success he achieved, in the careful planning of every action and in his domination of such afterwards famous people as Montgomery and Percival.

*Michael J. Costello*
*Lieutenant-General (Retd.)*
*1981*

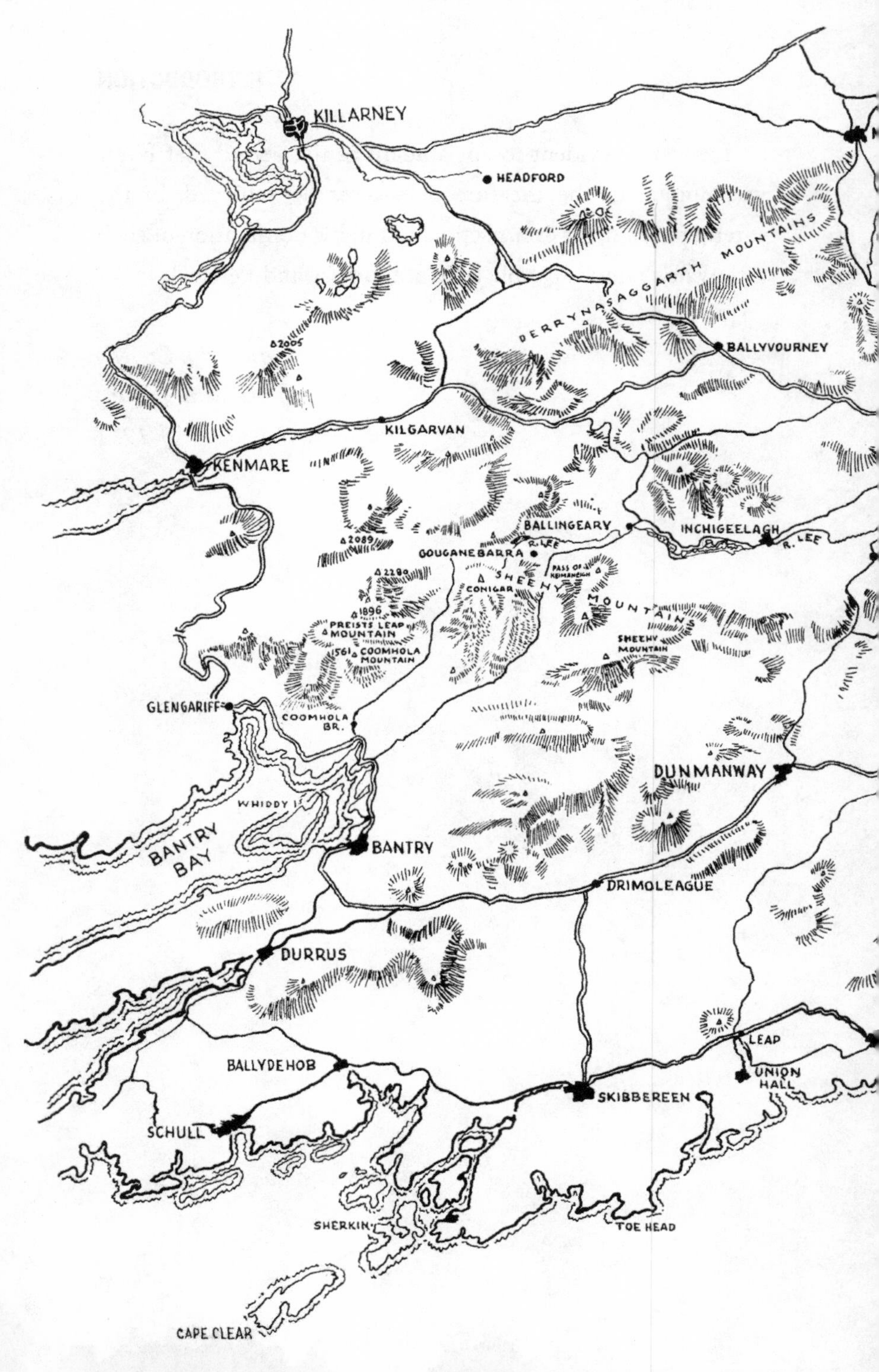

KILLARNEY
HEADFORD
DERRYNASAGGARTH MOUNTAINS
BALLYVOURNEY
2005
KILGARVAN
KENMARE
BALLINGEARY
INCHIGEELAGH
R. LEE
2089
GOUGANEBARRA
R. LEE
2280
PASS OF KEIMANEIGH
CONIGAR
SHEEHY MOUNTAINS
1896
PREISTS LEAP MOUNTAIN
1561 COOMHOLA MOUNTAIN
SHEEHY MOUNTAIN
GLENGARIFF
COOMHOLA BR.
DUNMANWAY
WHIDDY I.
BANTRY BAY
BANTRY
DRIMOLEAGUE
DURRUS
BALLYDEHOB
LEAP
UNION HALL
SKIBBEREEN
SCHULL
SHERKIN
TOE HEAD
CAPE CLEAR

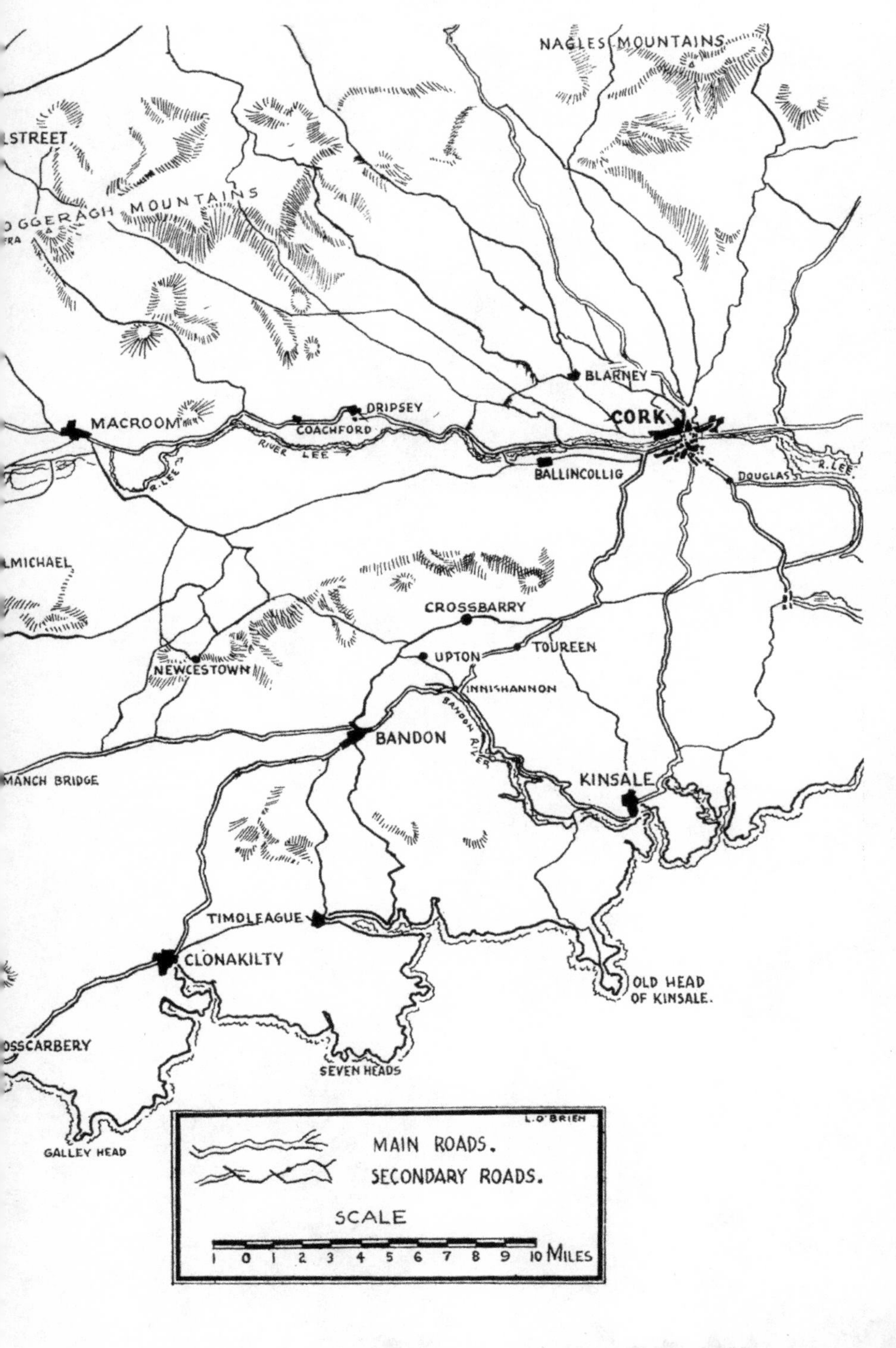
NAGLES MOUNTAINS
LSTREET
OGGERAGH MOUNTAINS
BLARNEY
MACROOM
DRIPSEY
COACHFORD
RIVER LEE
R. LEE
CORK
BALLINCOLLIG
DOUGLAS
R. LEE
LMICHAEL
CROSSBARRY
UPTON
TOUREEN
NEWCESTOWN
INNISHANNON
BANDON RIVER
BANDON
MANCH BRIDGE
KINSALE
TIMOLEAGUE
CLONAKILTY
OLD HEAD OF KINSALE.
OSSCARBERY
SEVEN HEADS
GALLEY HEAD
L. O'BRIEN
MAIN ROADS.
SECONDARY ROADS.
SCALE
1 0 1 2 3 4 5 6 7 8 9 10 MILES

# AUTHOR'S NOTE

THERE is something to be said for waiting a quarter of a century before writing a factual account of what I know of the most stirring page in Ireland's long and chequered story. The lapse of this period of time allows one to write of men and matters as they really were from 1919 to the Truce with Britain in July 1921, without being influenced by the tragic Civil War that followed. At the same time those guerilla days are sufficiently near for any reader who seeks confirmation to interview witnesses and examine the documents and newspaper issues of those days, which are still available.

No one has read this story in part or as a whole until it was sent to the publishers, except my wife who typed it and my solicitor who examined it for any unconscious libel. Therefore every opinion in it is mine alone and I have sought to tell only the truth.

As I have not written a reference book, I regret I cannot include the names of all and every West Cork man and woman whom I know gave service to the nation during those years of strife.

*T. B. B., CORK, 1948*

# 1

# THE GLORIOUS PROTEST

FOR me it began in far-off Mesopotamia, now called Iraq, that land of Biblical names and history, of vast deserts and date groves, scorching suns and hot winds, the land of Babylon, Baghdad and the Garden of Eden, where the rushing Euphrates and the mighty Tigris converge and flow down to the Persian Gulf.

It was there, in that land of the Arabs, then a battleground for the two contending imperialistic armies of Britain and Turkey, that I awoke to the echoes of guns being fired in the capital of my own country, Ireland. It was a rude awakening, guns being fired at the people of my own race by soldiers of the same army with which I was serving. The echo of these guns in Dublin was to drown into insignificance the clamour of all other guns during the remaining two and a half years of war.

This rude awakening came in the month of May 1916, when I was serving with the Mesopotamian Expeditionary Force. After futile and costly attempts to break through the tough ring of Turkish-German steel which encircled the British General Townshend and his thirty thousand beleaguered troops at Kut el Amara, our unit had been withdrawn to rest at a point twelve miles back. We were sheltering in a nullah out of view and range.

One evening I strolled down to the orderly tent outside which war communiqués were displayed. These one usually scanned in a casual manner, for even then war news was accepted in a most sceptical way. But this evening there was a 'Special' communiqué headed 'REBELLION IN DUBLIN'. It told of the shelling of the Dublin GPO and Liberty Hall, of hundreds of rebels killed, thousands arrested and leaders being executed. The communiqué covered a period of several weeks and contained news which up to then had been suppressed from overseas troops. I read this notice three or four times and now, thirty-two years later, I can recall it almost word for word.

Walking down the nullah my mind was torn with questionings. What was this Republic of which I now heard for the first time? Who were these leaders the British had executed after taking them prisoners: Tom Clarke, Padraic Pearse, James Connolly and all the others, none of whose names I had ever heard? What did it all mean?

In June 1915, in my seventeenth year, I had decided to see what this Great War was like. I cannot plead I went on the advice of John Redmond or any other politician, that if we fought for the British we would secure Home Rule for Ireland, nor can I say I understood what Home Rule meant. I was not influenced by the lurid appeal to fight to save Belgium or small nations. I knew nothing about nations, large or small. I went to the war for no other reason than that I wanted to see what war was like, to get a gun, to see new countries and to feel a grown man. Above all I went because I knew no Irish history and had no national consciousness. I had never been told of Wolfe Tone or Robert Emmet, though I did know all about the kings of England and when they had come to the British throne. I had never heard of the victory over the Sassenach at Benburb, but I could tell the dates of Waterloo and Trafalgar. I did not know of the spread of Christianity throughout Europe by Irish missionaries and scholars, but did I not know of the blessings of civilisation which Clive and the East India Company had brought to dark and heathen India? Thus, through the blood sacrifices of the men of 1916, had one Irish youth of eighteen been awakened to Irish nationality. Let it also be recorded that those sacrifices were equally necessary to awaken the minds of ninety per cent of the Irish people.

The Great War dragged on. Nineteen-seventeen saw a return from the borders of Asiatic Russia to Egypt, Palestine, Italy, France and, in 1919, to England. Back to Ireland after nearly four years' absence, I reached Cork in February 1919. In West Cork I read avidly the stories of past Irish history: of Eoghan Ruadh, Patrick Sarsfield, John Mitchel, Wolfe

Tone, Robert Emmet and the other Irish patriots who strove to end the British conquest. I read the history of the corpses of the Famine, of the killings of Irishmen without mercy, the burnings, lootings and the repeated attempts at the complete destruction of a weaker people. In all history there had never been so tragic a fate as that which Ireland had suffered at the hands of the English for those seven centuries. I also read the daily papers, weekly papers, periodicals and every available Republican sheet. Past numbers told the story of 1916, of the ruthless suppression of the Rising, of the executed, the dead, the jailed. Those of 1917 shadowed the gloom of the year after military defeat, while the 1918 issues mirrored rising morale, the coming together of the nation to defeat the conscription of Irishmen to fight for Britain and the overwhelming victory at the polls for the Republicans, who had pledged themselves to set up a parliament and government of an independent Irish Republic.

The 1916 Proclamation appeared to me to be a brief history in itself. In it were the call to arms, the Declaration of Rights, the history of the nation and of the six previous risings, the establishment of a provisional government, the call for discipline and the appeal to the Most High for His Blessing.

POBLACHT NA HEIREANN.<br>THE PROVISIONAL GOVERNMENT<br>OF THE<br>IRISH REPUBLIC<br>TO THE PEOPLE OF IRELAND.

IRISHMEN AND IRISHWOMEN: In the name of God and of the dead generations from which she receives her old tradition of nationhood, Ireland, through us, summons her children to her flag and strikes for her freedom.

Having organised and trained her manhood through her secret revolutionary organisation, the Irish Republican Brotherhood, and through her open military organisations, the Irish Volunteers and the Irish Citizen Army, having patiently perfected her discipline, having resolutely waited for the right moment to reveal itself, she now seizes that moment, and, supported by her exiled children in America and by gallant allies in Europe, but relying in the first on her own strength, she strikes in full confidence of victory.

We declare the right of the people of Ireland to the ownership of Ireland, and to the unfettered control of Irish destinies, to be sovereign and indefeasible. The long usurpation of that right by a foreign people and government has not extinguished the right, nor can it ever be extinguished except by the destruction of the Irish people. In every generation the Irish people have asserted their right to national freedom and sovereignty: six times during the past three hundred years they have asserted it in arms. Standing on that fundamental right and again asserting it in arms in the face of the world, we hereby proclaim the Irish Republic as a Sovereign Independent State, and we pledge our lives and the lives of our comrades-in-arms to the cause of its freedom, of its welfare, and of its exaltation among the nations.

The Irish Republic is entitled to, and hereby claims, the allegiance of every Irishman and Irishwoman. The Republic guarantees religious and civil liberty, equal rights and equal opportunities to all its citizens, and declares its resolve to pursue the happiness and prosperity of the whole nation and of all its parts, cherishing all the children of the nation equally, and oblivious of the differences carefully fostered by an alien government, which have divided a minority from the majority in the past.

Until our arms have brought the opportune moment for the establishment of a permanent National Government, representative of the whole people of Ireland and elected by the suffrages of all her men and women, the Provisional Government, hereby constituted, will administer the civil and military affairs of the Republic in trust for the people.

We place the cause of the Irish Republic under the protection of the Most High God, Whose blessing we invoke upon our arms, and we pray that no one who serves that cause will dishonour it by cowardice, inhumanity, or rapine. In this supreme hour the Irish nation must, by its valour and discipline and by the readiness of its children to sacrifice themselves for the common good, prove itself worthy of the august destiny to which it is called.

Signed on Behalf of the Provisional Government,

THOMAS J. CLARKE

SEAN Mac DIARMADA THOMAS MacDONAGH

| P. H. PEARSE | EAMONN CEANNT |
|---|---|
| JAMES CONNOLLY | JOSEPH PLUNKETT |

*Promulgated on Easter Sunday, 23rd April 1916, at Liberty Hall, Dublin.*

The beauty of those words enthralled me. Lincoln at Gettysburg does not surpass it, nor does any other recorded proclamation of history. Through it shines the grandeur and greatness of those signatories who were about to die with their pride, their glory and their faith in their long-conquered people.

Obviously, of all the events since the Rising of 1916, by far the most important was that which naturally followed the Republican victory at the general election of 1918, the Proclamation of Dáil Éireann setting up the government of the Irish Republic as the *de facto* government of Ireland in January 1919. The Rising of 1916 was a challenge in arms by a minority. This was a challenge by a lawfully established government elected by a great majority of the people. The national and the alien governments could not function side by side and one had to be destroyed. All history has proved that, in her dealings with Ireland, England had never allowed morality to govern her conduct. Force would be used to destroy the government of the Republic and to coerce the people into the old submission. There could be no doubt it would succeed unless the Irish people threw up a fighting force to counter it.

About the middle of 1919, whispers came of the Volunteers again secretly drilling and reorganising. Names leaked through of local leaders and eventually I approached Seán Buckley of Bandon, telling him who I was and that I wanted to join the IRA. Buckley told me to return again, and at a later meeting asked me not to parade as yet with the local company, but to act as an intelligence officer against the British military and their supporters in the Bandon area. So began my connection with the IRA.

# 2

# WEST CORK BRIGADE

WEST CORK is a poor land, where bogs and mountains predominate, but there are fertile stretches, such as those along the valley of the Bandon and in the vicinity of the towns of Clonakilty and Skibbereen. Those rich areas were in the hands of a small minority, and the large majority of the people had a hard struggle for existence. Families reared in poverty had nothing to look forward to but emigration to the United States, the Colonies, Great Britain, or to join the British Services. Before the European War of 1914–1918, few young men or girls who had reached the age of twenty remained, and so the poor part of the countryside was sparsely populated. The rich lands had been well planted by the conquerors, and an examination of the names of the occupiers is a history in itself. There predominated the descendants of the mercenary invaders who had defeated Red Hugh in the Battle of Kinsale in 1601. When Gaelic Ireland went down at that battle it was a tragedy for the whole Irish nation, but its consequences were more far-reaching to the Irish in West Cork than to those living in other parts. It was there the battle was fought and it was there the conqueror, in his first flush of victory, with fire and sword sought to destroy the natives. Those left alive were driven to the woods, the bogs and the wastelands, while the invaders settled in their homes and on their lands.

In 1919 the 'Big House' near all the towns was a feature of first importance in the lives of the people. In it lived the leading British loyalist, secure and affluent in his many acres, enclosed by high demesne walls. Around him lived his many labourers, grooms, gardeners and household servants, whose mission in life was to serve their lord and master. In the towns, many of the rich shopkeepers bowed before the 'great' family, and to them those in the big house were veritable gods. The sycophants and lickspittles, happy in their master's benevolence, never thought to question how he had acquired his thousand acres, his castle and his wealth, or thought of themselves as the descendants of the rightful owners of those robbed lands. The chief example of the dominant British loyalist was the Right Hon. The Earl of Bandon, KP.

Offshoots from the 'Big House' were a large number of farmers settled on the best land. Of the religion of Tone and Emmet, they would not consider themselves as Irish. Theirs was a privileged position upheld by British domination, and it was their mission in life to see that their privileged and aloof status was maintained. A small number of the bigger merchants and strong farmers, although Catholic in religion, aspired to become members of the loyalist society through motives of snobbery or gain. They were strong in wealth and not in numbers. The remaining civilian prop on which British power rested in West Cork was a large group of retired British naval and military officers. These lived in comfort, in groups, in the most beautiful parts of a lovely countryside. They, too, never considered themselves as Irish, and were soon to prove that their loyalty to British power was not simply a passive one. All these active supporters of British power held over half the wealth of the area, though they did not number one-tenth of the population.

During the Anglo-Irish War, British military and police forces in West Cork numbered about three thousand. These were reinforced as the fight against them developed. The largest British garrisons were stationed in Bandon, Clonakilty, Dunmanway, Skibbereen, Bantry and Castletownbere. In all, they occupied twenty fortified posts, structurally strong and situated at points of strategic importance. In the town of Bandon there were three enemy posts. At the end of North Main Street stood the military barracks. Eighty yards across from it a large hotel was commandeered to house one hundred and ten Black and Tans. A few hundred yards away at the end of South Main Street the regular RIC barracks was chiefly garrisoned by Black and Tans. In addition to the troops within the area, many thousands stationed outside the borders were used for operations in West Cork. They came from Cork, Ballincollig, Macroom and Kinsale.

Practically all those British troops had battle experience during the 1914–1918 war. They were highly trained and well accustomed to fighting and bloodshed. Armed with the most modern weapons, they had a plentiful supply of machine guns, field artillery, armoured cars, engineering material, signalling equipment and motor transport. The finances of the world's largest empire were behind them.

Arrayed against these military and civilian garrisons were three-quarters of the people of West Cork. The blood sacrifice of the 1916 patriots had awakened them to their national degradation and in the 1918 election only Republican candidates were nominated. It would be wrong to suggest that at the beginning of the Anglo-Irish War a majority of the people supported armed action against the British. They did not, mainly because they considered such a campaign as hopeless and suicidal. It is true, however, that when the issue was knit and the people saw with amazement that their own Volunteers were carrying the fight to the Sassenach, they rallied behind them. The savagery of the British and the deaths of their neighbours' children for the people's freedom roused them, and from the middle of 1920 they loyally supported the IRA. As was natural, a certain section was more enthusiastic in their support, and burdens were not equally shared.

From these people sprang the Irish Republican Army, the finest of the manhood of West Cork. Mostly young men of good physique, the IRA was virtually untrained and unarmed. Their unit was the Third West Cork Brigade, one of the three formed at the end of 1918 and in early 1919 to cover all Cork city and county. Its eastern boundary extended from west of the Old Head of Kinsale, north to a point two miles south of Waterfall. Here the boundary turned west and ran one mile south of Crookstown and Kilmichael, to the southern end of the Pass of Keimineigh on to the Kerry border, west of Glengarriff, to meet the sea after enclosing all the Castletownbere peninsula.

In the brigade there were seven battalions, organised around the chief towns; the First Battalion, Bandon; Second, Clonakilty; Third, Dunmanway; Fourth, Skibbereen; Fifth, Bantry; Sixth, Castletownbere; and Seventh, Schull. Each battalion was divided into a number of companies, which, in turn, were divided into sections, the smallest unit of the Irish Republican Army. Battalions, companies and sections were of unequal sizes and strengths. The Bandon Battalion had thirteen companies and was by far the strongest. Its personnel exceeded that of the combined Bantry and Castletownbere units. Likewise one company might have a roll of fifty members, while another might include over one hundred. The organisation was elastic, based on the factors of population and terrain, and no attempt was ever made to form units on an establishment basis as in regular armies. This was important as it allowed for the development of a fighting machine under changing conditions and growing enemy pressure. In all, the brigade had at its peak period about three thousand volunteers.

Unlike the enemy, the West Cork IRA had no experience of war. The members were untrained in the use of arms and were backward even in ordinary foot-drill. They had no tactical training, but they had a great desire to become efficient volunteers. They were practically unarmed. Even in the middle of 1920, the whole brigade armament was only thirty-five serviceable rifles, twenty automatics or revolvers, about thirty rounds of ammunition per rifle and ten rounds for each automatic or revolver. The Volunteers had no transport, signalling equipment or engineering material, machine guns or any other weapon whatever, except a small supply of explosives and some shotguns. They had no money and were an unpaid volunteer force. They had no barracks to which they could retire, and no stores to supply them with food. They had no propaganda department to blazon forth their objectives or to deny enemy slanders. Each brigade stood alone, without hope of outside reinforcements should disaster threaten it. Within the whole national movement the unit made its own war, gloried in its victories and stood up to its own defeats.

This was the force that was to attempt to break by armed action the British domination of seven centuries' duration. Behind it was a tradition of failures. Each century had seen the humiliating defeat of some Irishmen who had sought to break the British yoke. Worse still, tradition showed that, after its savage crushing in 1601, West Cork did not take a worthy part in the numerous risings, except when Tadhg O'Donovan mustered a handful of men in 1798 at Ballinascarthy in a gallant but hopeless attempt to help in the fight for freedom. And sadly it must be recorded that, when West Cork women and children died in 1846 and 1847 of hunger, while the British Ascendancy seized their food, not a West Cork man drove a pike through any one of the murderers of his family. Still, West Cork did produce in the nineteenth century that patriot who will ever be revered by the Irish people, the great O'Donovan Rossa.

In the summing up of the strengths of the contending Irish and British forces, the factor of morale must rank highest. There was no doubt whatever that the morale of the IRA stood far above that of the British. Greater experience, numbers and armaments of the British were indeed an important consideration, but this was far excelled by the willingness of the Volunteers to sacrifice themselves for a cause they knew to be right. Theirs was an aim higher than that of simple political freedom, for, perhaps without being fully able to express it, they knew that when they fought and gave their lives for the ending of their long-endured subjection, they did so for the dignity of man and all mankind.

## 3

# THE ATTACKS BEGIN

AT the general election in 1918, held under British auspices, seventy per cent of the electors of all Ireland voted for candidates pledged to abstain from the British parliament, and the setting up of the parliament and government of the Irish Republic in Dublin. When these members met in January 1919, in pursuance of their election programme and the declared will of the people, they established Dáil Éireann as the parliament of the Irish people. They further proclaimed the independence of the nation and the setting up of the *de facto* Government of the Irish Republic. They established parallel departments of state to those of the British and sought the people's allegiance and support for the new institutions of the Irish state. The issue was now clear. Two opposing governments could not function side by side; one would certainly be destroyed.

Observers of revolutionary epochs, and particularly those who decry the use of the political weapon in any form as an instrument for successful emancipation, should study well the three periods of the 1916–1921 endeavour. Firstly, the armed rising and the blood sacrifices of the 1916 patriots to awaken the nation, although there was no hope of military success; secondly, the contesting of the 1918 elections and the subsequent setting up of the national parliament and government; and thirdly, the 1920–21 guerilla warfare to prevent the destruction, by armed force and terrorism, of the institutions so set up.

Those three plans of action dovetailed perfectly. Without 1916 there would have been no Dáil Éireann; without Dáil Éireann there would, most likely, have been no sustained fight, with moral force behind it, in 1920–21; and without the guerilla warfare of 1920–21 Dáil Éireann would have been destroyed and the sacrifices of 1916 in vain. Looking back it seemed to me that the Master, moved to pity by the centuries of failures and oppression which Ireland had suffered, guided the footsteps of our leaders on the only road to success.

The January proclamation of Dáil Éireann had two messages for the Volunteers. Remembering the past records of British oppression, the Volunteers knew that the enemy would use military force to suppress the Government of Ireland and its administration if they could not otherwise destroy it. The Volunteers would either have to fight or surrender all that had been won. The other message was that Dáil Éireann had now formally, as the elected parliament of the Irish people, proclaimed the Volunteers as the people's army, subject to the newly elected Government of the Irish Republic. Henceforth, the Irish Volunteers were to be the Army of the Republic, with the moral and legal status of a lawfully organised army of a democratic government.

About the middle of 1919, the various state departments of the Irish Republic commenced to take shape. Soon representatives of the Republic were accredited to foreign lands, despite the lack of recognition by other established governments. Courts of Justice were established, subscriptions to a National Loan invited, local and municipal authorities, hitherto governed by Dublin Castle, came under Dáil Éireann, and industrial and agricultural programmes were formulated. As was expected, the British government took action. Dáil Éireann and all national organisations were proclaimed as illegal bodies and large military and Black and Tan reinforcements poured into Ireland to suppress the elected parliament of the people. In the opening months of 1920 the British raids, arrests and searches for arms and literature were in full swing, even though throughout 1919 neither police nor soldiers were fired on by the IRA in West Cork.

There were, however, two incidents which showed the awareness of the progressive elements of the IRA of the coming struggle and the desperate need for arms. In June 1919 there was some agrarian trouble in Kilbrittain. To protect the landlord's interests, the police at Kilbrittain were reinforced by a section of British military. Each evening a party of six soldiers and one policeman patrolled the road near the disputed estate. The Kilbrittain IRA were naturally on the side of the tenants and they made representations to have official IRA action taken against the British patrol. They failed to secure an official order but decided to act on their own. One evening in June, fourteen of the Kilbrittain Company, wearing masks, waited for the patrol of seven, rushed, disarmed and tied them up. No shots were fired, but one revolver, five rifles with ammunition and equipment were secured by the IRA. This Kilbrittain Company was eventually to prove itself the best company in Ireland. The other incident occurred in November 1919. A British naval ML boat lay in Bantry Bay. The IRA kept a close watch on the routine of the crew. On November 17th, a party of the Bantry IRA, under Maurice Donegan, boarded the naval boat, held up the sentry and guard and secured all the arms on board. Six rifles, ten revolvers, equipment and ammunition were taken and these, with the Kilbrittain spoils, were the main basis on which the West Cork Brigade armament was built.

It appeared at the opening of 1920 as if nothing could prevent all the known Volunteers from being arrested. Small parties of the RIC and small groups of military, led by a policeman who knew the people and the countryside intimately, were continuously raiding for arms and literature and attempting to arrest Volunteers. No armed resistance was being offered to them, but all wanted men evaded arrest as best they could. Not one shot had yet been fired at those patrols who were disrupting the whole IRA organisation, except when a few Volunteers shot a most aggressive policeman at Kilbrittain in December 1919.

However, on February 12th, 1920, attacks on the RIC and Black and Tans commenced. Three parties were assembled to attack barracks at Allihies, Farnivane and Timoleague – Tom Hales in charge at Farnivane, and his brother Seán at Timoleague. The Allihies attack was unsuccessful. The groups at Farnivane and Timoleague, through unforeseen circumstances, were unable to get close enough to push home the attack and were forced to retire after some shots had been fired. Durrus Barracks was also attacked by a party under Ted O'Sullivan's command, on March 31st, but in it, too, the garrison held out.

There was a lull until April 24th, when a sergeant of the DMP was shot dead near Clonakilty. On the 25th, a small party under the Battalion Adjutant, Jim O'Mahony, intercepted and shot dead a sergeant and constable on patrol near Upton. Two carbines and ammunition were taken. Next a group under Charlie Hurley's leadership attacked a police patrol from Timoleague at Ahawadda. Three police were killed, one wounded and all arms and ammunition were taken.

No further attacks took place until June 22nd, when Jack Fitzgerald, Company Captain, Kilbrittain, led a party into the coastguard station at Howes Strand, near Kilbrittain, and secured ten Ross rifles and equipment without resistance. The British immediately supplied another dozen rifles and ammunition to this station, and on July 2nd, a group under

Charlie Hurley again raided the station. The coastguards fired on the raiders, who replied. After some firing the IRA burst the door with sledges and the coastguards surrendered. There were no casualties on either side. The IRA secured all arms, ammunition and also a wireless installation.

In the Bantry area on June 12th, Ted O'Sullivan and a few IRA resumed the western attacks and a constable was shot dead at Anagashel, on the Bantry–Glengarriff road. On June 22nd, Maurice Donegan and five of his men attacked a patrol of five RIC at Clonee Wood, on the Bantry–Durrus road. One constable was killed and another wounded. Ralph Keyes and a few Volunteers shot dead a terrible ruffian of the RIC, right under the noses of the British garrison at Bantry. On the same day, Maurice Donegan, with a few Volunteers, was again on the warpath in Glengarriff, where one constable was shot dead. Down in Castletownbere, on July 25th, a party of IRA, under Billy O'Neill, attempted a raid on the coastguard station by a ruse. It failed, and four IRA were wounded. Two days later, on July 27th, a few IRA led by Jim (Spud) Murphy shot a constable dead in Clonakilty. There was some IRA activity in the Skibbereen area and RIC patrols were fired on.

On Sunday, July 25th, the most dangerous member of the British forces in West Cork was shot dead in Bandon, a sergeant of the RIC. He was chief intelligence officer for the British in the area, the man who controlled all political police intelligence, which, in effect, was the only accurate enemy intelligence. It was on his information that the raids and arrests were executed. He had for long known that his activities would eventually entail an attempt on his life and he took every precaution. He never travelled out with raiding parties and never appeared in public, practically living within the barracks. One journey he did undertake with regularity. Each Sunday he attended Mass at the nearby church, a hundred yards from his barracks. He was generally escorted to Mass by Black and Tans, who, on reaching the church gates, turned and went back to barracks. It was impossible to attack the sergeant between the barracks and the church gates. Inside the church gates about seventy steps led steeply upwards to the yard in front of the church porch. On the last Sunday of July 1920, the sergeant went to church. He climbed the steps, reached the yard and was proceeding towards the church porch, when, on receiving two revolver bullets, he staggered and fell dead into the porch of the church. His death was instantaneous. Those who shot him walked off without hindrance.

In the same month the Brigade OC, Tom Hales, and the Brigade Quartermaster, Pat Harte of Clonakilty, were arrested by British military and brought to Bandon Military Barracks. The Hales family were amongst the founders of the Volunteers in West Cork and were prominently associated with all the armed activities throughout the Anglo-Irish War. Several of the brothers had taken part in the 1916 mobilisation and had marched from Ballinadee to Macroom with the West Cork contingent. Tom was the first officer commanding the West Cork Brigade. The family had what is probably an All-Ireland record, as when Tom was serving a sentence of penal servitude in Pentonville, his three brothers were serving in the brigade flying column.

In Bandon, the British repeatedly beat up their two prisoners, Hales and Harte, in an effort to obtain information from them. After failing in this effort the Essex Regiment torture squad was called in. The two prisoners were stripped naked and the torture squad got to work with pincers and pliers, pulling out the hairs and crushing the nails of their helpless prisoners. When they had finished, Tom Hales was unconscious and Pat Harte completely insane, but the torture squad had failed to get any information. Pat Harte was transferred to a mental hospital and remained insane until he died a few years later. Tom Hales was sentenced to penal servitude and was held in Pentonville Jail until after the Treaty of 1921 was signed.

# 4

# TRAINING CAMP

IN May 1920 I had received a warning that the British suspected me. I had been temporarily resident in Bandon and, having little liking for being arrested or beaten up, I told Seán Buckley I was leaving the town, and I did so without delay. One day after Tom Hales had been arrested, Seán Buckley told me that the new Brigade OC, Charlie Hurley, wanted to see me. We met at Barrett's, Killeady, and Charlie asked me to take on training throughout the brigade area. He spoke in detail of the urgency of getting some trained men ready to defend themselves. Before long I was to learn that Charlie's Volunteer outlook was governed by twin ideas: train and fight. The brigade staff of which I was to become a member in August 1920 was composed of the following IRA officers:

Charlie Hurley, promoted over the heads of many officers to take charge of the brigade, had previously held the post of

Vice-OC of the Bandon Battalion. He was a remarkable man and a lovable personality. Born in Baurleigh, Kilbrittain, on March 19th, 1892, he went to work at an early age in a Bandon store. While there he studied for and passed the Boy Clerks' examination and was posted to Haulbowline. He served at Haulbowline from 1911 to 1915, when he was ordered to Liverpool on promotion. He refused to accept the transfer as it entailed conscription in the British armed forces, and he, being a member of the Irish Volunteers, Sinn Féin, the Gaelic League and the GAA, was well grounded in the faith of Irish Republicanism. He returned to West Cork and commenced to organise the Volunteers, but early in 1918 he was arrested. He was charged and found guilty of being in possession of the plans of the British fortifications at Bere Island. Sentenced to five years' penal servitude, he served part of it in Cork and Maryborough jails, but was released with other hunger strikers under what was known as the Cat and Mouse Act at the end of 1918. Release under this Act allowed the British to re-arrest any prisoner at any time they considered him fit to serve the unexpired portion of his sentence, without the formality of court proceedings. Back again in 1919 in West Cork, he worked day and night to organise the IRA, and it was he, above all others, who continually urged a fighting army policy.

Liam Deasy, the Brigade Adjutant, from Kilmacsimon Quay, Bandon, was one of five brother members of the IRA. From his boyhood he had been a member of the Volunteers and other national organisations. By the middle of 1920 he had travelled throughout the whole brigade area, organising units and arranging lines of communications. Whenever he could get away from his staff work he was with the flying column, to which he was a tower of strength. He was easy to co-operate with and was the best brigade adjutant in Ireland. Later he was to prove himself one of the best brigade OCs.

Seán Buckley was the Brigade Intelligence Officer and, as may be gathered already, was another pioneer of the Volunteer movement in West Cork. To us who were twenty-two, he appeared an elderly man, for his hair was grey and his mien was grave. He must then have been about forty-six years. He was quiet and reserved, but had an unexpected sense of humour. Wise in council, militant in outlook, he was a splendid staff officer and undertook many duties outside his own department of intelligence, which he kept going till the Truce. He worried continually about all our lives, but never about his own, although the British would most certainly have killed him had they laid their hands on him from mid-1920 onwards. In spite of his age and austere appearance, he was tough, carrying his gun and marching long distances with the best of us.

Dick Barrett was the Brigade Quartermaster, successor to Pat Harte. He was a careful and conscientious quartermaster and a sincere patriot. His duties as Principal of the Gurranes National School were a good cover for his IRA activities. A native of Hollyhill, Ballineen, he was a gay and cheery soul and gave great service to the IRA in West Cork, until his arrest in May 1921.

Later I was to meet Ted O'Sullivan, the Brigade Vice-OC. A native of the western end of the brigade, he was usually to be found in the Bantry and Castletownbere Battalion areas. He, too, was an old Volunteer and was engaged in all the earlier activities in his district. He was also to serve with the brigade flying column for many periods. Young, and of powerful physique, he was a hard-working and reliable officer. He was Brigade Vice-OC until the Truce.

Formal meetings of this staff, as such, were never held, and no decisions affecting military operations or brigade matters were ever taken by it. But there was the closest co-operation between all these officers, and many informal discussions about brigade matters took place when they could meet. But there were meetings of the brigade council, as distinct from the brigade staff. This council was composed of the brigade staff, the battalion commandants and usually one other member from each battalion staff. At these meetings reports were submitted by each battalion OC as to the strengths and armaments of his own and the enemy forces in his battalion area. He further reported on the training of his unit, the efficiency of his intelligence department, the attitude of the civilian population, enemy activities and the steps he was taking to resist such pressure. Those meetings enabled the brigade staff and the various battalion officers to get a view of the overall situation in the brigade area. Here, too, officers saw problems facing the battalion commander of a particular area, which might not yet have appeared in theirs, and they were able to judge of the effectiveness of his method of dealing with them. General policy and tactics were discussed at length at those meetings.

Battalion council meetings were also held in each battalion area. These were attended by the battalion staff, all company commanders and one or more company staff officers. At times, a brigade officer presided. The business was conducted on the same lines as that of the brigade council meeting. Still lower in the scale of organisation were company council meetings, where the company staff and section commanders met to deal with matters within the company area. A battalion staff officer usually attended and reported back to the battalion staff on the position of affairs of the companies.

There was always a great danger that any of those brigade meetings would be surrounded by the enemy, and that all the controlling officers would be killed or captured. It is unnecessary to emphasise the disaster of such a happening, and all possible precautions were taken, but still the danger was ever present. Looking back and being wise after the event, it might have been wiser to have brought one or two battalion staffs together for a meeting, with one brigade officer at one venue, and thus have avoided the possibility of the whole brigade staff and all the battalion commandants being wiped out in one swoop.

In the summer of 1920 enemy pressure increased. Two thousand extra British troops were landed at Bantry and distributed throughout West Cork. IRA attacks had slowed down and nothing was hampering the British movements.

One attempt was made on August 28th to stop the Essex Regiment, but it met with very bad luck. Seán Hales lay with a small party to ambush an enemy raiding patrol at Brinny. The Essex patrol, travelling across country, came in behind them and opened fire. The IRA withdrew only with great difficulty and were forced to retire. Lieutenant Tim Fitzgerald of Gaggin was killed. This fine, promising young officer's death added to the darkness of the outlook and all the brigade staff keenly felt his loss. Tim Fitzgerald was the first IRA Volunteer killed in West Cork.

Desultory training of companies proceeded irregularly. This was not satisfactory. A group of sixty or seventy men meeting for an hour once a week, with only a few rifles at most, could not be trained as efficient soldiers. One week's collective training is the minimum required to inculcate military discipline and to teach men elementary tactics. Assuming that the brigade staff could arrange a company camp for every week, it would take a year to train the whole brigade, and by that time, of course, all the IRA would have been wiped out. Accordingly, the idea of starting the training of each company in turn was dropped, and instead it was planned to train all battalion staff and company officers. These would then act as training officers to their own units.

At the time this training policy was being discussed, GHQ in Dublin had sent a communication to all brigades that a flying column should be started in each brigade. The idea was enthusiastically accepted in West Cork, but it was thought wiser to develop it a bit further. The West Cork training plan envisaged the organisation of five training camps of separate groups of officers, at short intervals, as an initial step. The first and second groups were to be composed of all battalion and company officers of the Bandon Battalion, which, on account of its size, had about twice as many officers as the next largest unit. These were to be trained at separate camps at Kilbrittain and Ballymurphy. Then a camp was to be held at Bantry, followed by one at Schull. The fifth and final camp was to be located in the Dunmanway area. After each of those camps, which, on mobilisation, automatically became flying columns, engagements were to be sought with the British. Thus, whilst fulfilling the object of spreading military training throughout and giving all officers some experience of action, the West Cork Brigade would maintain a flying column for active operations, and would take a worthy part, without delay, in the defence of the people against the aggressor. One hundred and fifty battalion and company officers were to pass through these camps and flying columns.

The great advantage of this plan was that instead of having within the brigade a small number of very highly trained and a large number of untrained officers and men, there would be a fairly large number of officers and men capable of bearing arms. This allowed for the expansion of the flying column to the size it eventually reached, that of about one hundred and ten men, about twice as large as the next biggest flying column in Ireland.

The first camp was held at the end of September. Thirty-five officers of the First Battalion and two from the Clonakilty Battalion assembled at O'Brien's, Clonbuig, Kilbrittain. The O'Brien boys were active members of the IRA and the girls prominent members of the Cumann na mBan. The officers of the Bandon Battalion were responsible for the scouts and stores, and the Kilbrittain Cumann na mBan actively helped the O'Brien girls in cooking and cleaning for the IRA throughout the whole week. The column slept in O'Brien's house and a large adjoining barn. Clonbuig was situated two and a half miles from the Black and Tan post at Kilbrittain, six miles from the Bandon and fifteen from the Kinsale enemy garrisons. Extensive security measures were taken against surprise. During the day an outer ring of unarmed scouts from the Kilbrittain Company were on duty, and after darkness the column placed armed sentries. Increased surveillance of enemy movements was arranged at all nearby posts, and from the time of arrival in camp, everyone was kept on the alert. Surprise of the column would be extremely difficult.

As the men arrived in camp, they were detailed to sections and section commanders appointed. Their first parade was to listen to a talk on the plan of defence and the security measures to be enforced. The men were told to act as if they were expecting attack at any hour of the day or night, and most detailed instructions were issued. For the next hour they practised occupying their defence positions, aiming and trigger pressing and moving in extended order as directed. It was an unorthodox approach to training, but the circumstances necessitated the departure. After all, if an attack had come, all that really would have mattered would have been that the men would obey orders, shoot straight and move in proper formation. Their ability to salute or to form fours smartly would not have been a consideration.

Day and night alarms were given. If the men called out of bed came too slowly or made too much noise, they had to commence all over again, until eventually they leaped from bed, dressed, equipped themselves and moved silently and swiftly, in proper order, to their defence positions within a period of three minutes. Were a man found without his rifle or equipment off parade, even a few yards from his billet, he was sharply reprimanded. All the time the word 'security' was dinned into these men. Their watchwords were discipline, speed, silence and mobility. Another instance: after the first hour on parade, the column was ordered to fall out for a few minutes' rest. The four sections moved towards one another in a large group in the middle of the field, and then sprawled on the ground. They were immediately ordered to fall in again, and were questioned as to what they thought the consequences would be if the British could line one of the ditches and open fire on them bunched together in the middle of a large field. They were reminded that this could happen should one scout fail in his duty or be captured by the enemy. These IRA officers were intelligent men and quickly realised that such a surprise was possible. Therefore, when they were instructed that, in all later breaks, sections would rest at different corners, and post sentries, they realised that it was not a finicky order, but an essential security measure.

From eight in the morning until six in the evening the men drilled and trained. Close order, extended order, arms drill and elementary tactics occupied the first four days. During the remaining three days more advanced movements were undertaken and special attention was given to 're-drilling.' In this each officer, in turn, took command of a section and handled it for an hour or so. Attack and defence exercises were a feature of the training, and after these, at a signal, all would come together to talk over and criticise the movements. Situations were envisaged of engaging the enemy at a stated strength, moving in a certain formation, and officers were appointed, in turn, to command the column. The officers showed an extraordinary keenness on all parades, but particularly for sham battles.

At night the column assembled from 7.30 to 9.30 p.m. in a large barn for a lecture or for written exercises. The lectures were not those which could be compiled from textbooks, since there were none that could tell this flying column how it could fight and continue to exist in the midst of enemy posts through the years ahead. IRA policy, flying column tactics and security measures, ambushes, town fighting, elementary signals, map reading and blackboard problems were all considered until the men's minds held nothing but the thought of war. At the final parade of the camp, a musketry course was fired. Only four rounds per man could be spared, and each round was fired under different conditions and at altered range. The shooting, on the whole, was good. This must have been heard at the Kilbrittain Black and Tan post, but no move was made to raid the district for some time afterwards.

Many statements have been made by ministers and generals in various countries on the necessity for long periods of training before even an infantry soldier is ready for action. This is utter nonsense when applied to volunteers for guerilla warfare. After only one week of collective training, this flying column of intelligent and courageous fighters was fit to meet an equal number of soldiers from any regular army in the world, and hold its own in battle, if not in barrack yard ceremonial. Its camp training now completed, the flying column was ready to seek out the enemy.

# 5

# THE FLYING COLUMN

FOR months preceding September 1920, many officers of the IRA throughout Ireland must have given thought to the policy and tactics which a flying column should adopt to ensure its existence. Strange as it may seem, it was accepted in West Cork that the paramount objective of any flying column, in the circumstances then prevailing, should be, not to fight, but to continue to exist. The very existence of such a column of armed men, even if it never struck a blow, was a continuous challenge to the enemy and forced him to maintain large garrisons to meet the threatened onslaught on his military forces, and for the security of his civil administration. Such a column moving around must seriously affect the morale of garrisons, for one day it would surely strike. It also remained the highest expression of our nationhood, the flying column of the army of the people.

But the flying column would attack whenever there were good grounds for believing that it would inflict more casualties on an enemy force than those it would itself suffer. It would choose its own battleground, and when possible would refuse battle if the circumstances were unfavourable. It would seek out the enemy and fight, but would not always accept an enemy challenge. It must avoid disaster at all costs, but a situation might arise, when, in the interest of defence of the whole movement, it would be prepared to lose man for man, provided that a column of limited size only was risked, and that sufficient armed and trained men remained to put a new column on the march. Consistent with those two unchangeable objects, the mission of the flying column was continually to harass, kill, capture and destroy the enemy forces; to keep in check his attempts to rebuild his badly shaken civil administration; to guard and protect the building of our own State institutions and the people who were establishing and using them.

The task of this spearhead of the People's Army was a heavy one, in view of the preponderance of the strength and resources of the enemy and our own weakness in numbers, materials and experience. Obviously, a loosely built, careless flying column could not exist a full week without disaster. Only the best types of volunteers, severely commanded, trained and disciplined, could fulfil its role. From its establishment the following factors prevailed in the West Cork column:

1. The command of the brigade flying column was absolute. The

column commander could not be interfered with by anyone. His decisions were personal, subject to no authority whatever, within or outside the column. His was the responsibility, and it was he who had to take the blame for any failure. No one could share his authority and no one should share his responsibility in the event of disaster.

2. Every battalion and company in the brigade and all their resources were to be at the disposal of the flying column. Without those units of organisation the flying column would be ineffective and its existence curtailed.

3. Only picked volunteers of the IRA would be accepted for service in the flying column. Unwilling men would be a danger. All officers of battalions and companies were expected to spend a period on column service, but they, too, were not compelled. However, any officer who shirked such service would soon be considered as unfit to continue to be an officer of the IRA.

4. The men who volunteered for the column were made aware of the strict discipline which would have to prevail. It would have to be severe. They had also to understand that mobility was one of the most essential considerations; that they would have to march long distances, eating whenever food was available, sleeping in outhouses, if no other accommodation could be secured, and generally living hard. Each man also knew that because of the odds against it the column continually faced destruction.

5. Column officers and section commanders were appointed by the column commander, irrespective of the ranks held by the men previous to their enrolment in the column. Thus a company lieutenant might be a column section commander and so over a battalion commandant, should the lieutenant be deemed the most suitable.

Amongst the brigade staff there was not one member anxious to undertake the responsibility of taking command of the brigade flying column. Each one of us was anxious to fight with it and urged the others to accept. It was only after much discussion, and strong and sustained pressure from the brigade OC, that I agreed to take the command.

The brigade flying column marched away from Clonbuig and lay in ambush at several places without result. Eventually it arrived at Balteenbrack and Ahakeera, a few miles east of Dunmanway, and its next attempt is a good instance of its efforts to engage the enemy. On October 9th it occupied positions on the Dunmanway–Ballineen road to attack a party of troops at Farranlobus, two and a half miles from Dunmanway. This patrol of British soldiers travelled daily from Dunmanway in a peculiar formation. First came about twenty cyclists, and after them, in a lorry, about twenty other soldiers. At times the cyclists would pass Farranlobus five minutes before the lorry-borne troops. On other occasions, there would be a twenty-minute interval between them. Consequently it was necessary that the cyclists should be dealt with without an exchange of shots, so that the troops following would not be aware of the ambush until they drove into the position and were attacked.

The attack on this party had to be arranged as follows. Three riflemen were sent four hundred yards directly behind the column, onto the high ground, from where they could fire on an enemy attempting to come in from either flank or from the rear. Nineteen riflemen under the column commander, who were to attack the cyclists with fixed bayonets, were placed behind the northern ditch of the road, extending about 80 yards, the estimated length of the enemy cyclist column. At a given signal this group was to jump the ditch, and each man was to attack the nearest soldier. No shots were to be fired by the IRA. The remaining group of fourteen, with the brigade OC in charge, were posted 150 yards further west, inside the same ditch at the northern side of the road. They were to attack the lorry as soon as it arrived in their midst. They were not to be diverted under any circumstances from that task, but it was hoped that the main IRA party would have dealt with the cyclists in time to aid this group.

The flying column waited in position until nightfall, but the enemy did not travel that day of all days, although they had done so for the previous six days. Disappointed, the column withdrew. It had now to disband, as all the rifles were required for the next camp, due to commence at Ballymurphy Upper.

The section of the Bandon Battalion was ordered to march to Newcestown and to transfer their rifles on the following day. When this party, under Seán Hales, reached Newcestown Cross, it halted. Most of the men had moved off and only about seven remained on the roadway. It was quite dark. Suddenly there was a blaze of light, and two lorries of enemy soldiers swept around a bend a few hundred yards away, and came towards the Cross. The IRA had just time to jump into a field and line the ditch. They fired a couple of volleys at the leading lorry. The lorries stopped, their lights were extinguished and confusion prevailed. The small IRA group fired more shots and quietly slipped away through the fields. One British officer had been killed and several soldiers wounded. This was an instance of the fortunes of war. The flying column had been seeking to engage the enemy for over a week and could not meet them. Now they arrived when nearly all the column had been disbanded. The small IRA section did exceedingly well in inflicting casualties after nearly being surprised.

As arranged, the training camp opened at Ballymurphy, in an empty farmhouse owned by our friend, Miss Forde. There were thirty-two new officers present, but a few others who had been at Clonbuig sought and were given permission to go through the course again. The routine was similar to that of previous camps. As at Kilbrittain, there was no enemy interference, although there were raids by the Ballincollig military within half a mile of one of the billets. The training completed, this column was also to look for an engagement with, it was hoped, better luck than that experienced by the previous column.

For several days before the camp opened, two, and at times three, lorries of the Essex travelled daily at 9 a.m. from Bandon to Cork and returned each evening. This was to be the first target for the new column. But just as the camp was about to open, Michael O'Neill and Jack Fitzgerald of Kilbrittain, two of the finest officers in the brigade, were arrested and brought to Bandon. It was almost certain they would be transferred to Cork, very probably with the convoy we wished to attack.

Any assault on a party escorting those prisoners meant certain death for O'Neill and Fitzgerald, either by our fire or by the enemy. Therefore, we had to postpone the attack on this target until the prisoners had arrived in Cork. Without much hope of success we lay in ambush on several days, some distance from where we proposed to attack the Bandon to Cork convoy, but the enemy did not appear. Had we continued to move around this district our presence might have become known and the regular daily routine of this particular convoy altered, so we disbanded temporarily until the prisoners had reached Cork.

During the few days that the column was temporarily disbanded, the brigade OC and I went in to Bandon to attempt to shoot Major Percival. This officer was easily the most viciously anti-Irish of all serving British officers. He was tireless in his attempts to destroy the spirit of the people and the organisation of the IRA. Day and night he raided homes and arrested numbers, including some who had no connection with the IRA. Intelligence reports stated that this man had, on the three previous nights, left the barracks at 7.45 p.m. and walked one hundred and fifty yards to a certain house, presumably for dinner. On the fourth night, we waited in adjoining doors at 7.30 p.m., sixty yards from the barracks. Off duty and on leisure bent, some soldiers and two officers passed at intervals, but did not notice us; they were easy targets, but the man we wanted did not come, although we waited until 8.20 p.m.

Disappointed, we trudged out of Bandon back to our headquarters, little thinking that Major Percival, who was to fail so dismally against the West Cork IRA, was later to become the commander of the pathetic surrender of 1941 at Singapore. We could not foresee that our target of that night would, as Lieutenant-General Percival, Commander-in-Chief of ninety thousand British troops, surrender himself, his army and many months' supplies, after a skirmish and without a real fight, to a much smaller force of Japanese.

On the following day we received a report that Percival had left the barracks at 6 p.m. that evening and was actually raiding IRA houses while we were waiting for him in Bandon.

# 6

# THE FIGHT AT TOUREEN

EVENTUALLY word came that Jack Fitzgerald and Michael O'Neill had been transferred, and on the night of October 21st, the column of thirty-two riflemen mobilised at Dan Delaney's, Ballinphellic. One memory of that night remains very vivid. About eight o'clock a group of the column was chatting in a large kitchen. Leaving them, I walked towards a small room, and, leaning against the frame, looked in. Sitting on the floor, his black head bent, intently putting the finishing touches to his beloved mine, was the brigade OC. Helping him was Paddy Crowley, Kilbrittain. Over against the wall stood Seán Hales talking to his friend, Dick Barrett. Since, I have often blessed a merciful Providence for refusing man the power to foresee the future, for all four of these were to die by the bullet, Paddy Crowley and Charlie by British, Seán Hales by IRA and Dick Barrett by Free State bullets.

At four in the morning of October 22nd, the flying column fell in and moved off to occupy positions at Toureen, on the main road seven and a half miles from Bandon and twelve from Cork. It arrived at about 7 a.m. at a large house, owned by a Mr Roberts, which stood about twenty yards back from the road. An advance party had already made all the occupants of the house prisoners, and as the farm workers arrived, they, too, were held. Mr Roberts got permission later to remove his wife to a neighbouring house, a few hundred yards back, as she was not well, and the shock of a fight might worsen her condition. Two armed men accompanied them and had the dual responsibility of ensuring that no person left the neighbour's house, and that the column would not be surprised from the rear.

The plan of attack was outlined and the signals explained to all. Unarmed men were to signal the approach of the lorries. Two riflemen were to cover the western flank of the column and a similar number to cover the eastern. These were placed several hundred yards from the main attacking party and were two hundred yards back from the road. Thus, six riflemen were used to protect the rear and the flanks.

On occasion there had been three lorries in the convoy, and while personally hoping for two, provision had to be made to attack a third. Five men were sent to occupy positions about sixty yards west of a point where the attack on the second lorry was to occur, to meet this conjectured eventuality. At worst these would hold off the soldiers of a third lorry while the first two were being dealt with. Afterwards they could be reinforced to complete their task.

Those necessary arrangements disposed of eleven riflemen, leaving only twenty-one to attack the first two lorries, which usually carried about thirty soldiers. Nine of these twenty-one, with Liam Deasy in charge, were placed eighty yards east of Roberts' house, inside the southern ditch of the road. Halfway between these and the house, and hidden behind a laurel hedge, were Charlie Hurley and two riflemen. He was to explode the mine under the first lorry, and then his small party and the eastern section were to open a combined attack on the occupants, if such was found necessary to ensure their surrender. Sixty yards west of the mine, and behind a large timber gate which opened from the farmyard onto the road, a section of ten riflemen was placed to attack the second lorry. They were under the direct command of the column commander. Ropes were fixed on the gate, which was to remain loosely closed until the tail of the first lorry had passed. Then the ropes were to be pulled immediately, and when the gate flew open, five men kneeling and five standing immediately behind them were to be ready to fire a volley at their target, at a distance of only five or six yards. This particular part of the plan was practised at least half-a-dozen times, so that there could be no slip-up. This section was expected to deal with the second lorry without help. By 8 a.m. all men were posted.

Shortly after 9 a.m. the scouts signalled the enemy approach from Bandon. Soon the noise of the lorries was heard and in a few minutes the first lorry passed the gate. The gates were pulled open and the IRA were waiting with levelled rifles. Almost immediately the second lorry appeared, and as her bonnet showed, the order to fire was given, and a three-pound bomb, made by the IRA GHQ, was thrown. The bomb, which landed right in the body of the lorry, did not explode, but the volley sounded as one long, loud shot. The lorry skidded to a halt on the side of the road twenty yards from the gate, and the soldiers leaped out, led by their officer, Captain Dickson, and the fight was on. The enemy opened fire as they sprawled on the road facing back to the gate section. Obviously none had been killed by the first volley, though several must have been wounded. From the gateway itself, they could not be fired at, so out onto the road some of the IRA had to go. Now a few IRA were lying facing the Essex, whose shooting certainly was not good. Volley after volley was fired by the IRA party on the road, and Charlie Hurley and a few others got some shots in from the rear of the British. Captain Dickson was shot through the head as he was firing his revolver and soon some more of the Essex were killed and wounded. Then a shout arose as the British survivors chanted, 'We surrender, we surrender', and raised their hands over their heads. Immediately the whistle to cease fire was blown. An order was given to the eastern and western sections to remain at their positions to prevent any further forces from coming in, and all others were instructed to get out to strip the enemy of their armament and equipment.

The brigade commander came onto the road. He was disgusted at the failure of the mine and the escape of the first lorry. He had pressed the exploder handle as the front of the lorry passed over the charge, but there was no explosion. The IRA east of the mine had remained behind the ditch, waiting for the explosion before standing up to join in the attack. Unfortunately, the lorry had passed before they realised the failure of the mine. Paddy Crowley and a few others fired after the lorry and thought they might have hit a few, but there was no confirmation of the casualties. The lorry sped on and never halted until it reached Cork Barracks. The Essex left their comrades to their fate, and were guilty of shameful desertion. Had those fifteen soldiers stopped their lorry five or six hundred yards from the ambush, they could have made matters awkward by getting into the field south of the road and advancing on the column flank. They would have been met by a small flanking party, which would have been reinforced in a few minutes by our eastern section, and a little later by the remainder of the column not needed to guard the prisoners. It is more than probable that the column would have dealt quickly with them, but that fact does not excuse their failure to stop and help their comrades.

Five of the enemy were dead, including Captain Dickson, four were wounded and six unhurt except for shock. Fourteen rifles, bayonets, equipment, some Mills bombs, fourteen hundred rounds, as well as the officers' revolvers and equipment were secured from them. Not one of the IRA was hit. The members of the column helped to make the wounded Essex comfortable and supplied bandages to the unwounded for their comrades. The dead were pulled away from the vicinity of the lorry and it was sprinkled with petrol. The unwounded Essex were then lined up and told that their ruffianism during raids, their beatings of helpless prisoners and their terrorism of the civilian population were well noted; that their torturings of prisoners, as in the case of Hales and Harte, were not forgotten. They were also reminded that, in September, they had arrested Lieutenant John Connolly, Bandon, an unarmed man, and after holding him for a week in barracks had taken him out to Bandon Park and had foully murdered him there. It was pointed out to them that on that day they had been treated as soldiers, but if they continued to torture and murder they could expect to be treated only as murderers. An Essex sergeant, who was now in charge, then thanked the IRA for their fair treatment and protested his innocence of murder and torture, stating he would carry the message to his officers and comrades.

Within fifteen minutes of the opening of the attack, the column had assembled in Roberts' farmyard, and as the flames from the burning lorry leaped high, it quickly moved off. Speed was essential, as enemy forces from Bandon or Cork could reach the scene of action in twenty minutes or half an hour. The column marched south across country to meet the Bandon River opposite Kilmacsimon Quay. A short halt was made near Chambers' Cross and it was there, when the column was about to resume its march, that Charlie Hurley spoke a few words to the men, and on behalf of the column, ceremoniously presented me with Captain Dickson's revolver and field equipment, an action typical of his generous character. Then the IRA moved off to Skough and dumped some of the captured arms, preparatory to their being brought back to Crosspound at a later date by Frank Neville of Raheen, Assistant Brigade Quartermaster.

We reached the Bandon River, opposite Kilmacsimon Quay, about 1 a.m., and there Liam Deasy's brothers were waiting with a large boat. A section embarked immediately, while the rest of the column deployed to cover their crossing. On reaching the other side, they pushed on for half a mile, to cover the landings of the remainder. The second section crossed and held the immediate vicinity of the landing quay. Soon the third and fourth sections were safely over and the march was resumed by road to Ballinadee, on to Kilbrittain, and there the column billeted for the night.

The men were in a cheerful mood after the day. I recognised that two mistakes had been made. The eastern section had not been warned of the possibility that the mine might not explode. They were posted sufficiently far from it to be able to remain standing behind the ditch, not crouched down, waiting for the explosion. Had this been done, they could have opened fire and have stopped the lorry before it passed their positions. The other mistake made was my throwing of the large bomb at the moving lorry only a few yards away. It should have been clear that this was more of a danger to the IRA than to the enemy, since the balance of probability was that it would hit the lorry or the soldiers, drop back on the roadway and explode at the feet of the IRA party.

On the following morning eight extra IRA were mobilised. Armed with captured material, they increased the strength of the column to forty men. Reports came in that the Essex had been loose in gangs of about forty the previous night, smashing up and terrorising the town of Bandon. They were led by the sergeant and a few more of the survivors of the Toureen ambush who had been so profuse with their promises of good behaviour. They sought out anyone known to be connected, even remotely, with the national movement, but all these had wisely cleared out when they had heard of the Toureen fight and its result. The reports also showed that the Black and Tans had mingled with the Essex for the night's rampage.

It was decided to move the column on that night to Bandon, to try and protect the citizens from a repetition of the assaults of the previous night. A parade was held, and after exercises in street fighting were carried out, the column went to billets to rest. At 6 p.m. they were again paraded and detailed instructions were given on the night's task. At 6.30 p.m. the men moved to the jumping-off point, one and a half miles south of Bandon. There the scouts were to report at 8.30 p.m. Several IRA agents reported on time. Apparently on the previous night, the Essex and the Tans, in their assaults, had not discriminated sufficiently in their victims, and British loyalists had suffered in person and property before they could make clear their hostility to the Irish Republican Army. These loyalists had complained to the British divisional headquarters in Cork, and on the day following the assaults the Essex had been confined to barracks. That night about four hundred of them in four formations, with full battle equipment, accompanied by armoured cars, were paraded through the town at 7 p.m. and kept on duty there till midnight. The higher authorities had probably ordered this as a gesture of respect for the law and as a token of punishment for the whole garrison. It was also a clever move to try and convey that the Black and Tans, and not the regular army, were responsible for the night's hooliganism.

The column waited until 11 p.m. Further reports were received that there was no change in the position, and the IRA then withdrew back to the Kilbrittain area. For several days the column circled Bandon, lying in ambush positions, but failed to make contact. It was then disbanded, as the rifles were required for two other camps arranged for Kealkil and the Schull Peninsula on successive weeks.

While waiting for the transfer of rifles to the Bantry Battalion, the brigade OC and I made another journey to a town in the area. This time our object was to shoot a judge who had arrived there. This man was notorious for harsh sentences on IRA prisoners in pre-court-martial days. Where another judge passed sentence of six months, this man gave three years to members of the IRA. Reports had come in that he had arrived with a large escort of Black and Tans and an armoured car. He was staying at a hotel. Our intelligence officer located his room at the back of the hotel and reported that on the first two nights the judge had gone to his room at approximately 11 p.m., switched on the lights and had gone straight to his window to see that the air space was to his liking. On the third night we went in.

Behind the hotel ran a railway line on a raised embankment. It passed nearly level with and a short distance from the judge's window. Taking our boots off, we walked noiselessly along the line, crawling the last hundred yards, to lie close together opposite the judge's window at 10.40 p.m. From the hotel ground floor came the sounds of revelry and the loud talk of the Black and Tans who were in the building and at the frontal approaches.

The room remained dark until 11.10, when the lights suddenly went on, but no figure appeared on the drawn blind. Five minutes passed, and then a figure appeared, walking slowly towards the window. I took aim and gently touched the trigger of a Peter the Painter automatic with a stock attached. Then the blind sprang up revealing a woman. The shock was terrible, and I have never fathomed yet why it did not cause the very, very light pressure required on the trigger to fire the bullet. We lay motionless while the woman peered out in to the darkness, as if trying to see the surroundings of a strange room. Then she drew the blind down.

Speechless, we crawled away about 70 yards. Charlie told me that immediately the figure appeared he had taken the first pressure on the trigger of his rifle and that he would have fired only he was waiting for me to give the agreed word 'Now', so that we could fire simultaneously. We walked away so happy we had not killed this woman that we quite forgot our failure to shoot the judge.

The following day we heard that on the previous evening the judge had asked to be moved to a larger room and that his baggage had been moved in that day. Someone else may be able to explain what prompted him to change his room that evening but, most certainly, something greater than ourselves caused Charlie Hurley and myself to delay pressing the triggers, thus saving an innocent woman's life. All our regrets would not have undone the tragic mistake.

This incident, and the Percival attempt, are recalled to show that in West Cork we were thinking clearly as to the value of targets. The death of Percival and this judge would have far exceeded in real value to our armed fight the deaths of fifty soldiers or Black and Tans. Percival was a leading instrument in the plan for our destruction, while the judge was an important prop to British power. This judge, technically a civilian, had large armed forces at his disposal. British law administrators and British military forces were complementary. I cannot remember any GHQ order to shoot judges, but there was neither morality nor common sense in risking the lives of the IRA to shoot private soldiers if far more important representatives of the oppressors were allowed to function unharmed.

I moved the following evening to the western camps. Fifty-five officers from the Bantry, Schull and Castletownbere Battalions attended these courses. The camps were undisturbed by enemy action, and although each group lay in ambush following training, no enemy forces were encountered. Some of the rifles were then sent on to the Dunmanway Battalion for the final training camp.

# 7

# MARCH TO KILMICHAEL

SIR Hamar Greenwood, British Chief Secretary for Ireland, announced in the House of Commons in August 1920 that the RIC continued to resign, and that, in addition to those already departed, five hundred and sixty others had walked out in the months of June and July. He also stated that his Black and Tans, made up of British ex-servicemen, were now not only filling the gaps created by RIC resignations, but were actually doubling the 1918 strength of the RIC. He gave many assurances that in a few weeks the military, Black and Tans, and a new force called the Auxiliaries, would wipe out in Ireland all resistance to British rule. One hundred and fifty of this new force of Auxiliaries arrived in Macroom in August 1920 and commandeered Macroom Castle as their barracks.

Of all the ruthless forces that occupied Ireland through the centuries, those Auxiliaries were surely the worst. They were recruited from ex-British officers who had held commissioned rank and had had active service on one or more fronts during the 1914–18 war. They were openly established as a terrorist body, with the avowed object of breaking by armed force Ireland's continued resistance to British rule. Their war ranks ranged from lieutenant to brigadier-general and they were publicised as the very pick of Britain's best fighters. Highly paid, and with no bothersome discipline, they were habitual looters. They were even dressed in a special uniform calculated to cow their opponents. Each carried a rifle, two revolvers, one strapped to each thigh, and two Mills bombs hung at the waist from their Sam Browne belts. It should be said in all fairness to the better type of British officers that they had refused to join this force.

Macroom was outside the West Cork IRA Brigade area, but the company of Auxiliaries stationed there seemed to concentrate, from the time of their arrival, on raiding south in our brigade area. Day after day they travelled in to Coppeen, Castletownkenneigh, Dunmanway and even south of the Bandon River. By November 1st, it seemed to me they were working on a plan to eliminate IRA resistance by terrorism in one district at a time, and then move on to repeat their activities in some other area. They had a special technique. Fast lorries of them would come roaring into a village, the occupants would jump out, firing shots and ordering all the inhabitants out of doors. No exceptions were allowed. Men and women, old and young, the sick and decrepit were lined up against the walls with their hands up, questioned and searched.

No raid was ever carried out by these ex-officers without their beating up with the butt ends of their revolvers at least a half-dozen people. They were no respecters of persons and seemed to particularly dislike the Catholic priests. Actually in cold blood they murdered the aged Very Rev. Canon Magnier, PP, Dunmanway, on one of their expeditions. For hours they would hold the little community prisoners, and on more than one occasion, in different villages, they stripped all the men naked in the presence of the assembled people of both sexes, and beat them mercilessly with belts and rifles. They commandeered without payment food and drink and they seldom returned sober to their barracks. Observing some man working at his bog or small field a few hundred yards from the road, they would stop their lorries and start their pleasant game. Laughing and shouting, four or five would take aim, not to hit him, but to spatter the earth or bog around him. The man would run wildly with the Auxies' bullets clipping the sods all about him. He would stumble and fall, rise again and continue to run for safety. But sometimes he would not rise as an Auxiliary bullet was sent through him to stop forever all his movements. Still laughing and joking, these gentlemen and officers would ride away. Why not? The corpse was only an Irish peasant, and probably a sympathiser with these rebels, and anyway what did it matter? One more or less made no difference, and it was part of their duty to strike terror into the hearts of all the Irish.

The Auxiliary force had been allowed to bluster through

the country for four or five months killing, beating, terrorising, and burning factories and homes. Strange as it may appear, not a single shot had been fired at them up to this by the IRA in any part of Ireland to halt their terror campaign. This fact had a very serious effect on the morale of the whole people as well as on the IRA. Stories were current that the 'Auxies' were super-fighters and all but invincible. There could be no further delay in challenging them.

On November 21st, a column of thirty-six riflemen were mobilised at Farrell's of Clogher, north-west of Dunmanway, for a week's training preparatory to opening the attack on this super-force. On that Sunday a brigade meeting was held at Curraghdrinagh, and although many battalion OCs reported the assaults of Auxiliaries in their districts, no mention was made that it was proposed to attack them on the following Sunday.

After the meeting I turned north to meet the new flying column. This unit was composed of new men, only one of whom had fought previously at Toureen, and only three had been through camp training. They were mostly quite untrained, but many appeared to be splendid natural fighters. They looked a fine body of the best type of Volunteers, and with some exceptions, lived up to this estimate afterwards. The column was divided into three sections, section commanders were appointed, and training started early on Monday morning. Training was interrupted three times by enemy military raiding parties who came so close that twice a fight was nearly forced on the IRA. The column had a definite objective on the following Sunday and was not to be diverted, so it was moved on and evasive action was taken. Starting on Monday at Togher, it was thirteen miles south-east of its first billets on the following Saturday when training was completed. On the Friday, accompanied by Michael McCarthy, Vice-Commandant of the Dunmanway Battalion, I rode on horseback to select the ambush position.

We returned to the flying column. That night Paddy O'Brien came to speak to me as I was pondering on the problem as to how best to ensure that the Auxiliaries would slow down before the attack opened. Paddy was wearing a fine IRA officer's tunic. Suddenly the thought came that the Auxiliaries could never have seen a man wearing one of these. If, on coming into the ambush position, they were to see a man wearing such a uniform, with an officer's field equipment such as I wore, they would be certain to slow down to investigate. Paddy O'Brien was told to change his tunic for my civilian coat for a couple of days.

At 2 a.m. on Sunday, the flying column of thirty-six riflemen fell in at O'Sullivan's, Ahilina. Each man was armed with a rifle and thirty-five rounds. A few had revolvers, and the commander had also two Mills bombs, which had been captured at Toureen. At 3 a.m. the men were told for the first time they were moving in to attack the Auxiliaries between Macroom and Dunmanway. Father O'Connell, PP, Ballineen, had ridden out to hear the men's confessions, and was waiting by the side of a ditch, some distance from the road. Silently, one by one, their rifles slung, the IRA went to him, and then returned to the ranks. Soon the priest came on the road. In a low voice, he spoke, 'Are the boys going to attack the Sassenach, Tom?' 'Yes, Father, we hope so.' He asked no further question, but said in a loud voice, 'Good luck, boys, I know you will win. God keep ye all. Now I will give you my Blessing.' He rode away into the darkness of the night.

The column started its march against lashing rain. Everyone was drenched, but the march continued by road, byroads and cross-country. Noiseless, silent, and only smoking in the cover of a ditch during the short rest halts, no one knew of its passing as it went towards Kilmichael. During a rest halt, when the column was three miles from its destination, Flyer Nyhan came up from the rear section to report that young Pat Deasy had followed the column all the way and was now fifty yards behind the last section. Pat, a lad of sixteen, was already Battalion Lieutenant of Signalling in the Bandon Battalion. Quiet and serious beyond his years, he was still a merry boy and a favourite with all the column. His enthusiasm for Volunteer work and training was exceptional, and, when all others were tired out, he could be seen practising arms drill outside his billet. He had been ill for two days previously, and before we left I had told him he would have to miss this fight. He was instructed to hand over his rifle and equipment to a local man selected to take his place in the column. He was also told to return to the Bandon Battalion area until he would be recalled in a week or two. Now, here he was again after trailing the column to within three miles of the ambush position.

Flyer Nyhan was ordered to bring him forward and Pat was asked most formally: 'Lieutenant Deasy, you have disobeyed orders. Why?' 'No, Commandant, honestly, I have not. I can go back to the Bandon area this way, but I thought if you saw I was able to march with the column you would let me wait for the fight. I am not sick. I could march twice as far again without a stop.' It was difficult to resist the plea in Pat's voice. It sounded as if his boyish pride was terribly hurt, so he was given back his rifle and his deputy sent home.

The column reached the ambush position at 8.15, as the late winter dawn crossed the sky. The ambush area was in the centre of a bleak and barren countryside, a bog land interspersed with heather and rocks. It was bad terrain for an ambushing unit because of the lack of roadside ditches and cover, but the column had to attack in some part of this road between Kilmichael Cross and Gleann Cross of three roads, a few miles to the south. The column could not engage the Auxiliaries on the Macroom side of Kilmichael, as enemy reinforcements could quickly arrive from their base. It could not select a position south of Gleann, because on the previous four Sundays, the terrorists had diverged from Gleann Cross to four different districts. There was no certainty of meeting them, except on the road between Kilmichael and Gleann, which they never once failed to travel.

The point of this road chosen for the attack was one and

a half miles south of Kilmichael. Here the north–south road surprisingly turns west–east for 150 yards and then resumes its north–south direction. There were no ditches on either side of the road but a number of scattered rocky eminences of varying sizes. No house was visible except one, 150 yards south of the road at the western entrance to the position. It was on this stretch of road it was hoped to attack the Auxiliaries.

Before being posted the whole column was paraded and informed of the plan of attack. They were also told that the positions they were about to occupy allowed of no retreat, the fight could only end in the smashing of the Auxiliaries or the destruction of the flying column. There was no plan for a retirement until the column marched away victoriously. This would be a fight to the end, and would be vital not only for West Cork, but for the whole nation. If the Auxiliaries were not broken that day in their first fight with the Irish Army, then the sufferings and degradations of the Irish race would surely continue until another generation arose. The Auxiliaries were killers without mercy. If they won, no prisoners would be brought back to Macroom. The alternative now was kill or be killed; see to it that it is those terrorists die and are broken.

All the positions were pointed out to the whole column, so that each man knew where his comrades were and what was expected of each group. The dispositions and details of the plan were:

1. The command post was situated at the extreme eastern end of

the ambuscade, and faced the oncoming lorries. It was a small, narrow wall of bare stones, so loosely built that there were many transparent spaces. It jutted out onto the northern side of the road, a good enfilading position but affording little cover. Behind this little stone wall were also three picked fighters: John (Flyer) Nyhan, Clonakilty; Jim (Spud) Murphy, also of Clonakilty; and Mick O'Herlihy of Union Hall. The attack was to be opened from here, and under no circumstances whatever was any man to allow himself to be seen until the commander had started the attack.

2. No. 1 Section of ten riflemen was placed on the back slope of a large heather-covered rock, ten feet high, about ten yards from the command post. This rock was a few yards from the northern edge of the road. By moving up on the crest of the rock as soon as the action commenced, the section would have a good field of fire.

3. No. 2 Section of ten riflemen occupied a rocky eminence at the western entrance to the ambush position on the northern side of the road, and about one hundred and fifty yards from No. 1 Section. Because of its actual position at the entrance, provision had to be made so that some men of this section could fire on the second lorry, if it had not come round the bend when the first shots were fired at the leading lorry. Seven men were placed so that they could fire if the lorry had come round the bend and three if it had not yet reached it. Michael McCarthy was placed in charge of this section.

4. No. 3 Section was divided. Stephen O'Neill, the section commander, and six riflemen occupied a chain of rocks about fifty yards south of the road. Their primary task was to prevent the Auxiliaries from obtaining fighting positions south of the road. If the Auxiliaries succeeded in doing this, it would be extremely difficult to dislodge them, but now O'Neill and his men would prevent such a possibility. This section was warned of the great

danger of their crossfire hitting their comrades north of the road and ordered to take the utmost care.

5. The remaining six riflemen of No. 3 Section had to be used as an insurance group. There was no guarantee the enemy would not include three, four or more lorries. Some riflemen, no matter how few, had to be ready to attack any lorries other than the first two. These men were placed sixty yards north of the ambush position, about twenty yards from the roadside. From here they could fire on a stretch of two hundred and fifty yards of the approach road.

6. Two unarmed scouts were posted one hundred and fifty and two hundred yards north of No. 2 Section, from where they were in a position to signal the enemy approach nearly a mile away. A third unarmed scout was a few hundred yards south of the command post to prevent surprise from the Dunmanway direction.

All the positions were occupied at 9 a.m. when up the road came John Lordan with his rifle at the trail. He had heard that the column was looking for action and had followed it. Now he asked if he could take part, and was posted to No. 2 Section. John was the Vice-OC of the Bandon Battalion, a fine type of Volunteer officer and a splendid fighter. He was a welcome addition to the flying column.

The column had no food. There was only one house nearby, and although these decent people sent down all their own food and a large bucket of tea, there was not enough for all. The men's clothes had been drenched by the previous night's rain and now it was intensely cold as they lay on the sodden heather.

Except for a few visits to the sections there was nothing to do but wait, think and shiver in the biting cold. The hours passed slowly. Towards evening the gloom deepened over the bleak Kilmichael countryside. Then at last at 4.05 p.m. the distant scout signalled the enemy's approach.

# 8

# DRILL AMIDST THE DEAD

AS soon as the signal was received the order – 'Lie flat and keep your heads down until firing commences' – was given twice. Then around the entrance bend, unconscious of the enemy behind them, riding on a sidecar pulled by a grey horse, came five fully armed IRA. These men should have reached the flying column on the previous Sunday, but failed to receive the mobilisation order in time. Now, as well as endangering their own lives, they very nearly upset the operation and endangered the whole column, for nobody could foresee the consequences if the Auxiliaries had come on them at the entrance to the ambuscade. Luckily there was a ditchless lane leading to the house and immediately the order was given, 'Gallop up the lane, the Auxies are here. Gallop, gallop.' The grey horse galloped, and in thirty seconds the small party disappeared from sight and were not to reappear until the fight was over.

Fifteen seconds later, the first lorry came around the bend into the ambush position at a fairly fast speed. For fifty yards it maintained its speed and then the driver, apparently observing the uniformed figure, gradually slowed it down until, at fifty yards from the command post, it looked as if it were about to stop. But it still came on slowly and, as it reached thirty-five yards from the small stone wall, the Mills bomb was thrown, an automatic barked and the whistle blew.

The bomb sailed through the air to land in the driver's seat of the uncovered lorry. As it exploded the rifle shots rang out. The lorry lurched drunkenly, but still came on impelled by its own weight, the foot brake no longer pressed as the driver was dead. On it came, the Auxiliaries firing their revolvers at the IRA who were pouring lead into them, and then the lorry stopped a few yards from the small stone wall. Some of the Auxiliaries were now fighting from the road and the fight became a hand-to-hand one. Revolvers were used at point-blank range and at times rifle butts replaced rifle shots. So close were the combatants that in one instance the pumping blood from an Auxiliary's severed artery struck one attacker full in the mouth before the Auxiliary hit the ground. The Auxiliaries were cursing and yelling as they fought, but the IRA were tight-lipped, as ruthlessly and coldly they outfought them.

It was not possible to see the efforts of the IRA except those near me. There Jim (Spud) Murphy, John (Flyer) Nyhan and Mick O'Herlihy were fighting splendidly. Once I got a side glimpse of Flyer's bayonet being driven through an Auxiliary, whom I had thought dead as I passed him, but who had risen to fire and miss me at four yards' range. There was no surrender called by those Auxiliaries and in less than five minutes they had been exterminated. All nine Auxiliaries were dead or dying, sprawled around the road near the little stone wall, except the driver and another, who, with the life smashed out of them, were huddled in the front of the lorry.

At the opening of the attack I had seen the second lorry come around the entrance bend, but did not know of the progress of the action at that part of the road. Now that we had finished with the first lot, we could see the second lorry stopped thirty yards at our side of No. 2 Section. The Auxiliaries were lying in small groups on the road firing back at No. 2 Section, at about twenty-five yards' range. Some men of No. 2 were engaging them. Waiting only to reload revolvers and pick up an Auxiliary's rifle and some clips of ammunition, the three riflemen from the command post, Murphy, Nyhan and O'Herlihy, were called on to attack the second party from the rear. In single file, we ran crouched up the side of the road. We had gone about fifty yards when we heard the Auxiliaries shout, 'We surrender.' We kept running along the grass edge of the road as they repeated the surrender cry, and actually saw some Auxiliaries throw away their rifles. Firing stopped, but we continued, still unobserved, to jog towards them. Then we saw three of our comrades on No. 2 Section stand up, one crouched and two upright. Suddenly the Auxiliaries were firing again with revolvers. One of our three men spun around before he fell, and Pat Deasy staggered before he, too, went down.

When this occurred, we had reached a point about twenty-five yards behind the enemy party and we dropped down as I gave the order, 'Rapid fire and do not stop until I tell you.' The four rifles opened a rapid fire and several of the enemy were hit before they realised they were being attacked from the rear. Two got to their feet and commenced to run back past No. 2 Section, but both were knocked down. Some of the survivors of our No. 2 Section had again joined in and the enemy, sandwiched between the two fires, were again shouting, 'We surrender.'

Having seen more than enough of their surrender tactics, I shouted the order, 'Keep firing on them. Keep firing, No. 2 Section. Everybody keep firing on them until the Cease Fire.' The small IRA group on the road was now standing up, firing as they advanced to within ten yards of the Auxiliaries. Then the 'Cease Fire' was given and there was an uncanny silence as the sound of the last shot died away.

I ran the short distance to where I had seen our men fall and scrambled up the rocky height. Michael McCarthy, Dunmanway, and Jim O'Sullivan, Knockawaddra, Rossmore, lay dead and, a few yards away, Pat Deasy was dying. As we bandaged him, his face grew pale, but he was quite conscious as I spoke. 'They are all dead, Pat. We will move you safely to a house in a few minutes and will get a doctor. Are you in pain?' He smiled as he replied, 'No, Commandant, but give me water.'

I knew enough first-aid to understand that any liquid might quickly kill him, so he was told he would get a cup of tea when he reached the house. I turned away and ordered all the survivors, except the two who were to remain with Pat, to get down to the road. The whistle blew, and the order 'Fall in at the double' was given. Down the road with rifles at the trail came the insurance party of six riflemen; out from behind their rocks doubled Stephen O'Neill and his men; and from behind their high positions slithered No. 1 Section hastening to join the others. After numbering off they reloaded. Four men were sent hurrying for a door to bear Pat Deasy away; six were ordered to protection positions; eighteen detailed to remove the armament and papers from the dead Auxiliaries; and the remainder to make the lorries ready for burning. The first unarmed scout to reach the scene of the fight hurried for a priest and doctor, the other two collected the personal effects of Michael McCarthy and Jim O'Sullivan and made preparations for the removal of the bodies of those gallant comrades.

Within seven or eight minutes Pat Deasy was borne away and the flying column 'fell in' with its task completed. Eighteen men carried the captured equipment over their own, the enemy rifles slung across their backs. One man had a sandbag full of the Auxiliaries' papers and notebooks. Jack Hennessey of Ballineen, whose head wound had to be dressed, reported his fitness to march. He was told to remain sitting on the roadside until the column moved.

The flying column came to attention, sloped arms and was inspected. Some showed the strain of the ordeal through which they had passed, and a few appeared on the point of collapse because of shock. It was of supreme importance that those men should be jerked back to their former efficiency, particularly as another engagement with the British might well occur during the retirement. They were harshly reprimanded, and then the column commenced to drill and march. The lorries were now ablaze. Like two huge torches, they lit up the countryside and the corpse-strewn, bloodstained road, as the flying column marched up and down, halted, drilled and marched again between them. For five minutes the eerie drill continued until the column halted in front of the rock where Michael McCarthy and Jim O'Sullivan lay. There it executed the 'Present Arms' as its farewell tribute to those fine Irish soldiers.

The column formed sections and the order of march was given. A half-an-hour after the opening of the fight, it moved away to the south, aiming to cross the Bandon River before the British held Manch Bridge. Soon it commenced to rain again and the men were drenched. The rain continued as the IRA marched through Shanacashel, Coolnagow, Balteenbrack, and arrived at the vicinity of dangerous Manch Bridge. With full precautions the Bandon River was crossed, and Granure, eleven miles south of Kilmichael, was reached at 11 p.m.

On the road back I had decided that the column could not be risked in numerous billets that night as was usual. Hourly the threat to it would develop as the British sought it out and endeavoured to surround it. The column would have to remain together in a single house, ready for instant action. Paddy O'Brien and Dan Hourihan had reported an empty labourer's cottage at Granure, and it was in front of this the column halted. The local Ballinacarriga Company had been mobilised before our arrival and the members were eagerly waiting to help. They posted an outer ring of scouts, provided candles, bread, butter, buckets of tea, and placed bundles of straw on the floor. They dumped the surplus rifles and equipment. All ammunition, bombs and revolvers were distributed to the flying column.

It was now 1 a.m. and the scouts and sentries were inspected. When I returned half an hour later the men were all sleeping in their wet clothes on the straw-covered floors. I looked at them and a thrill of pride ran through me as I thought that no army in the world could ever have more uncomplaining men. They had been practically thirty hours without food, marched twenty-six miles, were soaked through, nearly frozen on exposed rocks and had undergone a terrifying baptism of fire. Their discipline was of the finest. Compulsion or punishments were not required for this volunteer army; they risked their lives and uncomplainingly suffered.

I poked out a corner near the door and lay on the straw. I could not sleep as my mind worked rapidly. Lying on my back, staring up at the ceiling of the dimly lit kitchen, thoughts crowded in on me. The Auxiliaries had had it. They were looking for it for a long time. But they were now smashed and their reign of terror against West Cork men and women was ended. The IRA had outfought them, and not more than fifteen or sixteen of our riflemen had had the opportunity to fire at them because of their dispositions. The 'super' force! Who was this Colonel Crake who had commanded them and who now lay dead on the road? Close-quarter fighting did not suit them. It does not suit the Essex or the Tans. Keep close to them should be our motto, for generally they must be better shots than us because of their opportunities for practice and their war experience. There are no good or bad shots at ten yards' range. Our dead! Two of them might be alive now had I warned them of the bogus surrender trick which is as old as war itself. Why did I not warn them? I could not think of everything. Liam will be cut up but he will understand. Pat *would* come. What will Mick's and Jim's people say? War means death to some and can't happen without deaths. The Auxies paid, though. Could we have managed three lorries of them? A good enough haul, eighteen rifles, one thousand eight hundred rounds, thirty revolvers and ammunition. And the Mills bombs. They were badly wanted. We are well armed now. I must sleep. If they find us before day and come on us from the north we will have to ____. I must sleep. I must sleep as I want to be fresh when they come. Some day they will surround us. Sleep, sleep!

I awoke with a start as someone gently pressed my shoulder. It was Charlie. I looked at my wristwatch and saw that I had not slept for more than half an hour. We tiptoed to an outhouse so that the sleepers would not be disturbed. There, as we smoked, I told him of the fight. Charlie had been in the Clonakilty area, and on his way to us had heard some extraordinary rumours of what had happened. The best news he had got was that two Auxiliaries and six of the column were killed; the worst, that the whole column had been wiped out with no British losses.

We talked for an hour, and I went back to sleep more easily as Charlie had taken over charge of the sentries and scouts. Until morning he would prowl round, tireless and watchful. Again I thought of what an extraordinary army we were. Where in all the world would a brigadier walk alone and armed for fifteen miles to find a fighting unit and mount guard himself while it slept in safety? But then, there was only one Charlie Hurley, and there never was his equal in all the units that fought for freedom in 1920 and 1921.

On the following day the column was confined to the cottage while reports of intense enemy activity came in steadily. Large bodies of the British were gathering in Dunmanway, Ballineen, Bandon, Crookstown and Macroom before converging on Kilmichael. One unit of two hundred and fifty steel-helmeted soldiers, moving on to Dunmanway about noon, passed two hundred yards from the cottage, while the column stood at the alert. Other enemy units were moving at the same time a few miles away on to Manch Bridge. No risks were taken by them as it was nearly 4 p.m. when all their forces reached Kilmichael. The British were aware at 6 p.m. Sunday evening that the Auxiliaries had been ambushed, yet it was late evening on the following day before they ventured to the scene of the fight. It was clear enough to me that they thought a large IRA force was engaged and waiting for a stand-up fight with the British reinforcements. That morning Charlie moved east at my request to attend to several urgent matters, including the burial of our three dead comrades. When night came, while the British were concentrating north of the Bandon River, the column drove further south to Lyre. For three days it zigzagged, avoiding at times by only a few hundred yards, clashes with other fresh British troops who had been sent to West Cork. It was possible to engage one of those units, although there was a great probability that if the IRA had attacked again, the other enemy units, a few miles away, would have got at the rear or flanks of the column before a decision was reached.

During those days other British forces converging on Kilmichael, carried out large-scale reprisals around the ambush area. Shops and homes, hay barns, outhouses were destroyed at Kilmichael, Johnstown and Inchigeela. Proclamations were posted up and printed in the daily press:

NEW POLICE ORDER IN MACROOM.

December 1st, 1920.

Whereas foul murders of servants of the Crown have been carried out by disaffected persons, and whereas such persons immediately before the murders appeared to be peaceful and loyal people, but have produced pistols from their pockets, therefore it is ordered that all male inhabitants of Macroom and all males passing through Macroom shall not appear in public with their hands in their pockets. Any male infringing this order is liable to be shot at sight.

By Order.

AUXILIARY DIVISION, R.I.C.

Macroom Castle.

December 1st, 1920.

NOTICE

December 2nd, 1920.

The General Officer Commanding 17th Infantry Brigade, Cork, requests that all business premises and shops be closed between the hours of 11 a.m. and 2 p.m. Thursday, December 2nd, 1920, as a mark of respect for the Officers, Cadets and Constable of the Auxiliary Division R.I.C. killed in ambush near Kilmichael, 28th November, 1920, and whose Funeral Procession will be passing through the City on December 2nd.

F. R. EASTWOOD, MAJOR.

BRIGADE MAJOR, 17th Inf. Bde.

This 'request' was enforced on the unwilling citizens by large forces of military, Black and Tans, and Auxiliaries, who lined the funeral route through the city.

Later came the martial law proclamation on December 10th,

1920, from Field Marshal Lord French, Lord Lieutenant of Ireland.

> Because of attacks on Crown Forces culminating in an ambush, massacre, mutilation with axes of sixteen cadets, by a large body of men wearing trench helmets and disguised in the uniform of British soldiers, and who are still at large, now I do declare Martial Law proclaimed in:
>
> The County of Cork, East and West Riding, The City of Cork, Tipperary, North and South Riding, The City and County of Limerick.

Impartial students of guerilla warfare may agree that the Kilmichael ambush justified Field Marshal Lord French in proclaiming martial law in the south of Ireland. I anticipated such a step as a logical sequence. It was even welcomed, as it connoted our recognition by the enemy as an army in the field, instead of their previous pretence that our status was that of a gang of rebel murderers.

However, this proclamation was based on lies. Firstly, Lord French referred to sixteen casualties only, whereas the British government had officially announced their losses at Kilmichael as sixteen dead, one missing and one in a dying condition. Secondly, Lord French used the word 'cadets' to describe those hard-bitten terrorists, all veterans of the world war and who were ranked in the British official communiqué announcing their deaths as majors, captains, etc., etc. The calculated use of this misnomer 'cadet' was intended to arouse sympathy from the outside world. Thirdly, Lord French stated the attackers used British uniforms as a disguise. No officer or member of the IRA attacking force wore uniform of any kind, except the column commander who had an official IRA tunic. Fourthly, the proclamation alleges that the IRA mutilated the bodies of the Auxiliaries with axes. The foulest of all British weapons has ever been 'atrocity' propaganda. No axe was in possession of the IRA and no corpse was interfered with. This mutilation allegation was a vicious and calumnious lie. Well may one ask from where Lord French got his information. Of the eighteen Auxiliaries, sixteen were dead, one reported missing (after he had been shot, he crawled to the bog hole near the side of the road, where he died and his body sank out of sight) and one dying of wounds. The last-mentioned never regained consciousness before he died. There were no spectators to the fight.

To clinch this exposure of lying British propaganda, it is as well to state here that after the Truce with the British in July 1921, Sir Alfred Cope, then Assistant British Under-Secretary for Ireland, called on me in Cork for a written statement that the IRA had killed the Auxiliaries at Kilmichael, since this was essential before the British government could pay compensation to the dependants. He informed me that the British Government had no evidence as to how these men had met their deaths, as there were no survivors to testify in court and the dying Auxiliary had never recovered consciousness. Incidentally, he was refused any statement.

# 9

# HOSPITAL INTERLUDE

DURING the four days after Kilmichael, while the column zig-zagged, one appointment was uppermost in my mind. It was of such importance that it was the deciding factor in not attacking one of the enemy marching units. This appointment could, in my opinion, initiate an operation which would have far-reaching consequences, namely the capture of the military barracks and the destruction of the two large Black and Tan posts in Bandon. The appointment was for the night of December 3rd.

One of the oldest ruses in war is to send spies, posing as deserters, into enemy lines. The classic example is, I think, the American Civil War, when hundreds of these pseudo-deserters were discovered as spies by both armies and dealt with as such. This knowledge was uppermost in my mind, when a local company officer reported to me that he had arrested two men of the Essex Regiment wandering about in civilian clothes stating they were deserters from the Bandon garrison, and that they wanted help to get back to Britain. Knowing full well the risks, I instructed the company commander to bring them to me for interview on the Thursday night before the Kilmichael fight.

Bandon Military Barracks could be taken on any night that sixty picked IRA fighters were able to approach the guardroom at the main gate entrance without the alarm being raised. One sentry outside the unlocked wicket of this main gate was the only obstacle in the way. Could one soldier on this sentry duty be relied on, through bribery, or for any other reason, to allow an IRA storming party to approach the wicket without raising the alarm, the job could be done. Fifteen of the attackers could deal with the guard of eighteen, fifteen others race to the officers' quarters, and the other three sections of ten rush the armoured car park, the NCO quarters and to the top storey of the building, directly across the square from the main entrance. This storming unit would use revolvers and bombs. On its heels would follow other picked men with every rifle in the brigade. Outside the town would wait a thousand unarmed IRA in ten units, who on a signal would hurry in to strip the barracks. Simultaneously with the opening of the attack, Bandon would be isolated by the taking over of the telephone and telegraphic exchanges and the blocking of all roads.

In the military barracks were armaments and supplies for a small army. In addition to the arms of six hundred soldiers, there were a battery of eighteen-pounder guns, four armoured cars and twenty-five large lorries. There was a reserve magazine containing nearly one thousand rifles, two hundred and fifty thousand rounds of ammunition, an unknown quantity of machine guns, Mills bombs, shells, explosives and engineering equipment. Should this be captured, a formidable IRA striking force would be created overnight. Members of the IRA were available to shoulder the rifles, man the machine guns, handle the armoured cars, and a few were capable of using the eighteen-pounder field guns. With the eighteen-pounders and the armoured cars the two Black and Tan posts would be quickly blasted out of existence and the whole town would be in IRA hands as a base for further operation.

It is, of course, pure conjecture, whether a quickly organised IRA column of one thousand riflemen, armoured cars and field artillery would or would not surprise and capture Cork where at least five times the amount of armaments were stored. Should it succeed there is little doubt that an Irish army, which would take some stopping, would snowball through Munster before the British could bring over and concentrate sufficient forces to halt it. At worst, the newly equipped Irish army would destroy British garrisons in many towns, and would make their re-occupation a costly matter if attempted. Anyway Britain, with her worldwide commitments in 1920 and 1921, would have found great difficulty in sending over sufficient troops.

With all this as a distinct possibility, it is little wonder that for many months we were seeking a contact with some soldier of the Essex Regiment. Now here were two, probably spies, but one might be bribed and tested. I interviewed each separately. The second man appeared to be the more likely of the two for our requirements. After nearly half an hour of questioning, I told him I knew he was a spy, but if he were interested in a proposition which would gain him three thousand pounds and a safe passage to any other country, we could strike a bargain. He asked what I wanted, but was told that the details would not be divulged for the present. I was about to suggest that he should go back to his unit, take a small punishment which would be the result of his absence without leave, and as a test, act as an IRA spy at a salary of twenty pounds weekly, when he said: 'I have a brother, a sergeant in the Essex in Bandon and he is anxious to get out, but he is afraid of not being able to get a job back home. Could I talk to him as he would do anything for that amount of money?' Eventually it was agreed that he and I should meet his brother at 8.30 p.m. on December 3rd, one and a half miles from Bandon. He wrote a letter dictated by me making the appointment. He was closely watched as he wrote on paper supplied by us and that letter could not have conveyed any hidden message. It was posted by our messenger in Bandon. Before he was taken away, he was warned of the consequences of treachery and he undertook to keep this arrangement secret from the other deserter. Both were taken away by an escort who were instructed to continue to look on the prisoners as spies and to keep them closely guarded. On the following night a dispatch was sent to the OC of the Bandon

Company to meet me at 8 p.m. on December 3rd, at a point half a mile from the meeting place arranged for the sergeant and myself. The company captain was instructed to come alone and unarmed. Nothing else but this bare instruction was contained in the dispatch.

On Friday, December 3rd, the flying column was at Ahiohill. A motor car had come to pick up the guard of three riflemen and myself. We were to call for the sergeant's brother and drive to a point a mile from the meeting place with the Bandon Company captain. From there it was planned to approach the rendezvous cautiously, through the fields, with a gun against the back of the deserter, so it is practically certain we could not have been trapped.

During the action on the previous Sunday at Kilmichael, so sharp was the sudden spasm of pain that struck me, I thought I had been wounded in the chest. Several similar, but lesser, pains had occurred afterwards, but did not appear serious. Now, with my foot actually on the running board of the Ford car, something seemed to hit me violently in the chest again and I knew no more.

Two hours later a tragedy was being enacted near Bandon while I lay unconscious of my surroundings. Captain John Galvin, accompanied by Lieutenant Jim O'Donoghue and Section Commander Joe Begley, were walking towards the place where John Galvin was to report. When these three reached the actual spot where the Essex sergeant was to meet his brother, in all probability Jim O'Donoghue and Joe

Begley were about to turn back since John Galvin had specific instructions to come alone. However, at the point a large force of Essex in ambush position surrounded the young Volunteers and shot them dead. Finding my short note signed as brigade column commander, the Essex commander immediately sent troops to the meeting place mentioned in the note and these remained in ambush around there throughout the night.

It is perhaps just as well that there are no details of the treatment meted out to Galvin, Begley and O'Donoghue. The only certainty is that the three corpses were found the following morning lying on the road near where they had been intercepted. The bodies showed marks of ill-treatment. In the centre of each of their foreheads was a hole made by a revolver bullet. There were no other bullet holes, but their bodies showed the marks of ill-treatment before they were killed off by the savages who called themselves soldiers of the British King. Bandon mourned for those three fine young men who died for Ireland, while the Essex and the Black and Tans caroused to celebrate another famous British victory.

Of course, the two pseudo-deserters were spies. Acting under instructions to treat them as such, their IRA escort had lodged them under guard, not in friendly houses, but in British loyalist homes. Despite the vigilance of the guards, one of them dropped a note giving particulars of the brigade column commander's appointment near Bandon. This was conveyed by the loyalist to the enemy, and hence the deaths of the three Bandon Volunteers. Some time after, the two British spies were brought to Kilbree, Clonakilty, and there they were executed.

When I regained consciousness some hours after my collapse, a priest was anointing me, and a doctor was also in attendance. The doctor said that through injury my heart was seriously displaced and that under no circumstances could I be moved for some days. For four days I lay, nearly motionless, in McCarthy's, Kilmoylerane. Miss Christina McCarthy, now Mrs O'Donovan, and Pat O'Mahony, then Company Adjutant, now a Superintendent of the Gardaí, attended me day and night. Later, Miss Mary Lordan, Newcestown, a nurse, came on duty. During these dark days, as I lay helpless, whenever I awoke day or night, one of these Cumann na mBan girls or Pat O'Mahony was with me, watching and waiting. Dr Fehilly of Ballineen was also tireless in his attentions. All these knew the risks they ran if the British came, but they never wavered, and their kindness will always remain an unforgettable memory. On the fifth day, Dr Fehilly allowed me to be removed. Wrapped in blankets, I was lifted into a motor car and, accompanied by Miss Lordan in her nurse's uniform, set out for the Mercy Home in Cork. We travelled a circuitous route and passed several enemy convoys, but reached our destination safely.

Sister Mary Mercy was the nun in charge of the home. She was the only person there who knew who I was, but later the two nurses, Miss Collins, now a nun, and Miss O'Sullivan, now Mrs Michael Cremin, were aware of my identity. Both the doctors, Dr J. J. Kearney and the late Dr P. T. O'Sullivan,

Tom Barry at the age of 22, by then commanding the West Cork Brigade flying column.

A bridge near Kinsale blown up by the IRA.

Auxiliaries outside Union Quay Barracks.

Civilians being searched for arms. Possession meant death.

The funeral of six men killed by the British at Clogheen, near Cork, passing military and Black and Tans.

Major A. E. Percival, DSO, 1st Battalion, Essex Regiment.

Brigadier-General Frank P. Crozier, DSO, Commander of the Auxiliary Division RIC.

Major-General Sir Peter Strickland, GOC 6th Division.

Macroom Castle, which housed a company of Auxiliaries.

Bloodhounds used to track IRA men.

Auxiliaries at Kent (Glanmire) rail terminus, Cork.

The wireless section of the British garrison at Bandon.

Tom Hales,
first Commandant of Cork 3 Brigade.

Liam Deasy,
third Commandant of Cork 3 Brigade.

Charlie Hurley,
second Commandant of Cork 3 Brigade.

Dick Barrett,
Quartermaster of Cork 3 Brigade.

*Above:* A group of Auxiliaries.

*Left:* Dr Cohalan, Bishop of Cork, after visiting Terence MacSwiney, then on hunger strike in Brixton Prison, London.

knew me also. Like the West Cork people, all of these treated me with unfailing kindness, and there was never a leakage of my presence there, through loose talk or otherwise. Each day I watched the doctors mark with an indelible pencil the progress of the return of my heart to its normal position, while I tried to obey their directions to lie flat and keep still.

On the night of December 11th, the British burned part of Cork city. Sister Mary's face was troubled as she made arrangements to remove the bedridden patients. She feared the hospital and home would also be burned by the rabble of drunken military, Black and Tans and Auxiliaries who were loose in the city, but the terrorists appeared satisfied when they had burned out a large part of the main thoroughfare.

It was while I was in hospital that the Bishop of Cork issued his decree declaring that anyone taking part in an ambush was guilty of murder and would incur the censure of excommunication. Let nobody minimise the gravity of such a decree in a Catholic country. Every Volunteer in the West Cork Brigade was a Catholic and, with few exceptions, deeply religious. Dr Cohalan's decree applied to territory including a large part of our brigade area, as it extended from the city to Bantry. My own reaction was one of anger. Everyone knew that if the IRA laid down their arms as requested by the Bishop at least 200 members in Cork city and county would be killed off within a week by the British forces. Yet Dr Cohalan did not even extract a promise from the British commanding officer that there would be no executions or murders if the fight for independence stopped. For days I brooded over the decree, knowing full well how deeply religious the IRA were. However, in the event, every active service man in our brigade continued the fight, most priests continued to administer the Sacraments and the IRA practised their religion as before.

There was a great questioning of Dr Cohalan's action. Cork Corporation members boldly challenged the ethics of his decree. Dr Alfred O'Rahilly, one of the most learned men in Europe and probably the greatest lay exponent of Catholic Action and Sociology in Ireland, replied to the Bishop in detail, and completely clarified the position for anyone in doubt.

About eight o'clock on the night of December 15th, Charlie Hurley walked into my room. He wore his grey cap and a trench coat, which covered the two guns slung round his waist. He had walked in twelve miles and had travelled through the city, which was infested by enemy gangs, but was as unconcerned as if he were calling next door to our own headquarters. As we shook hands I said, 'You lunatic, what brought you in here?'

He replied he had come in with an extra magazine and some ammunition for my Colt automatic. He would be gone in an hour and clear of the city before curfew; but he did not leave until six the following morning. After his tea, he lay on the bed and we talked of many things. When he came in his eyes were hurt and anxious, and I knew he was worried about something of which he had not yet spoken. After about an hour, I said, 'Come on, out with it. You are hiding something, but I am nearly better, and I will only start worrying if you do not tell me what is wrong.' He paused for a long time and then he told me.

On the night I fell ill, Charlie had taken over the brigade flying column and moved it away from Ahiohill. Twelve men were added to it and these were armed with some of the captured Kilmichael rifles. Five days later, on December 8th, he had brought the column into positions at Gaggin to ambush a party of eight Black and Tans, who regularly travelled from Clonakilty to Bandon in a single lorry. The column was in position about two hours when the lorry came into the ambush. A section commander misinterpreted Charlie Hurley's orders and allowed the lorry to pass on to the next section, as he understood this was the plan of attack. This was not so, and the second section was not ready to open fire when the lorry speeded through. Only a few shots were fired at it and none of the Black and Tans were hit.

Charlie wisely retired the column. The lorry rushed on for about half a mile, and then the Black and Tans, evidently believing, because of the few shots fired at them, that they were sniped at by only one or two men, stopped the lorry. They got into the fields and came on the unsuspecting column's flank as it retired. The Black and Tans, surprised at the strength of the IRA force, fired a few volleys, ran back to the lorry and drove rapidly on to Bandon. The few volleys killed Lieutenant Michael McLean of Schull and caused some confusion in the ranks of the column. A few of the IRA behaved very badly and one nearly caused a panic before the brigade OC regained control.

Charlie was worried over this reverse and wrongly blamed himself for the enemy's escape and Michael McLean's death. Historians, on behalf of the State, are now writing on the armed struggle during that period, so it is as well to state here that later on we examined the positions in company with Charlie's section commanders and from them heard of Charlie Hurley's orders on that day. Nothing could be clearer than that Charlie did place the IRA properly and that he issued correct instructions. The misinterpretation of orders was not Charlie's fault but just one of those things that happen. Charlie made only one mistake: not shooting on the spot the man who nearly caused the panic. Later on this coward was dismissed from the IRA and ordered out of the country.

A few days before December 28th, I had been allowed out of bed to walk gently around the room at short spells. On that morning both my doctors assured me that my heart was back in position, but that any exertion for about six months might have serious consequences. They advised a long sea trip to Australia. I told them I would let them know my plans on the following day. They refused any payment for their services and Sister Mary Mercy was indignant when asked for my account. That night at nine o'clock I slipped out of the home and set off alone for brigade headquarters, twelve miles away.

Once clear of the city I breathed more easily. Underneath the Viaduct, through Waterfall, I plodded on to the Mountain. There I took to the fields as a short cut, but got jittery. The lands here are wild and sparsely populated. The thought came to me that after all the doctors might be right, and if I dropped dead it might be weeks before my body would be found and by then the rats, which I knew to be numerous, would have eaten me. Illogically this possibility horrified me, so I turned back to the road and reached headquarters, O'Mahony's of Belrose, at 2 a.m. on December 29th, three weeks after I had left West Cork. The O'Mahonys always left one window in the sitting room unclasped so that we could come and go without disturbing the household. After getting into the sitting room, I removed my boots and tiptoed upstairs to the large bedroom reserved for us. When I lit a match, Charlie jumped up.

'Mother of God, how did you get here?'

'I walked the whole twelve miles so I must be cured. Shove over there and give me the warm place.'

# 10

# THE MURDER CAMPAIGN

THE year 1920 closed with the struggle well defined between Ireland and her ancient enemy. Now there could be no turning back. All Ireland had accepted to some degree the challenge of the growing British Terror, although some areas were wholly lacking in the offensive spirit. Bad leadership was responsible in non-fighting districts for lack of reply to British aggression since there was some fine material in every brigade. Some of the early commanders of the Volunteers never visualised that an armed fight would develop. They anticipated the continuation of the IRA as a flag wagging, speech-making and parading organisation, confining its activities to those harmless pursuits and its sacrifices to short terms in jail. The year 1920 was a grim reminder to those men that a new phase had commenced, and that nothing really mattered then, but to fight back against the armed terrorism of the occupying force.

Some of the incompetent and non-fighting officers had gracefully departed or were superseded, but others had hidden themselves and hung on to their commands. Safe in their dumps, they shamefully neglected to 'fight' their units, and so relieve to some extent the enemy pressure in areas like West Cork. Some actually actively prevented their officers from attacking the enemy so that their areas would be quiet and free from enemy counteraction. At least a dozen counties had some such figureheads, who were surely greater traitors to Ireland in her hour of need than any spies or informers. This explains why some battalions of the IRA never caused a single casualty to the British during the whole Anglo-Irish conflict.

By the end of the year 1920 the nation was deeply stirred and angry. The British murder campaign had grown steadily, and scores of unarmed members of the IRA and their supporters had been 'unofficially' killed by crown forces. Official hangings had commenced and Kevin Barry had died in Mountjoy Jail, dangling in the noose of a British rope. The torturing and beating of members of the IRA and civilians had roused a bitter hatred. Irish towns, villages, factories, creameries and homes had been burned out or blown up by high explosives. National institutions and organisations were banned and declared illegal. Farm implements and the wheels of carts were taken by the enemy so that the land could not be worked. The use of motor cars and pedal cycles was not allowed except under permit.

Proclamation by General Nevil Macready, Commander-in-Chief of the British forces in Ireland, December 10th, 1920:

EXTRACTS:

NOTE WELL,

That a state of armed insurrection exists. The forces of the Crown in Ireland are hereby declared on active service.

Any unauthorised person found in possession of arms, ammunition or explosives will be liable on conviction by a Military Court to suffer Death.

Harbouring any person who has taken part … is guilty of levying war against His Majesty the King, and is liable on conviction by a Military Court to suffer Death.

No person must stand or loiter in the streets except in pursuit of his lawful occupation.

All meetings or assemblies in public places are forbidden and for the purpose of this Order six adults will be considered a meeting.

All occupiers of houses must keep affixed to the inner side of the outer door a list of the occupants setting forth their names, sex, age and occupation.

Although outside happenings by reason of their savagery forced themselves in on us, West Cork had to contend with more than its share of British terrorism. Canon Magnier, Dunmanway, Young Crowley of Bantry, a cripple, and Denis O'Regan of Castlefreke, another civilian, were arrested and deliberately murdered. Five members of the IRA – Connolly, Galvin, O'Donoghue, Begley and Timothy Crowley – were also taken and coldly executed without trial or charge. Most of those men had never been mobilised for action against the British, but this fact did not save them from ill-treatment and death. Many IRA prisoners had survived torture, and in all about one hundred had been arrested and jailed. The homes of members of the IRA and their supporters had been burned to the ground and the residents of towns and villages had been terrorised.

Against this formidable list the West Cork Brigade had nothing to show, as we were not competitors in terrorism, as yet. Not one member of the British armed forces off duty and unarmed had been fired on by us up to December 31st, 1920. Fifty-one members of the British armed forces, up to that date, had been captured by the West Cork IRA and had been released immediately after their arms had been taken. Not one home of a British supporter was burned in 1920, nor was there any instance in West Cork where a British loyalist's property was interfered with or commandeered.

But in actual fighting the West Cork Brigade of the IRA was most certainly on top. The British losses in West Cork, according to their own official statements, published in the daily press of 1920 and excluding their wounded, were forty-one killed in action. The IRA losses in action for that period were five killed. Likewise the West Cork Brigade had captured up to December 31st, from the enemy, seventy-six rifles, forty-four revolvers, a large amount of ammunition, explosives, bombs and equipment. Against this the British did not succeed in taking a rifle or revolver in action, or in raids on homes. Those figures which can be checked prove conclusively that in the fighting between the armed forces the West Cork Brigade was easily master, whereas in the killings of unarmed men, torturings, burnings and general terrorism, the British occupying forces excelled.

The British were now being forced to operate in far larger units. At the opening of 1920, three or four police or half a dozen soldiers would boldly leave their barracks and travel miles into the country to effect arrests or carry out raids. At its close, the enemy never ventured to operate unless at a strength of one hundred. Motor transport was only used in large convoys now at irregular intervals, while their cycle patrols ceased. Their weaker Black and Tan posts had been evacuated, although there were about three times the number of enemy troops now holding West Cork than in January 1920. So uncertain were the British of their future that Royal Navy personnel were posted to their chief West Cork garrisons in December 1920, to set up and maintain wireless communications with divisional headquarters in Cork city.

As fighting had developed the support of the civilian population had grown behind the Irish Republican Army. The Irish Republican Courts were used extensively by the people instead of the boycotted British ones. Subscriptions to the National Loan issued by the Irish government were fairly generous and widespread, while British collectors ceased attempts to collect taxes. Republican police maintained order all over West Cork, except in the larger occupied towns, while the enemy police dropped all pretence to function as a normal police force. Irish civil administration was anything but complete, but nevertheless it existed in every battalion area. Through 1919 and 1920 Seán Buckley had laboured hard to build it, in addition to carrying out his duties as Brigade Intelligence Officer. Important as this work was it was only very secondary to the armed action effort as the year 1920 closed and all officers were now concentrated on military duties. Despite some failures and inevitable weaknesses the Republican government's civil administration was to remain an important factor in the nation's struggle until the Truce with Britain.

The women's auxiliary, the Cumann na mBan, was now well organised. No work was too dangerous or too strenuous for those fine women, numbering in West Cork about five hundred. Without the aid of this organisation the army would have found it very difficult to carry on.

Within the ranks of the West Cork IRA itself a splendid unity prevailed. Stories had seeped in of dissension in some units in other counties. Invariably these were non-fighting units which were not pulling their weight in the fight for freedom. It was a moot point as to whether those squabbling officers were so busy fighting each other that they had no time to bother the enemy, or whether their disinclination to engage the British left them with so much time on their hands that they started fighting one another. Whatever the cause, it was well known that such dissensions destroyed the effectiveness of several brigades. One is happy to record that in the West Cork Brigade no such bickerings or dissensions ever existed. The brigade staff set an example of good comradeship that could not be surpassed. We were a happy family, bound together by close ties. The dividing lines of our various duties were not clearly drawn, and each officer did the work nearest to hand without feeling that he was infringing on another officer's prerogative. Every member of the staff gave top priority to the task of destroying the enemy, and no one worried if he fought as a rifleman, a section commander or in any other rank during an action with the enemy.

The principal factor in this harmony and smooth co-operation was undoubtedly the characters of the senior officers of the brigade and the battalions. Neither pettiness nor jealousy was to be found in those men. To them nothing mattered but the pursuit of the movement for freedom. Another reason was that the officers were not engaged in politics as such, which was one of the causes of dissension in some other units. A third reason was that all those officers were so fully employed that there was no time for bothering about little grievances, real or imaginary.

As the old year faded out we talked of the future. Charlie Hurley had disbanded the flying column some days after the Gaggin affray. No attacks on the enemy had been carried out since that date. Because of this fact and the publication of Bishop Cohalan's excommunication decree, urgent action was indicated. Otherwise, the people and the IRA itself would be justified in giving credence to enemy stories that the West Cork IRA had shot its bolt and was a spent force. Therein lay the danger of demoralisation, defeat and death. The proper policy was crystal clear to all the officers. Each battalion was instructed to send on riflemen to form another brigade flying column, which was to mobilise on January 18th. Meanwhile, the Bandon Battalion section was to assemble immediately to carry out the first attack of the New Year.

# 11

# THE FIGHT GOES ON

KILBRITTAIN Black and Tan post was the first objective. This barracks was strongly held, fortified, steel-shuttered and encircled by barbed-wire entanglements. The only hope of capturing it was by exploding a mine against a wall or door and storming the breach immediately after the explosion. The mine was made. It consisted of thirty pounds of gelignite and gun cotton encased in a wooden box. It had an electric detonator, connected by forty yards of electric cable to an exploder. The attacking party totalled twenty-eight riflemen and some officers. It moved into the outskirts of Kilbrittain village after midnight on January 3rd. Ten riflemen were detailed for protection duty against enemy reinforcements. The remaining eighteen with officers moved cautiously up the village towards the target and halted. Forty yards from the barracks, the mine-laying party crawled forward up to the barbed wire. Great difficulty was experienced in getting the mine up against the wall, underneath the ground-floor window next to the door. It was a slow job as all noise had to be avoided, otherwise heavy fire would be drawn on the exposed IRA. Eventually the mine was placed satisfactorily and the small group crawled back to the remainder of the storming party. The order was whispered to get ready and the plunger of the exploder was pressed home, but the mine did not explode. Again and again the plunger was pressed until it was obvious that the mine was a failure.

An attempt was made to draw the mine back from the barracks, but it became tangled in the barbed wire and some noise was made. This alarmed the garrison, who opened fire. Knowing that the barracks was impervious to rifle bullets, and bearing in mind the scarcity of ammunition, only about fifty rounds were fired before the withdrawal of the attackers.

Again, on the night of January 15th, a second attempt was made to take this post. This time an ordinary detonator with a fuse attached was used instead of the electric detonator. The mine was again successfully laid and the long fuse lit. It spluttered and the fire rushed until it reached the top of the box. We waited for the explosion, but again there was a failure. A few IRA riflemen opened fire on the mine in an attempt to explode it while others fired at the door and the steel-shuttered windows. The box was hit several times, but the mine did not explode. After the first shots the garrison replied and the IRA remained on for about twenty minutes firing occasional shots and hoping against hope that the mine could be exploded.

Then they were withdrawn. An hour later, when three miles away, we could still hear the garrison's shots echoing through the night.

Charlie Hurley and I left the Kilbrittain area on the evening of the 16th, to return to brigade headquarters to deal with some matters, before joining the brigade flying column, which was to mobilise on January 18th at Shanaway. Our route lay across Innishannon Bridge, a few hundred yards from the Black and Tan barracks. Innishannon Barracks was a distinct thorn in the side of the IRA, as it controlled the only bridge across the river between Bandon and Kinsale, a distance of about fifteen miles. If it could be destroyed, it would solve to a large extent the difficulties of communications between the thirteen companies of the Bandon Battalion, as then Innishannon Bridge could be crossed with little danger of surprise. The only alternative to this crossing was by boat at Collier's Quay or Kilmacsimon Quay or to travel a distance west of Bandon town.

Apart from the effort to destroy the barracks, the problem of dealing with immediate reinforcements had to be considered. The strong Bandon garrisons were only a short four miles away and reinforcements, including armoured cars and light artillery, could, if unimpeded, reach Innishannon in a short time. They could travel either by the direct road south of the river or by the northern (Brinny) road, which was not much longer. The assault on the barracks might also give an opportunity for another attack on the relieving forces and a double blow might well be struck. A feint attack should draw those reinforcements and give an indication as to the time it would take to get them under way and indicate also the road they would travel. As the IRA rifles were limited, an ambush could be laid on one road only – although all the roads surrounding Innishannon would have to be held, however weakly – this indication as to the route was more important than even learning the time it would take the reinforcements to reach the scene of the attack.

Charlie and I crossed the bridge and walked down the deserted village street to deliver this feint attack at 1 a.m. on January 17th. Keeping close to the houses we walked in single file to within twenty yards of the barracks and fired six rounds each from our automatics at the door and steel-shuttered windows. We turned and ran back down the street to the corner where the road turned off for our headquarters. As we ran the garrison opened fire and sent up alarm rockets, which lit up the sky. The first conclusion from our experiment was that this garrison was on the alert. We reached high ground about a mile from the village and waited, while the din of rifle fire continued below. Fifty minutes after we had fired on the barracks the lights of a number of enemy lorries appeared on the northern (Brinny) road as reinforcements hurried to the village where the garrison was still blazing away. We took to the fields and set out for Belrose, well satisfied that we had acquired useful data for the coming attack on this post.

Between the 5th and 12th of January, Charlie Hurley, Liam Deasy, Seán Buckley and I moved around the brigade to inspect various companies, and to examine the effects of

Bishop Cohalan's excommunication decree. Companies were paraded and we spoke to the Volunteers. At the end of each address, the men were told if they had any religious scruples about carrying on, they were free to leave the IRA. Any man so affected was invited to step from the ranks, but none did so.

After the Bishop's decree, the British, counting on confusion in the IRA ranks, put on the pressure. Units of Black and Tans, Auxiliaries and military were daily raiding the countryside. They made many arrests of unarmed Volunteers and civilians. The Essex Regiment added two more to their many murders of unarmed people. They arrested Patrick Donovan of Culnigh, Timoleague, and Daniel Hegarty, Clashfluck, Timoleague, both Volunteers. Pat Donovan was murdered on the 17th and Denis Hegarty on January 21st. Because of this widespread enemy activity, the holding of those parades was a difficult matter. Travelling to one of them Liam Deasy and I ran into a round-up near Castletown-Kenneigh and were nearly trapped, but our luck held, and we got away.

On the morning of the 18th, Charlie Hurley, Liam Deasy and I reached the flying column's assembly place. That day all the riflemen paraded. They numbered seventy and included some new men. This was the strongest flying column mobilised up to then, but each rifleman had only about fifty rounds of ammunition. The column was divided into seven sections of ten and section commanders were appointed. Two days were occupied with training drills and exercises, the column moving short distances each night. On the morning of the 22nd it was moved into ambush positions at Mawbeg, on the main road between Bandon and Ballineen.

Reports had been received that several days each week five lorries of the Essex travelled this road from Bandon in the forenoon. On the previous night an enemy spy from Castletown-Kenneigh had been arrested, court-martialled and found guilty. Details of this spy's activities and conviction as well as others of his kind will be given later. At eight o'clock on the morning of the 22nd he was shot and his body labelled 'Shot by the I.R.A., Spies and Informers Beware.' He was the first of many to be so labelled in West Cork.

The spy's body lay on the roadside all the morning. Concealed in their ambush positions alongside the road, the IRA watched passers-by stop, read the large label and then hurry away. It was anticipated that those people would spread the news in Bandon, and that it would surely reach the ears of the Black and Tans and military who would be certain to come out to investigate. We waited for seven hours, but still the enemy did not appear. At 3.30 in the evening the column was withdrawn four miles where it billeted for the night.

On the following morning, the 23rd, before dawn we moved towards Bandon and occupied ambush positions near Laragh, about three and a half miles from the town. This part of the area was continually subjected to heavy raiding and there appeared to be a good chance to engage the Essex. On the previous evening another court martial was held on a man from Carhue. A self-confessed informer, he was convicted and sentenced to death. On the morning of the 24th he, too, was shot and his labelled body lay all day a little over three miles from Bandon. On this occasion we sent in friendly people to spread the news that this spy's labelled body lay on the roadside.

We waited until 3 p.m. when one of our intelligence people arrived to report that the police and military were aware since 11 a.m. of our presence in the district. He reported that a certain man whom the Black and Tans considered as pro-British, but who was actually one of our friends, had spoken to a police sergeant about a rumour concerning the dead spy. The police sergeant replied he had already heard the story and that the military were also aware of it. But both police and military, according to the sergeant, had been told on the previous day that lying around in ambush near the body were hundreds of the IRA waiting for the soldiers and police to come out. The sergeant said both bodies were being used as bait by the IRA, but they would not trap the military.

At four o'clock we withdrew a few miles for food. That night the flying column crossed the Bandon River at Baxter's Bridge, and in the early hours of the 24th reached billets. On that evening it moved into Crossmahon, a few miles south of Bandon, where it was informed of its task for the night. This was an attack on a curfew party of the Essex in the centre of the town of Bandon.

The curfew order needs some explanation. Its origin goes back to medieval times when it was instituted against robber bands who operated after darkness. Now it was resurrected and for about six months had been enforced in various West Cork towns. Ostensibly directed against the IRA, it was in reality an official act of terrorism against all the residents of the town to which it was applied. The 'curfew' times were announced by the competent British military authority as being applicable between certain hours, say 8 p.m. to 6 a.m. on the following day. All citizens were ordered, under pain of being shot at sight, not to leave their homes during these hours. It did not excuse any resident to explain that he had to leave his house to get a priest or doctor for a dying relative. Nor were the British liable for any compensation if they shot down a breadwinner who was proved completely innocent of IRA sympathies. The legal powers of the occupying British forces in this as in all other matters were completely unlimited. No British courts could restrain the military authorities since martial law had been declared. No inquests were allowed.

Far from being a hindrance to the IRA in a military sense, this curfew imposition was in effect a help to us. It cleared the streets of all except enemy forces and so allowed us to attack without fear of shooting our own people. No 'wanted' Bandon IRA man lived in the town so their movements were not proscribed. And many residents who were not supporters of the IRA became bitterly anti-British after a few weeks' experience of the curfew order. But even so, this curfew of the Irish people by a gang of foreign hooligans was to us a humiliating reality. I had seen our people in broad daylight pinned into their homes like a lot of dumb animals, peering fearfully from their windows for the British enforcing patrol. And I was to see their joy on many occasions when the West Cork Brigade flying column challenged this curfew, masked the three barracks and patrolled the town. Then the people would open their doors, come out into the streets not directly under fire from enemy posts, and visit their neighbours. The youngsters would even dance on the footpaths and the streets would wear the air of carnival. This would continue until shooting started when all would scurry back to their homes, cheering and shouting encouragement to the IRA.

The Bandon Company of the IRA had reported that the curfew patrol left the military barracks nightly about 10.30 p.m. It consisted of one officer and forty-four other ranks, steel helmeted and with full battle equipment. It invariably marched in close formation, carrying the rifles at the slope. It regularly travelled the same route from the barracks, down North Main Street, across Bandon Bridge, up South Main Street, on to the end of Castle Road, where it turned back to South Main Street, through Shannon Street to the end of Boyle Street. It was planned to attack this patrol as it entered Shannon Street for the first inspection at between 11.05 and 11.20 p.m.

# 12

# BARRACK ATTACKS

AT Crossmahon the flying column was divided. The brigade OC, with twenty riflemen (and a mine which might come in useful should an armoured car emerge), guided by Captain Frank Hurley of Laragh, moved off to cross the river by a footbridge in Castle Bernard Park. The two sections were to occupy positions seventy yards from the military barracks, and a little over one hundred yards from the Black and Tan post at the Devonshire Arms Hotel. They were to remain concealed until the attack on the curfew patrol commenced, when they were to open fire on both enemy posts. This should ensure that the main body of the flying column would have sufficient time to destroy the patrol, without the intervention of the remainder of the garrisons. Another 'masking' section of ten riflemen, under Liam Deasy, moved off to carry out a similar task against the third enemy post, the Black and

Tan barracks at the western end of South Main Street. Both masking parties, as well as the main body of the column, were to reach their positions punctually at 11.05 p.m. The attack on the three posts was to be maintained for seven minutes, after which those sections were to retire. The main body of the column was to withdraw when ordered to do so by the column commander.

In bright moonlight the main body reached Shannon Street punctually. Ten riflemen occupied the raised iron bridge near Lee's Hotel, which was a splendid enfilading position. The remaining thirty occupied houses and the corners of two lanes which branched south from the South Main Street end of Shannon Street. The men were well schooled as to their actions. All were to remain concealed until the enemy patrol came well into the ambuscade. Then, at the bursting of a Mills bomb or the blast of a whistle, fire was to be opened. At two blasts of the whistle all firing was to cease and thirty riflemen were to rush onto the road, to secure the enemy arms and equipment, while the iron bridge section covered their action. At three blasts, the thirty riflemen were to retire back Warner's Lane, past a small barricade erected to stop armoured cars, to a rendezvous a mile away. Five minutes later the enfilading section, which was to cover the retirement, was to follow on.

Midnight passed and no curfew patrol appeared. At 2 a.m. it looked as if the enemy knew we were in possession of the town and around his barracks, and that there would be no curfew patrol that night. As usual I placed myself in the position of enemy commander and asked what action we would take were the positions reversed. The answer was easy. If a commander had knowledge of a strong attacking force outside his posts, he should not show any signs of that knowledge. Troops would be kept quietly on the alert and divisional headquarters in Cork would be notified. Troops from the surrounding garrisons, Cork, Ballincollig, Macroom, Skibbereen, Clonakilty and Kinsale would be ordered out to encircle completely the town of Bandon in a two-mile diameter. At dawn the circle would be narrowed and the Bandon garrison would make a sortie. The column would be trapped and destroyed.

At 2.55 a.m. I felt that the limit of our justifiable risk had been reached. I fired several shots as a signal to the 'masking' sections, who at once opened fire on all the posts. The reply was immediate. The cracking of our thirty rifles was drowned in the far heavier enemy fire, the rat-a-tat-tat of their many machine guns dominating the symphony of the action. The main body of the column, except for the ten riflemen on the iron bridge, was ordered to withdraw. At 3 a.m., not knowing how Charlie's and Liam's sections were faring, those men were ordered to fire several volleys in the direction of the posts to create a diversion. Although I hated the use of ammunition when no target was in sight, it was not completely wasted. At 3.03 a.m. this section also retired. Rejoining the main body we met Deasy's section. His party had arrived near the barracks punctually and had fired at it for the stipulated time. Although the enemy reply was very heavy, it had suffered no casualties.

The fifty riflemen moved off immediately to Collier's Quay where a boat was waiting to ferry them north of the Bandon River. Billets, about eight miles from Bandon, were reached at 6.30 a.m. as dawn broke. Later that day Charlie's two sections rejoined us, but one man was missing. He was Volunteer Daniel O'Reilly, Granassig, Kilbrittain, a splendid young Volunteer. He had been killed during the attack and his body remained where it fell, not far from the military barracks at Bandon.

The British officially announced the attacks, but did not state they had any losses. Stories reached us that many of them were hit in the first few minutes, before they got to their security positions, but we could not confirm those reports. Be that as it may, Dan O'Reilly's death was not in vain, for there were many gains:

(a) The brigade flying column had carried out an attack which would not be contemplated some months before. The occupation of the main enemy garrison town of West Cork for four hours, and the close-quarter attack on all three barracks by seventy riflemen against seven hundred and fifty heavily armed enemy troops, was an assurance that the IRA column was both capable and confident.

(b) There would be a heightening of morale all over the West Cork IRA Brigade. Our supporters in the town would not feel unprotected, waverers would come out on our side and British loyalists would think twice before acting against us or disobeying the decrees of the Government of the Irish Republic.

(c) The enemy were perturbed at the effrontery of the IRA at this attempt to engage them in their main fortress. The attack pointed the way for many other visits by large or small units of the IRA and kept the garrisons on their toes during the nights. Those troops who were either attacked or sniped by night were not capable of the strenuous work of operating over a countryside the following day. This was the beginning of a harassing campaign in Bandon, which told heavily towards the end as it wore down the nerves of the enemy and shook his morale. Bandon was their main nerve centre and every blow struck there was worth two in any other West Cork town.

On the following night, January 26th, we moved to within two miles of Innishannon. Here eighteen riflemen under Ted O'Sullivan were ordered to occupy ambush positions at Brinny, and to attack any British who might appear. The remainder moved on and halted close to Innishannon village. Ten were sent to hold the Cork–Innishannon road and ten others to hold the direct Bandon–Innishannon road. When it was considered that those protection parties were in position, thirty-two moved on to the village to attack the Black and Tan barracks. This post was even stronger than that at Kilbrittain. It stood away from the village street, surrounded by rolls of barbed wire, except for a narrow pathway up to the front porch. There was no 'blind' side as all four were loopholed for defence, as were the steel shutters which covered the windows. Like Kilbrittain Barracks, it too was impervious to bullets, and if the mine again failed, there was no other means of taking it.

In the village three small parties of four riflemen went to

positions covering the sides and rear of the post. Their task was to keep the enemy from breaking out in their direction and to open fire on the upper windows as soon as the attack commenced. The remaining twenty men were in two sections, ten with revolvers to rush the barracks if the door was blown down, and the others to follow on when called to do so. These were halted thirty yards from the barrack porch. In bright moonlight two of the column took the mine and quietly walked across the open space to the barrack porch. The mine was laid against the door and the two tiptoed back to where the storming party waited. The exploder plunger was driven home, but the charge failed to go off. We cursed another mine failure.

The order to fire was given and some thirty rifles fired a volley at the steel-shuttered windows and the doors. The garrison replied and, as on the night of the feint attack, sent up rocket after rocket as alarm signals to the nearby Bandon garrison. Again there was nothing we could do except waste ammunition or withdraw from the attack, so four riflemen were left to keep on sniping the barracks in order to force the garrison to keep firing and so leave the reinforcements under the impression that the attack was still on. The remainder of the column hurried back towards Brinny to strengthen the ambushing sections.

But the British reinforcements did not appear. Apparently having been brought on a wild goose chase the night of the 16th they decided that this was another bogus attack to disturb their rest. The feint attack which I thought would give us such valuable information did not now seem such a good idea. I regretted ever having thought of it, for it certainly was the reason the enemy from Bandon did not travel to Innishannon on that night.

This was the third mine failure within the month. Some thought there was a jinx on our attempts to breach the barracks, but I had no illusions about the reason. We were simply incapable of properly making a mine. I had no knowledge then of the theory or mechanics of explosive mines, although I did feel capable of handling them tactically once they were properly constructed. I had to rely on other officers who had given some study to the matter, but they too were only experimenting and hoping for the best. The fault was chiefly mine as I was brigade training officer before I became brigade column commander, and I should have gone to GHQ myself or have sent some other officers to learn about explosives. Had I done so I have little doubt that both Kilbrittain and Innishannon Barracks would have been captured. In support of this assertion it can be pointed out that when we found a new man capable of making a mine properly, which partly breached the porch and door of Rosscarbery Barracks, a far stronger enemy post than those two, those men who had failed at Kilbrittain and Innishannon pushed the attack home and after three hours' fighting shot and bombed the stronger garrison out and destroyed the barracks.

Therefore it is well that those failures should be placed in their proper perspective. There was nothing wrong with the plans or the tactics of the attacks. There was nothing wrong with the courage of the men who walked into the towns and up to the doors and windows of those enemy posts. The failures of the many mines we laid were most discouraging, but they were only the logical result of our complete ignorance of high explosives.

The mine was the only weapon the IRA had in its armoury to breach a barrack door or wall. Rifle and revolver bullets were about as useful as snowballs against those strong enemy posts. All the garrison had to do was to man the loopholed walls and windows in complete safety and shoot down any attackers who approached. The IRA had the materials for making mines, but it lacked the trained men to assemble them properly. I learned in January 1921 that no guerilla force should attempt to operate without having ten per cent of its personnel capable of constructing, laying and detonating effective mines. Later I was to raise that percentage to twenty-five.

Of all the tests of men's courage in guerilla warfare, that of carrying a mine across an open space on a bright night, and properly placing it against an enemy post is, in my opinion, the greatest. There is the initial waiting, when imagination can run riot. Next the approach and the steady walk up to the post with the mine, the fuse sizzling or the electric cable trailing. One expects a hail of bullets, and the dominant fear is that one of those will explode the mine, scattering its bearer into small pieces. There is a tendency to run quickly with the dangerous box, throw it against the wall or door and get the job over, instead of walking calmly and placing the mine gently and methodically in its proper place. During the return walk there is still the expectation of a few bullets through one's back. Coolness as well as courage is required for such work. For all other tasks except this the brigade column commander detailed the men he considered most suitable. But for placing mines, volunteers were invariably asked to step forward. Usually four or five times the number required volunteered, so in effect the commander had to select men.

It was a point of honour that officers only were accepted for mine-placing work, and this was held to with rare exceptions. One of those exceptions must be mentioned, for the Volunteer, a man unknown except to his comrades, was to die for Ireland, not long after the Innishannon attempt. This was Peter Monahan, born in Scotland of Irish parents. After the 1914–1918 war his regiment was transferred to Ireland. When Peter realised the nature of his work here he promptly contacted the IRA and came over to us, bringing his rifle with him. Blood triumphed over his environment and training and he was to remain until his death as fine a Volunteer as was in the ranks of the West Cork Brigade. A clean, brave and intelligent man, he was to die fighting the British on March 19th, at Crossbarry, a worthy comrade and a good Irishman.

Reaching billets on the morning of the 27th from the Innishannon attack, the column rested throughout the day, and marched that night to billets near Newcestown, reaching them on the morning of the 28th. Again on that night Bandon garrisons were attacked by two sections of the flying column. This attack was on a smaller scale than on the 24th, and was primarily intended as a harassing action, aimed to disturb all enemy posts and to prevent their resting. On this occasion the IRA had no casualty.

On the morning of the 29th, the column was reduced in strength to forty riflemen so that it would not be too unwieldy for its projected programme. Charlie Hurley and Liam Deasy went off to deal with some other duties, and the men from the western battalions, led by Seán Lehane, Seán O'Driscoll, Gibbs Ross and Jim Hayes, were sent back to their units to await recall. That night we moved south to enter the 2nd Battalion (Clonakilty) area.

# 13

# THE BURGATIA BATTLE

ON the night of January 31st, an informer from Desertserges was arrested by the flying column, court-martialled and sentenced to death. He was shot and labelled on February 1st. On that night the column left Ahiohill to march by a circuitous route to Burgatia House, Rosscarbery. Jim Hurley marched with me to talk on matters affecting his battalion area, through which we were now travelling. Hurley was then about eighteen and a half years, probably the youngest, and certainly one of the best battalion commanders in Ireland. He had been battalion adjutant, and had succeeded Dan Harte, who had a breakdown in health at the end of 1920. Jim Hurley had served with the flying column on previous occasions and was continually appealing to me to bring the column to his battalion area, and now here it was marching to billets before attempting to destroy Rosscarbery Barracks.

The billets, in this case, were a British loyalist's large house at Burgatia, a mile from the enemy post at Rosscarbery. It was planned to reach this house at three on the morning of the 2nd, rest there during the day, and move off to attack at midnight. This decision to billet for twenty-one hours, within a mile of the enemy post, may on the surface appear to have been over-daring and rash, but an examination of all the circumstances may alter that view. In favour of the decision the following circumstances were considered:

(a) The flying column had to be fresh for this attack, because it was anticipated that it would be a stiff and long struggle, occupying many hours. There was also the probability that the column would have to meet enemy relieving forces and to fight a retiring action all through the following day.

(b) Although many fine people resided in the ten mile approaches to Rosscarbery, there were nests of British loyalists. A continual worry to the column commander on such missions was that one of those informers would see the flying column pass, and slip away to report to the British that the IRA were moving towards Rosscarbery or some other enemy barracks. Should this happen the garrison would be waiting to shoot down the column and reinforcements would hurry to the scene.

(c) The telephone wires could not be cut until a few minutes before the attack opened, as the enemy security measures included an hour to hour check up, day and night, from barracks to barracks. If any garrison found itself cut off from telephonic communication, it immediately prepared against attack.

(d) Were the column reported to the enemy as moving on the morning of February 2nd, towards Rosscarbery, the British would never consider that it was lying in a British loyalist's house, a mile from the village. They might raid generally round the countryside, but would not search Burgatia House. Indeed, they were likely to imagine that they had received false information or that the column had passed west or turned north.

(e) The owner of Burgatia House was a leading loyalist, charged with espionage against the IRA and with secretly carrying all the Black and Tan mails between Rosscarbery and Clonakilty. He was due for arrest and trial. All his household, staff and visitors, could be held as prisoners and not released until the attack was over.

In short, the decision to billet at Burgatia House ensured that the column would be fresh for the attack, that no advance information of its movements would reach the enemy, that it was safe from casual raiding parties and that an enemy agent would not only be arrested, but would have to feed the flying column for twenty-four hours.

Against the decision was the proximity of the house to the enemy post. There was a possibility that some of the Black and Tans might pay a friendly visit and were this to occur the attack on the barracks could not take place. But the worst feature of all was the situation of the house from the defensive viewpoint. It could be surrounded very easily and quickly converted into a trap for the occupying IRA column. The house stood one hundred and fifty yards south of the main Rosscarbery–Clonakilty road. Behind it, a few hundred yards further south, the Atlantic ocean surged against high cliffs. A few hundred yards to the east branched the road to Owenahincha Strand and Castlefreke. To the west a few hundred yards was the wooded demesne of another large residence, Creggane House. The fields around Burgatia House were large, and if even a section of enemy riflemen occupied the wood to the west, and others the roads east and south, they could keep the column held in until strong reinforcements arrived. Another bad feature was that since our sentries had to be kept hidden close to and around the house itself to escape observation, they could not see the enemy approach until they were only a hundred and fifty yards away.

The column occupied Burgatia House at 3 a.m. Jack Corkery, a splendid officer, who gave great service in the West Cork Brigade from 1916 to the end, posted sentries. Tadhg O'Sullivan, later to become brigade quartermaster, took charge of the feeding of the men. He was by far the best quartermaster I have ever met. He had a knack of producing food, cigarettes, boots, overcoats or anything else he was asked for, in a most surprising manner. He spent a lot of time with the brigade flying column. Tadhg's face now beamed with pleasure as he saw the hungry column start on the substantial feed he had procured for them. The house was well stocked with eggs and bacon, and the quartermaster's idea of a reasonable supper was four rashers and four fried eggs for each man, with tea and bread and butter galore. The Volunteers appeared to enjoy their first experience of eating at the expense of one of their enemies. Up to then, the custom was to billet at friendly houses. This was not only unfair but stupid, as our supporters were being hard hit to feed the active service IRA while the enemy supporters were under no expense. From February 1921 this was changed. Whenever possible British loyalists' houses were used as billets for the flying column and our own people got a chance to recover. Incidentally, this served also to check any act of hostility by such loyalists, and indeed, in certain cases, the discipline and good behaviour of the IRA column made non-supporters become our good friends.

The owner, a prisoner under close arrest, was brought for trial in the morning. Confronted with evidence and questioned for an hour, he admitted that he had been secretly carrying dispatches between the Rosscarbery and Clonakilty enemy garrisons. His defence was that as the mails were unsafe owing to IRA raids, the Black and Tans would have to travel daily with those messages had he not volunteered to bring them. This would endanger the Black and Tans as they were almost certain to be ambushed, and he wanted to save their lives. On the charge of attempting to organise an espionage ring for the British he quibbled, stating he was only trying to organise an anti-Sinn Féin party in the interests of peace. The evidence against him of spying was strong but not entirely conclusive.

By all rules this man deserved the death penalty. Guilty of treason and treachery to the elected government of his own country, he had confessed to aiding actively the enemy armed forces in the guise of a civilian. His excuse for his espionage activities was a poor one, but luckily for him he had not caused the death of any member of the IRA up to the time of his arrest. Mainly because of this he was not sentenced to death, but ordered to leave the country within twenty-four hours. His house was to be burned and his lands and possessions were declared forfeited to the state. Until the Government of the Republic could decide as to their permanent disposition, his lands were to be divided amongst his workers and other local landless men, as sanctioned by the West Cork Brigade. He appeared to be surprised and relieved that he was not to be shot.

He had hardly been returned to his room when Jack Corkery announced that the sentries had held up the postman calling to deliver letters. This was an unwelcome intrusion, for this man was not considered friendly, although there was no evidence of actual hostility against him. If the postman were held a prisoner a search would be made for him, and he would surely be tracked to Burgatia House. If he were released and allowed to travel his rounds, he might mention our presence, or at worst, he might deliberately inform the enemy, although it was difficult to believe anyone capable of such treachery.

He was brought in for a talk. He was an ex-British regular soldier who had served previous to and through the 1914–1918 war. He was emphatic that he was not hostile to the IRA although he was not an active supporter of the independence movement. It was none of his business and he did not want to be mixed up in anything. If he was released he would travel his rounds and never divulge to anyone the presence of the IRA at Burgatia House. Holding a Bible in his hand, he solemnly swore not to inform anyone of our presence for twenty-four hours. I took the plunge and released him at 12.30 p.m.

At 2.30 Tom Moloney and James Hayes, two of the best Volunteers of the local company, arrived. They reported that there was no unusual enemy activity in the town up to 2 p.m. An hour later they were sent back and told to report again after dark. At 4 p.m. the sentries reported that Black and Tans carrying rifles were moving along the road in front of the house and that lorries of enemy military were also arriving. In a few minutes it was reported that some Black and Tans were moving in the woods on our western flank. The column immediately took up the already allocated defence positions around the house and within it. The Volunteers had the strictest orders not to show themselves or reply to any enemy fire until the whistle signal was given. It was clear that the enemy was acting on accurate information and our position looked bad. There was no escape to the south as the Atlantic barred the way and the enemy were already north and west of the column. There was only a possibility that the way to the east was still open, as although the British were not yet visible in that direction they could be lining fire positions on the Owenahincha Road, out of view of Burgatia House. If this proved to be correct the encirclement would be completed, and there appeared to be little else the IRA column could do but wait two hours until darkness and then attempt a breakthrough. But there were two major considerations against waiting. One was the shortage of rifle ammunition. If the column, which had only forty rounds for each rifle, had to fight off British assaults for two hours, it would have no ammunition left for an attempted breakthrough. This shortage of .303 was a haunting nightmare to the commander since the flying column was first formed. Visions of such an encirclement as was now in progress were ever present, and one imagined the last IRA rounds being fired and then the butchering as the helpless column was being finished off. The other consideration was the certainty that, by the time darkness had set in, large British reinforcements would have arrived for the kill and the flying column would have to fight its way through many times the number of the initial encircling force.

A few minutes after they were spotted the British opened fire from the road wall and the woods, smashing the windows but hitting none of the IRA, who lay securely under cover. They continued to volley as I directed one section to prepare to double to the east, to hold the Owenahincha Road at all costs until the remainder of the column passed through. Another section of six riflemen, under Jim Murphy, was detailed to be ready to push west and north to cross the main road if the British retired in disorder. He was to remain in position, holding a gap for seven minutes, so that if the section probing to the east met with opposition, the column could escape north into better fighting country. Thus the flying column would have an alternative line of retirement. The order to move could not be given to those probing sections as yet, because the enemy was certain to observe them from his firing positions. It was planned to lull the British into a sense of false security by withholding any reply to their fire, draw them towards the house from their safe positions, surprise them with heavy fire and, while they were retreating in disorder, push out two sections to probe and hold the escape lines.

After the enemy had been firing for a few minutes, some emerged and moved cautiously towards the house. Periodically they halted, lay down, fired and receiving no answer advanced a further short distance. They appeared puzzled at this lack of reply and some must have thought that the IRA column was but an informer's dream. One group was advancing up the avenue. They were bolder than the others and it was clear we would have to open fire on them before their comrades had come as close as we had hoped. As they advanced still closer, the whistle was blown and thirty IRA rifles opened fire. As the British turned and ran, the order was given to the probing sections to move and they doubled off to the east and west. The remainder of the column kept on firing on the retreating British, who ran helter-skelter back to the road and woods. The enemy did not even halt at their original fire positions, but crossed the road into the fields a quarter of a mile away from Burgatia House, where they re-formed later. Some few of them had fallen and lay close to the ground.

The success of the column's waiting tactics to surprise

and demoralise the encirclers was beyond all expectations. Without any doubt all the IRA could have followed and kept the British on the retreat had they so desired. But I was not only satisfied but very thankful to be allowed to escape from a position that had looked bad before the British had retreated. Hearing no sounds of shooting from the east, Section Nos 2 and 3 were ordered to proceed as rapidly as possible past the advance section to a point over two miles away. They brought with them our only casualty – Volunteer Brennan, who was badly wounded in the leg – the mine and a saddled horse commandeered from the loyalist. This horse was to serve with the column until its death some months afterwards. The remaining sections continued firing at the positions into which the enemy had disappeared. Five minutes later this covering section was also withdrawn, and the whole column, except Jim Murphy's section, which was to rejoin us later, united at a rendezvous two miles east of Burgatia House. As we reached this assembly point we could hear the noise of another rifle attack being opened on our late billet by the reorganised British. We continued to move east without delay, avoiding the main road so as not to clash with their reinforcements. Safely over Kilruane Bridge, the flying column was sent on to billet at Kilbree, within two miles of the Clonakilty garrison, as such a location was deemed to be outside the starting point for the enemy round-up expected at latest at dawn on the following day. Jim Hurley and Con O'Leary, Company Captain of Ardfield, and I, with three rifles, returned towards Burgatia and approached the house in darkness. After cautiously circling the building we entered through an unlocked back door and found the house unoccupied. Piling furniture and beds high in two large rooms and sprinkling well with paraffin, we set the building on fire and moved quickly towards Rosscarbery, where we knew the enemy troops and Black and Tans had assembled. Half a mile from the village we waited behind a ditch to fire on them as they travelled out to investigate the burning building. We waited for over an hour but they did not appear, although the blaze of the burning building lit up the darkness and was visible for many miles. At 10 p.m. we again moved on to Shorten's Cross over by the church, up the School Hill and down into the outskirts of Rosscarbery. We halted at Caim Hill. Below us a hundred yards near the 'Star' were a few of many lorries and a hundred yards further on was the Black and Tan barracks.

Crouched behind a wall, we could see steel-helmeted soldiers occasionally as they moved into the glare of the headlights of one of the lorries, which for some reason or other remained lighted. We opened fire on the soldiers and then at the back of the barracks. We had fired about five rounds each before their weak answering fire commenced, but by the time we had used ten or twelve, their reply was not alone heavy, but fairly accurate. Evidently the flashes from our rifles had been observed and the enemy were knocking sparks off the stone wall as they blazed away in our direction. Sheltered by the wall we ran up the hill and back down by the school, on to Cahermore Cross, through Sam's Cross and so to Kilbree, where we found the flying column at 4 a.m.

The question as to whether I was wise in occupying Burgatia House is, I suppose, a debatable one. That we had come through safely and the reasons why we avoided defeat, are less debatable. Over and above all was the incredible stupidity of the British to attack frontally and from a flank, without closing the only other line of escape. Had they done this, remained on the defensive, and awaited reinforcements, the column could hardly have got through without appalling losses, if at all. Secondly, the decision to hold the IRA fire was sound and indeed essential. Had we replied to their opening fire they would have stayed on the defensive and not suffered the subsequent surprise and the headlong retreat which gave us our opportunity. Thirdly, the cool and disciplined behaviour of those officers and men of the flying column throughout the action, and particularly during the time when they must have thought they were trapped and were not allowed to fire back. Had any of those IRA disobeyed orders or 'panicked' the end would have been very different.

The return to burn Burgatia House and to fire on the enemy in Rosscarbery was not an act of bravado, but part of a calculated policy. The owner had been told that his house was to be burned, and if we had waited to carry out this sentence, the house would be heavily guarded, or more likely another well-nigh impregnable enemy barracks. It had to be done that night or not at all. The attack on the enemy in Rosscarbery was equally imperative as a matter of prestige. Nothing could alter the fact that the flying column had to retreat from Burgatia House and some counteraction had to be attempted that night. The overwhelmingly powerful British propaganda was sure to claim that our retirement was a defeat, which it certainly was not. But the fact that some of the column had some hours after the retirement returned, burned the house and fired on their enemies in the town, was likely to place the engagement in its true light.

The *Cork Examiner* of the following day contained the British version of the fight. The British stated that one hundred and fifty members of the IRA under Michael Collins had assembled to attack Rosscarbery Barracks, and that six were killed and their bodies carried away. It was only when court claims for compensation were made at a later date, that some of their losses were allowed to leak out. More interesting in view of the many published British calumnies on the behaviour of the IRA was the statement of the wife of the owner of Burgatia House, published in the *Cork Examiner* of February 4th, 1921:

> Asked about the demeanour of the men, Mrs. ____ said they were all right and did not treat her roughly. Most of the men seemed to be very hungry and were cooking all night in the kitchen. She was kept 17 hours in her bedroom. She was released when the first shot was fired and was ordered to the basement for shelter. Mrs. ____'s narrative was supported by her husband. He added that shortly before firing began, he was blindfolded and questioned as to how many men servants he had. He was led into a large

> room to be 'courtmartialled' by three men, one of whom sat in an armchair and said he was an officer. Mr. ____ had no opinion to offer about the burning of his house.

The household left Ireland immediately. The postman was also evacuated by the British military reinforcements. After I had released him, he had curtailed his rounds, returned to the Rosscarbery post office, dumped his postbag and run straight to the Black and Tan barracks to inform on the flying column. We traced him to England but he kept moving from city to city. He returned to Belfast for a short period, but again crossed to Britain where we heard he died later.

# 14

# DESCENT ON SKIBBEREEN

THE British commenced the anticipated round-up on the morning of the 3rd and the column lay all that day behind them in billets near Clonakilty. At one o'clock on the following morning it marched after them, reaching Reenascreena before dawn when they had already raided that district. For two days the column trailed them as they scoured the countryside. We were far safer moving behind those strong forces than in front of them; nevertheless the column had to tread warily. It was as if one were venturing out on a frozen lake, stepping cautiously, testing the ice and constantly expecting a weak patch to break and precipitate the skater into the icy waters. All through the existence of the flying column this policy proved its worth when evading action with overwhelmingly powerful British forces.

On the 6th I left the flying column to return east to attend a brigade council meeting at John O'Mahony's, Ballinavard, Kilmeen, Clonakilty. This meeting commenced about three in the evening and continued for twelve hours. When the usual routine of reports from battalions on staff duties, organisation, training, intelligence and armaments was dealt with, three directives occupied the meeting for many hours. These were so indicative of our efforts to develop and extend the fight against the British that they are given here in some detail.

The first was that of spies and informers. It was clear to us long before the close of 1920 that the enemy had a fairly extensive spy service amongst civilians throughout the brigade area. Accurate information only could have enabled the British to kill several and capture many West Cork members of the IRA. We had up to the time of this meeting shot four of those agents, but we knew that as yet we had barely dented their organisation. Unless this ring of spies and informers was destroyed, the existence of the West Cork IRA would soon be terminated. Therefore, battalion commanders were ordered not to kill, but to procure evidence of the guilt of suspected persons without delay.

The second directive was to intensify raids on mail carriers and post offices for letters to members of the British Army, police officers and suspected persons. In particular we wanted the home addresses of the Auxiliaries, the Black and Tans and the Essex Regiment. Battalion commanders were instructed to ensure that there would be no looseness in those matters. Letters were to be opened only by a responsible battalion officer, and anything learned of the intimate affairs of suspected persons was to be kept strictly secret. Everything of importance was to be forwarded to the senior brigade officers.

The third directive to all battalions concerned the destruction of railways and roads. This matter was not as simple as it may appear on the surface. We had the personnel to destroy all roads and the whole railway communications system within the brigade area in a few nights, had we so desired. This would have paralysed the enemy transport services, forcing him to operate on foot until extensive repairs were carried out. But the destruction of roads and railways to that extent would also be a double-edged weapon, reacting against our own people, preventing their movements too, stopping the transport of essential goods, destroying trade, causing unemployment and shortages. In a critical situation we would not have hesitated to carry out this complete destruction, but up to February 1921 the need had not arisen. And the IRA had always to remember that the ordinary people were the bastion on which it was built, and that no unnecessary distress should be caused to them. A blow against the people was a blow struck against the IRA itself.

A detailed plan had to be drafted for each battalion. After careful consideration of all the circumstances, certain railway bridges and road bridges were selected for destruction. In addition to these, many roads were to be effectively trenched. Wherever a road bridge was to be destroyed or a road cut, the local IRA had to provide an alternative route for the residents of the district. This was effected mainly by cutting an opening in the ditch before and behind the road break, large enough for a horse and cart, but not a military vehicle, to pass through. Immediately inside those openings, two hundred square yards of ground was to be dug up to a depth of over a foot, so that if the enemy extended the opening, the wheels of his armoured cars and lorries would sink in the muddy fields, fail to grip, and thus bog down the military vehicle. The main line of the Cork, Bandon and South Coast Railway was not to be damaged, as it was the supply line for the people of West Cork, but all branch lines from it were to be put out of service. While this was an inconvenience to a number of people, their supplies could be drawn by horse cart from the nearest main line station. In all seventy-three separate breaches, road and rail, were scheduled for the nights of the 16th, 17th and 18th of February.

After the brigade meeting, I travelled back to the flying column. On the following morning the tactics of the column again changed over from the defensive to the offensive, as all the enemy reinforcements had returned to their own stations and the local garrisons had resumed raiding activities. We occupied Leap village, after receiving information that a company of the Skibbereen garrison was about to raid it, but they did not come nearer than three miles to the village on that day.

On the following morning we marched for Skibbereen. This town had then a population of nearly three thousand. Its inhabitants were a race apart from the sturdy people of West

Cork. They were different and with a few exceptions were spineless, slouching through life meek and tame, prepared to accept ruling and domination from any clique or country, provided they were left to vegetate in peace. Like the opium eaters of the East they were incapable of enthusiasm or effort for anything more strenuous than promenading or gossip, so it is little wonder that there were only four members of the IRA in the whole town, three of whom had been arrested. About a dozen other inhabitants were Sinn Féiners. The town was cursed with two cliques. One was the strong British loyalist group, which lorded it over the supine natives. The other was the more despicable group of local native politicians, who, invoking the names of Parnell, Redmond, Caitlin ni Houlihan and Mother Ireland, degraded the public life of this unfortunate town. These cringed to the army of occupation, and the loyalists deprecated, so very carefully, the national struggle for freedom, and pursued their petty meannesses under the guise of what they called Catholicism. They were not dangerous to the Republican movement as they lacked the energy and gumption to be actively hostile to anything. They were, however, it must be admitted, a true reflex of the people they represented, because if Satan himself appeared in the Skibbereen of 1920–21, the great majority would doff their hats to him, and if he wagged his tail once in anger, he was sure to be elected high in the poll to the Skibbereen District Council.

No one can explain the origin of the blight that destroyed

the spirit of man in the majority of the dwellers of that town. It was not a modern one, for Skibbereen can claim that in the so-called famine of 1846–47 more Skibbereen men died and saw their wives and children die of starvation than in any other town in Ireland, while the British Ascendancy were allowed to seize their food without the slightest opposition. O'Donovan Rossa even failed to make the male population of Skibbereen stand upright. A native of Rosscarbery, he went to work in Skibbereen and founded the 'Phoenix Society', but he had to rely chiefly for active support on the manhood of the parishes around the town.

Because of this no praise is too high for the four Volunteers and their dozen supporters who tried to keep the flag of resistance to the British flying within the town of Skibbereen. There were some splendid Volunteers in the surrounding districts. Led by Con Connolly, Sam Kingston, Pat O'Driscoll, Paddy O'Sullivan, Mick O'Donovan, Tim O'Sullivan, Pat Sheehy, Stephen Holland, Dan O'Brien, Pat Cadogan, Stephen O'Brien, Cornelius Bohane, Christy Kelly and Dan O'Neill, they did fine work during the national struggle. This battalion had several first-class company captains, notably Dan O'Donovan of Leap and Daniel O'Driscoll of Drimoleague.

Skibbereen was garrisoned by several companies of the King's Liverpool Regiment and about eighty Black and Tans. The military commander was Colonel Hudson, a good type of British officer. Up to the time of the departure of the King's Liverpools after the Truce, the behaviour of Colonel Hudson, his officers and men was exemplary in all the circumstances. They committed no murders, treated their prisoners humanely, and never burned a house except under a martial law direction from the British divisional headquarters. Colonel Hudson appeared to have a contempt for the Black and Tan garrison, and on many occasions saved IRA prisoners from ill-treatment and even death. On November 30th, 1920, Maurice Donegan, Ralph Keyes, Seán Cotter and Cornelius O'Sullivan were arrested. When they were brought in the Black and Tans howled for their blood, but Colonel Hudson asserted his authority, took the prisoners into his custody, treated them decently and had them sent on to a military internment camp. There is little doubt but that the colonel saved their lives.

It should be clearly understood that this regiment was very active against us and continuously raided the countryside. They were our enemies, but fair ones. In my opinion, because of the better type which officered them, the King's Liverpools were far more dangerous to meet in action than Percival's murderous Essex, or the King's Own Scottish Borderers, who were also stationed in our area.

Let the *Cork Examiner* of February 11th give the daily press version of our visit to the town of Skibbereen:

> A large force of civilians, 150 to 200, swooped down on Skibbereen to-night (9th) and held a large portion of the town for two hours. Shortly before 9 p.m. a number of armed men took possession of the corner of Ilen Street and Bridge Street and held

> up everyone passing into the town. One group was made to sing 'The Soldier's Song.' Several hundred men, women and children and even soldiers were held up in this way. This continued until after ten o'clock when the raiders fired several volleys and left. They commandeered horses and sidecars, the property of Mr. Minihane. In one of those they took away three soldiers whom they blindfolded. At 4 a.m. the soldiers returned with one horse, none the worse for their enforced absence. The sentry at the Town Hall was fired at but the bullet passed over his head.

The daily newspaper, the *Cork Examiner*, was not a supporter of the IRA and it was also subject to British censorship, so some of the details of its report require correction. The strength of the flying column had been increased to fifty-five riflemen and not one hundred and fifty. Forty-three of those were placed in ambush positions a little over half a mile from the town. Twelve men and the flying column commander moved into Skibbereen, hoping to engage a patrol. This group searched the streets to within a hundred yards of the military and Black and Tan posts but encountered no armed enemy. The enemy posts were then fired on and the small IRA party retired back a short distance to the Ilen Street–Bridge Street corner. The nearby street lamps were shot away so as to darken our defensive positions. Hundreds of residents attempting to get to their homes had to be held up by us for their own safety, as they would be in danger of being caught between two fires if the British emerged to engage us. Some unarmed soldiers of the King's Regiment were also taken prisoners. Naturally these were frightened at first, but I assured them of their safety and good treatment and that they would be returned to barracks on the following morning. Three of them were put on a sidecar and sent off under escort to Maguire's of Caheragh. The quartermaster received instructions to feed them well and buy them a drink. Those soldiers knew they were being treated so because of their fair attitude to IRA prisoners. During the night they were well looked after by their escort and were given numerous drinks. All three were keen singers and learned verses of our national songs from their escort, with which they regaled the residents of Skibbereen as they drove back merrily to their barracks on the following morning.

Among the civilians held were a few leaders of the Skibbereen District Council. One in particular was lectured strongly, as this council was practically the only one in Munster which still sent the minutes of its meetings to Dublin Castle and not to the Department of Home Affairs of our own government. He snivelled quite a lot, saying he was not responsible but he would raise the matter at the next meeting of the Skibbereen District Council. One of the IRA party suggested to this local politician that he might like to prove his loyalty to the Irish Republic by standing up on an empty porter barrel at the corner and singing 'The Soldier's Song'. True to Skibbereen form this gentleman promptly did so in his cracked voice to the gaping crowd of his constituents, who knew quite well, as we did, that the singer detested everything that 'The Soldier's Song' symbolised.

For two hours we held most of the town. Shots were occasionally fired towards the enemy posts while hundreds of the held-up residents, crouching behind safe corners, looked on in amazement at this impertinence by a handful of the IRA. Everything was done to draw out the military, but all failed. Instead, after the first shots, all their outside sentries were withdrawn into the buildings. Exactly two hours after our entry into the town, final volleys were fired and we moved back to the main ambush position. I now felt sure that they would have to make at least the gesture of following us as prestige demanded some such move. But we waited in vain for over four hours. Not alone did they not follow us, but they did not emerge from their barracks until the following day.

The flying column reached billets at dawn on the 10th, and that evening we circled north. In the forenoon of Saturday February 12th, I borrowed a respectable overcoat, and a member of the Cumann na mBan drove with me in a fast horse and trap through Drimoleague, so that I could get some idea of the surroundings of the Black and Tan barracks there. It looked formidable and there was little cover around it for an attacking party. That night thirty riflemen of the column were brought into Drimoleague to attempt the destruction of this barracks, although I was anything but optimistic about the effectiveness of our mine after past failures.

The story of the attempt is soon told. The mine was properly laid against the barrack door and the exploder plunger driven home. A weak explosion followed which did not even burst the timber box encasing the explosives. We fired about sixty rounds altogether at the impregnable post, and to save expenditure of our precious ammunition withdrew within five minutes of the mine failure. The only luck we had in this attempt, apart from suffering no casualties through enemy return fire, was that one of our bullets must have gone through a narrow loophole, as the British officially announced that a Sergeant Bransfield had been wounded during the attack. Going back down the road I vowed never again to risk one man's life in such attacks until I was definitely assured that we had a properly constructed mine which would be effective.

The flying column moved rapidly east and then south to avoid another round-up, and on the morning of the 16th a dispatch reached me with very bad news. It concerned a train ambush at Upton Station on the previous day. Lieutenant Patrick O'Sullivan, Raheen, Upton, Lieutenant John Phelan, whose parents lived in Liverpool, and Section Commander Batt Falvey of Ballymurphy, Upton, were killed in action. Lieutenant Daniel O'Mahony of Belrose (our headquarters for such a long time) was seriously wounded and Charlie Hurley himself was wounded in the face. Six civilians, including a woman, had been killed during the fight. In that day's press the British had announced officially that six soldiers were wounded during the Upton attack. I reached Charlie early the following morning and his eyes were again sad and worried as they looked at me from his bandaged face.

Subsequently I heard the account of the action from

Charlie and later from Tom Kelleher. During the ten days previous to February 15th, except Sunday, twenty soldiers of the Essex travelled each day in one carriage on the evening train from Cork to Bandon. Charlie decided to attack this inviting target. He mustered thirteen others, including Tom Kelleher, Flor Begley and Denis Doolan. Seven had rifles and each of the other seven had either one or two revolvers or automatics. On February 15th those soldiers left Cork as usual in one compartment, but at Kinsale Junction they were joined by about thirty others who distributed themselves in five or six groups throughout the train, and mingled with the civilian passengers. All were heavily armed. Two IRA scouts had been detailed to join the train at Kinsale Junction so that when it reached Upton they could signal to the attacking party the position of the carriage in which the enemy were travelling. Through a regrettable misadventure those two men did not travel, and when the train stopped at Upton Station a few of the IRA party opened the attack on a group of soldiers in the carriage in front of them.

The British replied and the unequal fight was on. Before Charlie could extricate his party, three were killed and Dan O'Mahony, soon to die, and he himself wounded. Through some miracle the nine unwounded and the two wounded got away across country in small parties, with the British following close up behind. Eventually the IRA reached safety but only when all were exhausted. There can be little doubt that Charlie Hurley, physically weak owing to his wound, would never have avoided death on that day were it not for the loyalty and courage of the man who helped him, Tom Kelleher. Likewise, Dan O'Mahony was helped by the others during their retreat. The attack at Upton was an IRA reverse, but it did not fail through the lack of courage or the sincerity of the men who tried and lost.

Again, what will the Irish state historians write of this attempt on the British at Upton on February 15th, 1921? I do not know, but it is easy to anticipate an opinion that the attack should not have been attempted by Charlie Hurley with the meagre forces and armament at his disposal. It will be forgotten that had the IRA scouts travelled as arranged, or had there been no extra troops distributed throughout the train, the attack, in all probability, would have been a success. Charlie Hurley was not alone a fearless soldier, but a good field commander. He was at least the equal in this respect of any other officer in the south of Ireland. He was no military genius, but neither was any one of the rest of us. But this great patriot and lion-hearted soldier seemed to be dogged by bad luck, and for a long period nothing would go right for him. It was uncanny, and he was very much aware himself of this hoodoo. Although he tried to hide it, one could see that the Upton reverse had seared him. A strange mixture of gentleness and ruthlessness, of compassion and of sternness, he mourned deeply for his dead comrades of the Upton train attack and for the dead civilians, whom he did not know, until he followed them a month later riddled by British bullets. Why Charlie took this to heart so much none of us could ever understand, for had any other one of us been in charge the result, in the circumstances, would have been no better, and perhaps much worse.

# 15

# THE TWELVE DARK DAYS

I RETURNED to the flying column on that evening, the 17th, and received more bad news. Four other Volunteers had been killed by the British in the Kilbrittain Company area. They were Volunteer Con McCarthy, Kilanetig, Ballinadee; Volunteer John McGrath, Rathclarin, Kilbrittain; Volunteer Timothy Connolly, Fearnagerk, Kilbrittain; and Volunteer Jeremiah O'Neill, Knockpogue, Kilbrittain. Those four IRA men were cutting a trench in the road at Crois na Leanbh, Kilbrittain, when they were surprised by a force of the Essex Regiment and all four were shot dead. How the Essex succeeded in surprising them is not known, for true to form this British regiment left no one alive to tell the story. The bodies of the four boys were found on the morning of the 16th stretched together near the unfinished cutting. All were shot through the head.

Two of those Volunteers undoubtedly had rifles as there were strict orders that in the general destruction of communications scheduled for those nights, working parties were to be protected against surprise. This order cannot have been enforced at Crois na Leanbh. Perhaps the two riflemen came in to help the other two in the digging, but that is only conjecture. Anyway, those four were dead, and they died for Ireland as surely as did their comrades at Kilmichael or in any other major engagement. Their deaths were a heavy price to pay for emphasising once more the lesson that was continually being dinned into the minds of the West Cork IRA from the commencement of hostilities: security and more security.

The *Cork Examiner* issues of February 17th and 18th bore testimony as to how effectively the West Cork IRA had carried out the instructions to destroy communications. Its issue of the 19th stated: 'Owing to the blowing up of bridges, all vehicular traffic in several districts of West Cork is still very dislocated.' In all, seventy breaches were made in railway lines, bridges and roads throughout the area. There was no interference with our destruction parties except that at Crois na Leanbh.

The first half of February 1921 was a black period for the brigade, for in twelve days we had lost eleven officers and men killed. In addition to the three at Upton and the four at Crois na Leanbh, three others were murdered and one was accidentally shot dead. Lieutenant Patrick Crowley, Kilbrittain, who was due for promotion to rank of battalion commandant, a pioneer of the movement and a most intelligent and courageous officer, was killed on February 4th at Maryboro', Timoleague. He was ill in bed at O'Neill's house when the Essex raided the district in strength. There was little hope of hiding him in that house of all others, for the O'Neill brothers and sisters were famous throughout the south of Ireland for their active services in the national struggle. Paddy ran from the house but was fired on, wounded, and then the Essex, recognising him, finished him off on the ground.

The second to die during this twelve-day period was Section Commander Patrick O'Driscoll, of Mohana, Skibbereen. When I returned from the brigade council meeting on the morning of the 7th, at five o'clock, I went to bed. Worried about the safety of the flying column, I got up again at 7 a.m. to visit the sentries and have a general look around. In addition to sentries, as a further security measure, the flying column was always protected against surprise by an outer ring of scouts drawn from the local company. It was the practice to arm those scouts with revolvers from the flying column, so that if unable to slip back to the billets to report an approaching enemy, they could fire shots and give the alarm. After visiting the column sentries, I went to inspect this outer ring of scouts, just as a relief was in progress. Pat O'Driscoll was relieving another man as I came up. To ensure that Pat knew his full responsibilities, I asked the man coming off duty to detail his duties for the relief scout. They stood only a foot apart, facing each other, and

I was close to both as the scout commenced his statement of duties. About halfway through his recital, a shot rang out and Pat O'Driscoll swayed towards me. Catching him I lowered him gently, but he was dead before I placed him on the ground. I turned to the man who had shot him. His face was a mask of consternation and he had dropped the Webley revolver. I spoke to him, but he could not answer and then, with a moan, he, too, collapsed, for the man he had accidentally shot was his best friend. I had not noticed him unconsciously fingering the trigger of his revolver, which had a very light spring, as he detailed his duties. It was unpleasant for me to feel that it was the presence of the column commander which had made the scout so nervous that, unknowingly, he had pressed the trigger and shot Pat O'Driscoll. Incidentally, the only other fatal accidents with firearms in West Cork during the Anglo-Irish War were those which caused the deaths of Captain Jeremiah O'Mahony of Coppeen and Volunteer Timothy Whooley of Currycrowley, Ballineen. Jeremiah O'Mahony, a first-class officer who had fought valiantly at Kilmichael, was accidentally shot when cleaning his rifle in December 1920, at his home at Paddock, Enniskeane. Young Timothy Whooley, an active and efficient Volunteer, died under similar circumstances on March 22nd, 1921, near Shannonvale, Clonakilty.

The third and fourth deaths of that dark twelve-day period were the brothers, Volunteers Patrick and James Coffey of Breaghna, Enniskeane, who were murdered in bed by Auxiliaries and Black and Tans on February 14th. Those two boys were unarmed, and were splendid Volunteers. The murderers on this occasion were led directly to the room where their victims were sleeping by two masked civilians, obviously local men and members of the British espionage circle.

Thus, eleven members of our brigade had been killed in twelve days, while we had failed to kill a single one of the killers. It is true that there was a number of them wounded, and it was not our fault as we had tried hard enough to engage them at Skibbereen, Drimoleague and at other places. The morale of any unit was bound to suffer if fatal casualties continued to be caused to it, while none were being inflicted on its enemies. There was, too, a limit to the number of fatal casualties which any area could endure. So the column lay in ambush around Bandon on the 19th and 21st for the Essex, but without results.

It was now clear that the column would have to go into Bandon town if the account with the Essex was to be squared in the immediate future. Furthermore it would have to go in before curfew time, which was 10 p.m. There was a consuming hate in our hearts for those Essex soldiers. Their brutalities when killing defenceless IRA prisoners were incredible. They never showed mercy to the wounded, the sick or the unarmed. There was never a unit in any army in any campaign which had disgraced the profession of arms as did those vulgar monsters who were the dregs of the underworld of London.

They had almost killed in us, too, the virtue of mercy. From January 1921 I was to know no pity for this Essex Regiment, though I was to grant mercy to other British forces who were our prisoners, but against whom murders were not proved. The orders issued by me in 1921 were to shoot every member of the Essex at sight, armed or unarmed, and not to accept their surrender under any circumstances. Up to then those troops were immune from attack when unarmed and off duty. On their return from a foray where they might have killed unarmed Irishmen and burned out houses, they would go out immune to public houses or promenade outside the suburbs with the few unfortunate women who alone would consort with them. They felt they were safe while unarmed as we had tried to play the game of war by the rules accepted by the civilised world. But now immunity was at an end.

Napoleon is reputed to have said, 'There are two levers for moving men: interest and fear.' There is surely a third and higher one, but that is not germane to this account of terror and counter-terror. No appeals could stop the inhumanities of the Essex Regiment, and the West Cork IRA had but one lever left: that of fear. From February 1921 terror would be met by counter-terror. The Essex, the Auxiliaries and all British terrorist forces would be destroyed as far as our strength was capable of killing them. Units like the King's Liverpool Regiment, who had behaved reasonably, were not to be interfered with when unarmed and off duty.

On the afternoon of February 23rd, forty-four members of the flying column were moved to within two miles of Bandon. Here they were split into a main party of thirty and two sections of seven each. Nearly all carried revolvers in addition to rifles.

The two smaller sections were to enter the suburbs from the Dunmanway road end at 8.30, and when shooting started in the town they were to flush out and shoot any Essex they could find. The main party was to enter the town by Cork Road, primarily to attack the patrol of forty-four which paraded the town nightly before curfew. The point of attack was to be the junction of North Main Street and Bandon Bridge. Several houses, including the Bank and the Freemason Lodge, known as the Allin Institute, were to be occupied by the column. These houses were two hundred yards from the military barracks, and somewhat less from the Black and Tan post at the Devonshire Arms Hotel. The third enemy post was about three hundred yards on the other side of the town at the end of the South Main Street.

Arriving at 8.20 p.m. in Cork Road, two hundred yards from the place of attack, the flying column was halted and residents were not allowed to move into the centre of the town. They were told to stay indoors for their own safety. I had decided to enter the town first to endeavour to locate the patrol. During my absence John Lordan was to take charge and Mick Crowley was to follow me at a distance of thirty yards. His duty was to signal back to the main party when it was considered time that they should move into the ambush positions. Mick was to halt at the corner of Watergate Street and remain in touch with the main party. The fact that the column commander undertook this task of locating the patrol should not be misunderstood. It was not a question of his being more competent than any other officer or man he might select to do this work. The reason was that the accurate timing of the entry of the main party to its ambush stations was all important, and nobody could be responsible for this decision but the commander. If the column went in long before the patrol was to pass, their presence would certainly become known to the enemy. Even if no one deliberately informed, residents, by putting up shutters, closing doors and scurrying to safety, would indicate our presence.

We dared not occupy positions more than five minutes before the arrival of the patrol. Had I sent some other officer in, a delay in decision would be inevitable until he returned. By going in myself the decision could be made immediately I had learned the whereabouts of the patrol. The risk I was taking was no greater than that of any column member. Against my doing so was the fact that as I was wearing an IRA uniform – tunic, pants, leggings and full field equipment – I was certain to be recognised by the townspeople, but this could not be helped. The moon was so bright that the light was that of early dusk on a summer's day.

Leaving Mick Crowley near the Allin Institute, I walked across Bandon Bridge, past many civilians who knew me. Near the post office I met some of our supporters. Telling them I was trying to get out of the town as I was alone, I asked where the patrol was. They gave me all particulars, saying it should pass back over the bridge towards the barracks in about five or seven minutes. This was a stroke of luck. I left them to return and instruct Mick Crowley to bring the column into their ambush positions. As I came to within four or five yards of North Main Street corner, I heard sounds of English voices, laughter and the footsteps of marching men, coming from immediately around the corner. I knew they were British armed forces, but I had no idea as to their numbers nor whether they were soldiers or Black and Tans.

The human mind in such a situation is capable of many diverse thoughts within a few moments. I thought of the official enemy order to all Black and Tans that revolvers were not to be carried in holsters, but in the hands or stuck loosely in tunics between the second and third buttons. I thought of escape from this bunch of killers, but the cowardly strain that is in me as in all other men was quickly subdued when my reason flashed the warning that if I turned and ran I would certainly be shot in the back before I had crossed the exposed bridge to the cover of houses on the other side. I thought, 'Here it is at last', as standing in the middle of the footpath I saw five Black and Tans walking in line, two on the footpath, and three on the road, round the corner a few yards away.

The gunfight commenced, and that fearless and most competent officer, Mick Crowley, joined in from his position. The first to fall was the terrorist who was already swinging his revolver in his hand as he came into view. A second staggered across the road and also fell to the ground. I missed a third with a left-handed snap shot as he sprinted past to the other side of the road. The fourth had bolted back for the barracks as the first shot was fired. The fifth, who was yelling unintelligibly, as indeed were all the others, had dropped to the ground unhurt. Now he leaped up and ran round the corner before I could fire at him. Then I was guilty of the most senseless act of my life, for I ran after him. He had a seven yards' start as I turned the corner. He was of medium height but heavily built and his revolver was in his right hand as he thundered on towards the barracks. I gained rapidly on him and when only three or four paces behind, I pushed the short Webley revolver I had in my left hand into my tunic pocket, retaining the Colt automatic in the right. I have never understood since why I did not shoot him in that race up North Main Street as I was never more than a few yards behind him and I could not have missed him had I pulled the trigger. But call it blood lust arising out of hate, madness or what you will, I wanted to get my hands on him, hence the freeing of my left hand of the Webley revolver. It never occurred to me, and apparently not to him, that all he had to do to ensure his safety was to turn and pull the trigger. Sixty yards from the scene of the gunfight I grabbed his left shoulder with my left hand. Fright crazed he squealed and turned like a hare in the nearest door, which I shot past before turning to follow him. As I ran into the small shop he was entering the kitchen immediately behind. Jumping the low counter gate, I too was in the kitchen a few yards from him, when common sense returned and I fired. His revolver clattered to the ground as he fell dead, but he was shot again to make certain that his terrorist days were over.

I now looked at the other occupants of the small kitchen. The woman had collapsed, and at first I thought that the bullet had passed through the Black and Tan and killed her too, but she had only fainted. Turning to the oldish man still sitting motionless in his chair, I got another surprise, for he was John Marshall, one of our special intelligence agents, who had come out to the country on many occasions to report directly to me. Of all the houses in Bandon, this Black and Tan would choose that of one of our intelligence officers in which to die. Marshall still lives in Bandon, hale and hearty at the age of eighty-four. After informing him that he could tell the British any story he considered best and that he could say he recognised me if it kept him out of trouble with the enemy, I ran out to the shop door. The engines of the armoured cars in the nearby military barracks square were roaring and the sounds of some shots came in from the Dunmanway road. But most disturbing of all were the shots coming up the street, which was my only way out. Those bullets knocking sparks off the flagstones were being fired by my own column. Mick Crowley had called it in and led by himself and John Lordan, were searching for their commanding officer, who had disappeared. They were attempting a clearance of any enemy who might still be on the street before pushing on towards the barracks. I hesitated at the doorway for a moment only. Although I had the horrible thought of being killed by bullets from my own men, the fear of the British armoured cars coming at us forced me to rush into the street and shout at the column that it was I and to stop shooting. Racing back, I immediately retired them up Cork Road and out of the town. Four hundred yards outside the town we occupied ambush positions in the hope that the enemy would follow us up. We waited for an hour and a half but they did not appear.

Reaching the rendezvous three miles from Bandon, we found the other two sections waiting. They had flushed out some unarmed Essex, shot two dead and wounded a few others who were running for their barracks. They also had two naval warrant officers of the Bandon garrison prisoners. I interviewed those British navy men. They were armed members of a foreign army of occupation, but were not guilty of the murder of unarmed Irishmen. Before releasing them unharmed, I read them a signed letter, which they promised to deliver to the commanding officer of the Essex in Bandon. There was no copy made of this communication, but it was on the following lines:

> 1. The Essex Regiment has murdered the following unarmed officers and men of the West Cork IRA while they were defenceless prisoners: Lieutenant John Connolly, Captain John Galvin, Lieutenant James O'Donoghue, Section Commander Joseph Begley, Volunteer Patrick Donovan, Volunteer Denis Hegarty and Lieutenant Patrick Crowley. It has also murdered whilst prisoners Volunteer Cornelius McCarthy, Volunteer John McGrath, Volunteer Timothy Crowley and Volunteer Jeremiah O'Neill. Only two of those men were armed when captured.

2. The Essex Regiment has attempted the murders of several members of the IRA.

3. The Essex Regiment has tortured many IRA prisoners and attempted the rape of Irishwomen.

4. The Essex Regiment has burned and destroyed nearly fifty West Cork homes, long before such burnings had become the official policy of the British military government in Ireland.

5. The shoot-up of the occupying forces, including the Essex Regiment, in Bandon tonight will be accepted by you as indicating that henceforth your unit, in common with other terrorists, will be subject to reprisals for every outrage committed by it.

After the release of the naval men, the flying column retired to billets at Newcestown. Although we had not engaged the military patrol, we had killed four of the enemy, wounded four others, and had not ourselves suffered any casualty. This reality of death to the enemy was all that mattered, for as surely as a subject people never got an iota of freedom from the British imperialists without killing British troops, so too was it a fact that the only way to make British troops behave with even a modicum of decency, was to pump those principles of humanity into their bodies with bullets attached. We also took heart from our knowledge that those five Black and Tan warriors, when faced with a fight on their own doorstep, had given a disgraceful exhibition of cowardice and panic. In all they had not fired more than three shots. The pendulum had swung again, and the British were once more at the receiving end. The IRA had evened up to some extent its February account with them.

The daily press of Thursday, February 24th, carried the official British communiqué giving the names of their dead as Constable Frederick W. Perrier, Constable P. J. Kerins, Corporal Stubbs and Private Knight. It gave no details of those we knew for certain were wounded. Needless to say the official statement said they were attacked by a large body of men. It also recorded the release of the naval wireless men. We knew of Perrier by name as a ruffian and a bully, but we did not know until later that it was he who died in Marshall's house.

## 16

# EXECUTION OF SPIES

THIS chapter dealing with British spies and informers has been rewritten. At first I listed the names and addresses of those sixteen British agents who were shot by the West Cork Brigade of the IRA. Then the thought came of the pain such a listing would bring to those traitors' descendants and relatives who are still living. Innocent men and women should not suffer for the sins of their fathers. Already they must have suffered much, and indeed, in truth, one felt for the wives and families of those informers then, though one had no pity for the spies themselves. Therefore, no names will be given in this account of the activities and deaths of those Irish-born traitors. However, the files of the daily press of the first six months of 1921 will supply all particulars, including the official British announcements of the deaths of their agents in West Cork.

Since in 1920 the RIC had resigned in large numbers and

the most actively hostile of those remaining had been shot by the IRA, spies and informers were practically the only source of enemy intelligence. These were the bloodhounds who nosed out the victims for the British murder gangs. From June 1920 they were a menace to the very existence of the Army of the Republic. They had been responsible for the deaths of several members of the IRA and the ill-treatment and arrest of hundreds of others. We had many reports about their activities, but we had hesitated too long to strike at them and we, the brigade officers, must always bear a certain responsibility for the needless deaths of many of our own Volunteers. By January 1921 not a single senior officer was in any doubt as to the seriousness of the menace of this ring of spies. Either those spies and informers would die or the IRA would be wiped out. There was no alternative. The IRA struck on the morning of January 22nd and again on the 24th and by the end of February twelve of those traitors were shot dead. Four others were also shot in the ensuing months before the Truce.

Two resided in the Innishannon, two in the Skibbereen, two in the Timoleague, and one each in the Upton, Carhue, Castletown-Kenneigh, Desertserges, Gaggin, Kilbrittain, Clonakilty, Ballineen, Rosscarbery and Bandon areas. Those British agents can be classified under three headings: paid spies, unpaid informers and ex-British officers. British gold circulated freely throughout Ireland in those years and the enemy paid well for information about the IRA. Those who took this blood money were invariably the most vicious and degraded of the population. The unpaid informers came from the wealthier landowning class who hated the Republican movement and all it stood for. The British organised those to seek out information, and they were more dangerous and successful in their treacherous activity than the paid spy. The reason for this was that such men were usually well educated and intelligent, and some were sincere believers in the policy of British domination and Irish subjection. The remaining class of hostile agents, the ex-British officers, were no less dangerous than the paid spy and unpaid informer. There was a large number of retired British military and naval officers resident in West Cork, and some, while posing as civilians, worked feverishly to destroy the IRA. Nominally retired, they were back again in the active service of king and country.

All the sixteen were not arrested and court-martialled. Some could not be arrested as they were under enemy surveillance, others were armed and tried to fight when the IRA attempted their arrests. The Ballineen spy seriously wounded the officer in charge of the IRA arresting party, before he himself was killed. Both Innishannon spies tried to fight, and one of them succeeded in drilling two holes in the clothes of the arresting IRA officer. One Timoleague spy drew two guns before he was killed. All the guns used by the agents were supplied by the British. Some were shot in their homes and others were intercepted when travelling. Despite suggestions to the contrary, the brigade never sought GHQ sanction for any of those executions. How could it? We had no jails to hold those men, and we dared not put all our evidence in writing because it might be captured en route or at GHQ and expose to certain death our own informants. GHQ during all the conflict never knew of the killing of an informer in West Cork until it read of it in a newspaper. How could those staff officers in Dublin offices judge better as to the guilt of an informer than the officers who had effectively to combat in the field the nefarious results of the traitors' activities? We were not concerned with law and procedures, but with justice and the continued existence of the Irish Republican Army. Here it should be stated that never once did GHQ question orally or in writing any of those executions. There was a tight rein kept on all battalions and no spy was executed without a brigade officer's sanction. There were cases where battalion officers arrested alleged informers, but on investigation by the brigade those men were released. Even at this distance of time, all the conclusive evidence against the executed West Cork traitors cannot be made public, because a fair amount of the testimony on which their deaths were decreed came from some who are still vulnerable to British reprisals. But an instance of the evidence against a paid spy, an unpaid informer and an ex-British officer, can be given here as only IRA personnel were involved in the procuring of the evidence.

The first is 'A' of Castletown-Kenneigh, aged about thirty, an ex-British soldier, a Catholic and a paid British spy. It will be recalled that the brigade flying column lay in ambush at Mawbeg on January 22nd. At twelve o'clock on the previous night three senior officers left the flying column to travel six miles to inspect the ambush area. They rode three horses and came on to the main road near the ambush positions at 1 a.m. The night was bright and they rode slowly along, endeavouring to gauge the size of fields, strength of ditches, the position of houses, byroads and the other factors which influence the selection of an ambush site. After travelling a few hundred yards the leading horse shied violently, nearly throwing his rider, and it was only when the horse was turned round and forced back that the leading rider observed a man lying on the grass by the roadside. Dismounting, he shook the man, who awoke, sat up and looked at the IRA officer. In reply to a question as to what he was doing there, the man again looked at the IRA officer and said: 'It is all right, sir. I am one of yere own and I have just left Bandon Barracks. The Major knows me well, as I work for him.' He then gave his name and address. Then the officer realised that because he was wearing full field equipment over his trench coat he had been mistaken for a British officer. 'A' was not drunk, but was obviously recovering from the effects of liquor. The second IRA officer was then called up and asked if he had ever seen 'A' in Bandon Barracks. He replied that he had not. 'A' was then told he would have to be examined further before he would be released, as he might be a 'Shinner', the British nickname for an Irish Republican. He was asked to walk along to the byroad, where the talk could proceed with less danger of observation from passers-by. During the next twenty minutes he told the two officers the sordid story of his treachery over a nine-month period. It all came out: the arrests he had been responsible for, the coups he had missed, his list of local IRA who were still evading arrest and the amount of pay he was receiving: 'Five pounds every week, and sometimes more, if I have good news.' That day, after reporting to the British battalion intelligence officer, 'A' had been drinking in the military canteen until after curfew hour. Then, free from observation, the Essex had driven him six miles and dropped him near where we had found him. Overcome by liquor, he had lain down before completing his journey home and had fallen asleep.

Then one of the IRA officers was sent back to bring up the third, alleged to be a prisoner, who would not give any particulars about himself. When 'A' was asked if he recognised this prisoner, he called the questioning officer aside and said, 'I do not know his name, but he is one of them. I saw him with the Lordans and others and he is high up in them.'

The spy was then told that the prisoner would be brought to Bandon Barracks where he would be forced to talk. At this 'A' got very excited and again calling the officer aside said, 'You can't bring this fellow into Bandon as he might know me and get a message out about me. Shoot him. Shoot him now, here.'

The IRA officer replied that he did not like shooting prisoners himself and he would wait until some of his troops came up. Then the spy showed the viciousness of his character for he eagerly volunteered to do the shooting. He asked for the officer's gun and reached greedily for it, but the time had come to tell him that the play had ended. This spy was a Catholic and the local priest was called to minister to him before he was shot on the roadside at Mawbeg seven hours later. Strange are the ways of destiny. Incidents which appear of little importance may cause death to some and allow life to remain with others. In all probability, but for the shy of a nervous horse, this spy would still be alive and many other members of the IRA would have met their deaths as a result of his activities.

The second instance is of 'B', aged over forty, a large farmer, a Protestant and an unpaid informer. Unlike 'A', who was not under suspicion, this informer had been the subject of many adverse reports by the local IRA. On the evening following the execution of 'A' an IRA officer called at 'B's' house, leaving three of his men concealed outside it. The officer was wearing an Auxiliary's tasselled beret obtained at Kilmichael, a trench coat, leggings and equipment, and was readily accepted by 'B' as a newly arrived officer of the Dunmanway Auxiliaries. 'B' waved away the trimly uniformed maid who had opened the door and ushered the visitor into the drawing room, where he invited him to join in a whiskey and soda. This was refused by the officer, who explained that he never drank spirits until after dinner. An offer of tea was also refused on the grounds that some Auxiliary officers were waiting on the road and that the visitor had not much time since the raiding party was on an urgent job. Then 'B' said it took the authorities long enough to come out in answer to the message he had sent two days before. The IRA officer replied it was to check on that information he had called and, producing a notebook, he asked 'B' to repeat the message. 'B' then stated that his message was about three of the IRA he had seen crossing country, two of whom carried rifles. He had tracked them to a barn where they slept in a bed of hay and blankets. He named two of the men, described where the barn was situated and suggested the best time and manner they could be surrounded. He again grumbled about the delays in acting on his previous message, and said that the IRA would have been finished in his locality long ago if the military and police acted quicker on the information that had been sent to them. He remarked it was strange that the Essex could act quickly in other districts, as they did when they finished those two Republican ruffians a few days previously near Courtmacsherry. Warming to his subject as he poured his second drink, he said it was a scandal that so many IRA were still at large in the locality. He correctly named the ranks of many local IRA and then went on to speak of several of the senior officers, including his visitor, about whom he had heard but did not know personally. He referred to them as 'The Big Shots'. The IRA officer tried to draw him about his associates and the informer let two names drop as reliable men who were helping the authorities.

At the end of half an hour when 'B' was drinking his third whiskey and had switched back to discussing the battalion officers, the end came. The informer had asserted that John Lordan was the Battalion OC of the Bandon Battalion, and the officer, feeling that he could expect no further useful information, was considering whether to shoot the informer as he sat drinking or to arrest him. Then the visitor remarked that his information was that Lordan was Vice-OC and not the OC. This was strongly contradicted by the informer, who said he knew better and that Lordan was the boss. To this the IRA officer replied, 'But I still say you are wrong for, you know, I am ________, whom you have already mentioned as a Big Shot, and John Lordan's senior officer.'

It was several seconds before 'B' realised the full significance of those words. The glass fell from his hand, his jaw dropped and a pallor spread over his face. He quickly obeyed the order to place his hands on the table, but was still stunned when the party of IRA who were outside appeared in answer to a whistle blast, to lead him away. That night he was court-martialled. He admitted making all those statements about his treacherous activities, but did not further incriminate his associates. He was shot a few hours later.

The third instance is that of 'C' of Innishannon, aged about thirty-seven, a retired lieutenant-colonel of the British Army. This Britisher was not only an important organiser of espionage against the IRA, but guided in person raiding parties of the Essex Regiment. He wore a mask and was dressed as a civilian during many of his early expeditions with the raiders, but one night, in the house of one of his victims, his mask slipped. From that night in December 1920 we wanted him very badly, but he knew he was in danger and practically lived with the British military officers in barracks. When on occasions he ventured back to Innishannon, he was invariably guarded by Black and Tans and his movements were most irregular. On the night of May 30th he went home to sleep at Innishannon, and on the following morning two of the column went to shoot him. Stealthily approaching 'C's' house, they hid in the laurels until he came out of the hall door and crossed to his garage. One of the IRA then walked up to him, spoke and shot him three times as he tried to pull his gun. The two Volunteers then ran for the gate, but fire was opened on them by the guard of four Black and Tans who were on duty in the house. Returning the fire with revolvers, they reached the road to retire in safety at their leisure, as the Black and Tans made no attempt to emerge from the house to pursue them. The death of this 'retired' lieutenant-colonel was greatly welcomed. He had long been a menace to the IRA and the people of that locality.

In addition to the sixteen who were killed, many other hostile loyalists fled to Britain. One of the latter was a Protestant minister, head of an intelligence group, the organiser and transmitter of all information collected by his section to the British. One night three members of the flying column went to shoot him, but observing their approach, he got out by the back door and escaped into the darkness. Before morning he had made his way to Ballincollig Military Barracks, where so often he had previously given his information, and within twenty-four hours he was escorted to England. To our knowledge he never returned to Ireland.

There were soon to be satisfactory indications that our

counter-attacks on the British murder gangs and informers had succeeded. The first was an official notice, published and extensively posted up over the Dunmanway and Bandon areas on the night of February 16th. This clearly indicated that we had disrupted their civilian intelligence and were getting the right men. This official notice read as follows:

> In order to prevent outrages by strangers taking place in Dunmanway and district, it has been decided that six male inhabitants shall be held responsible for each week for informing the O.C. Auxiliary Police at the Workhouse, Dunmanway, of any suspicious stranger arriving in the Town, or of any occurrence or circumstance which points to contemplated outrage. This plan is further intended to protect other inhabitants from intimidation and to render it possible for any LOYALIST to give information without the rebels being able to trace its source. The following individuals will be held responsible for providing information from and including 16th February, 1921, up to and including 22nd February, 1921 … Should any outrage occur in Dunmanway, or within two miles of the Market Square, the whole of the above mentioned will be placed under arrest.
>
> Lieut.-Col., 1st D.Q.,
> K. Company, Aux. Div., R.I.C.
> Dunmanway.
>
> Removal of this notice will entail punishment for the entire District Council.

An even more pointed consequence of our counter-attacks was the extraordinary drop in our casualty list. The enemy, deprived of the guidance of their civilian agents, were now raiding blindly, and the Essex, after their Bandon lesson, were more careful about murdering IRA prisoners. In one month from January 17th to February 16th, 1921, as a result of information given to the British, nine members of the IRA were captured and murdered within a twelve-mile radius of Bandon. But from that date for a period of nearly three months up to May 8th not one IRA man was murdered. Indeed, omitting the IRA who were killed in action on the morning of the Crossbarry fight, the West Cork Brigade only lost in all seven officers and men from February 16th until the end of hostilities at the Truce on July 11th, 1921. There can be no doubt as to why the death toll of the West Cork IRA dropped so amazingly. It was solely because British terror was met by a not less effective IRA counter-terror. We were now hard, cold and ruthless, as our enemy had been since hostilities began. The British were met with their own weapons. They had gone down in the mire to destroy us and our nation, and down after them we had to go to stop them. The step was not an easy one, for one's mind was darkened and one's outlook made bleak by the decisions which had to be taken.

The British imperialists down the ages owe in the main, their successful conquests of many peoples to the technique of 'divide and conquer.' They have consistently urged class against class, district against district, creed against creed, and in the resultant chaos of warring sects and factions, they established themselves and maintained their rule of exploitation. So in

1920 and 1921 they fanned the flame of religious intolerance between Catholics and Protestants. Whenever one of their agents not of the faith of the majority was shot, they announced his death as 'Mr X, a Protestant'. But, although the West Cork Brigade shot five Catholics who were British agents in quick succession, never once did the term 'Catholic' appear after those men's names in the British announcements of their deaths. This was in keeping with the general British propaganda to make the Protestants of Ireland believe that they and their faith would be victimised and destroyed under a Republican government of Ireland. With some of those Protestants, unfortunately, they succeeded only too well. When one of the West Cork informers was asked why he had betrayed to the British IRA neighbours who, he had agreed, had never shown anything but friendliness and goodwill towards him, he replied, 'Would you fight for the Pope?' Astounded, his questioner asked what that had to do with his informing activity for the British. Then the informer explained, 'I am a Protestant and the King of England is the Head of my Church. You are fighting to drive out his soldiers and himself. If you do this you will drive out the Protestant religion, too, and so I being a Protestant was right to help the English against you.' As this man was about to die, it was not worthwhile explaining to him that most of the Republican leaders of the past were members of the Protestant faith: Tone, Emmet, Lord Edward Fitzgerald, Russell, Henry Joy McCracken; that Parnell was a Protestant and that the Proclamation of 1916, the political bible of the IRA, enshrined the promise 'the Republic guarantees religious and civil liberty, equal rights and opportunities to all its citizens'.

Religious bigotry is the result of ignorance and all the Protestant population were not infected with it. The majority of West Cork Protestants lived at peace throughout the whole struggle and were not interfered with by the IRA. We did not press for their support, although we would have welcomed it. We had no doubt that nearly all of them disagreed with our campaign, but we accepted their right to their own opinions as to the wisdom of our cause or the tactics we employed. What we did demand was that they, in common with Catholics, should not commit any hostile act against us and that they should not actively aid the British troops or administration. The majority of the Protestants accepted this position, and let it be said that we found them men of honour whose word was their bond. Aloof from the national struggle, they did not stand with our enemy and they lived their days at peace with their neighbours in spite of all British propaganda and the bigotry and intolerance of the very small section of bigoted Catholics. Alas, religious bigotry was not confined to the Protestants, for the ignorant and petty-minded Catholics, too, had their fair share of this ancient curse.

# 17

# FIRE WITH FIRE

THE Irish Republican Army's counters to the activities of British murder gangs and espionage agents were not the only ones the situation demanded. The enemy campaign included other instruments, the chief of which was that of the fire terror. From the middle of 1920, fire-raising gangs accompanied raiding parties and roved over West Cork, burning to the ground the homes of IRA men or those suspected of actively supporting the IRA. I think the first home burned by them was that of Seán Buckley in Bandon in July 1920. From that date the destruction of Republican homesteads was an important plank of British terrorist policy, aimed to intimidate the Irish people into their old submission. Farmhouses, labourers' cottages and shops went up in flames as the British fire gangs passed, leaving desolation and misery in their wake. It was pitiable to see the plight of some of our people thus rendered homeless. Memories are still vivid of many mothers with young families camped under a tarpaulin tent in the yard, or living in a patched-up henhouse on a bitter winter's night, beside the ruins of their burnt-out homes. Other victims of the British fire terror crowded in on kindly neighbours who had so far escaped, but who knew not the minute nor the hour when they, too, would be compelled to watch the destruction of their homes by the swaggering bullies who seemed to enjoy their work so well.

The British are, of course, a people well practised down the centuries in the use of fire as an instrument of terror. It has been said that they reached the peak of perfection in this art in Ireland after the Rising of 1798, but I do not think this is correct. Surely they excelled in the war for the conquest of South Africa, when they failed to defeat in the field a handful of Boer riflemen, but succeeded in forcing their surrender by the mass burnings of Boer homesteads and the imprisonment, under appalling conditions, of Boer women and children, many thousands of whom died. So in 1920 and 1921 the British would use against the Irish the instrument which was so successful against the Boers, previous generations of the Irish and other subject races. There was, however, one all-important factor which the British evidently forgot to take into consideration. While the South Africans had no British loyalists' homes which could be destroyed as reprisals, Ireland was studded with the castles, mansions and residences of the British Ascendancy who had made their homes here. The West

Cork Brigade was slow to commence a campaign of counter-burnings, but eventually action was taken. A note was sent to the British military commander in West Cork, informing him that for every Republican home destroyed from that date, the homes of two British loyalists would be burned to the ground.

The British ignored this threat, and two nights afterwards burned out a small farmhouse and a labourer's cottage. The following night the IRA burned out four large loyalists' residences in the same neighbourhood. The British countered this by burning four farmhouses and we promptly burned out the eight largest loyalists' homes in that vicinity. And so the British terror and the IRA counter-terror went on. Castles, mansions and residences were sent up in flames by the IRA immediately after the British fire gangs had razed the homes of Irish Republicans. Our people were suffering in this competition of terror, but the British loyalists were paying dearly, the demesne walls were tumbling and the British Ascendancy was being destroyed. Our only fear was that, as time went on, there would be no more loyalists' homes to destroy, for we intended to go on to the bitter end. If the Republicans of West Cork were to be homeless and without shelter, then so too would be the British supporters. West Cork might become a barren land of desolation and misery, but at least the Britishers would have more than their full share of the sufferings.

Very soon after our campaign of counter-burnings commenced, an outcry arose from the British loyalists themselves, demanding that the British forces should cease destroying Republican homes, as otherwise they too would be treated likewise. Those Britishers had sat for many months smugly watching their Republican neighbours' homes going up in flames, and no expression of pity or appeal for clemency ever escaped them. The native Irish were being justly chastised for their refusal to bow to British overlordship and would soon be brought to heel again. But now it was their turn to watch the flames from their own homes light the darkness of the West Cork skies, and their appeals to the British forces to stop their burning campaign were long and loud. From this IRA counter-terror the British could not protect them, for the IRA never once failed to carry out in full the programme of reprisal. British peers in their House of Lords and members of the House of Commons, dyed-in-the-wool imperialists, who would gladly have destroyed the home of every Irish nationalist, echoed those appeals. They declared they were speaking on behalf of British loyalists in Ireland and pointed out that the British burnings were suicidal and bad policy, as the IRA destroyed two large mansions for every farmhouse or cottage burned by the British. They instanced where, following the destruction by the British of two small farmhouses worth less than a thousand pounds, four large houses of British loyalists worth twenty thousand pounds were destroyed by the IRA. This outcry had its effect, and although British burnings were never officially called off, they were slowed down considerably and even halted for a time. Once again the British had reacted to the only sure method of meeting their terrorism: an effective counter-terror; and hundred of homes of West Cork Republicans were saved from destruction.

One result of the IRA counteractions was the attempts made by the British loyalists to sell out their Irish properties and leave West Cork for residence in Britain. Those attempts also were defeated as the IRA completely banned all sales of residences and properties unless by permit from the West Cork Brigade. All sales came to a standstill, consequent on the posting up throughout West Cork of notice to this effect. No auctioneer would attempt to sell, and no buyer could be tempted to purchase loyalists' residences and land even at 'knock down' prices. Let those Britishers flee, but they would leave without the proceeds of their Irish properties. Some with guilty consciences did leave, and so although the brigade had no administrative machinery, or the time to set up such, we encouraged local landless men to settle on the lands and to use them. In some cases the Republican Army itself took over livestock and sold it for the benefit of the Brigade Arms Fund. As an instance, the *Cork Examiner* of April 29th, 1921, has the following news item:

> Twenty-four calves, twenty-three young cattle, eighty sheep and four horses were taken from the lands of _____ recently shot dead.

Active hostility to the IRA and active support of the British forces were now not only dangerous games but also very expensive ones.

Yet another problem of British intimidation presented itself in the early March of 1921. One day, accompanied by Mick Crowley and two other riflemen, I left the flying column in billets and travelled about seven miles to Castletown-Kenneigh on brigade business. We called to our good friends, the Misses Nyhan, in that village, where we were told that on that morning a company of Auxiliaries from Dunmanway had occupied the village of Ballineen in force. The Auxiliaries had rounded up all the men of the village and formed them into what they called a 'Civil Guard', whose main functions would be to report on IRA movements and to fill in all road cuts made by the IRA in that locality. Blood-curdling threats of 'shooting by roster' were made by the British should the newly formed Civil Guard fail in its duties. As we listened a local scout ran in to tell us that the new Civil Guard, under heavy Auxiliary escort, had commenced their first task, filling in a large trench a mile and a half from Castletown-Kenneigh. This British move to use our own countrymen against us was a serious matter, and unless it was nipped in the bud it could grow and develop into a menace. In the last analysis it mattered not that those civilians were victims of British terror and unwilling co-operators with the Auxiliaries. What the IRA had to realise was that those men were being used against it, and that this body called the Civil Guard could not, under any circumstances, be allowed to carry out the British instructions. If civilians, no matter how sympathetic they were to the IRA, allowed themselves to be used, because of threats, to fill in trenches or supply information, then it was only a short step to the arming of such people as an auxiliary force to the British troops.

The four of us moved on to a small hill about four hundred yards from the road cut, and down below we saw two dozen civilians with shovels filling in the large deep trench. Their escort was in position lying behind the adjoining fences, and all that could be seen of them were their berets and the barrels of their rifles. As this was the first 'operation' of the Civil Guard, the riflemen were instructed to avoid wounding them, but to spatter the earth sufficiently close to them so that they would clearly understand that we meant business. After the first IRA volley directed at the Auxiliaries, fire was switched onto the trench. The Auxiliaries replied and the new Civil Guard broke and scattered all over the countryside. Later we were to learn that when the Auxiliaries eventually succeeded in rounding up some of their new force, those men bluntly told them that no matter what the consequences would be, they would not carry out British instructions, that were they to be shot, they would far prefer to be killed by the Auxiliaries than by the IRA. This ended the Civil Guard in West Cork and no further attempts were made to re-establish it. It was a stroke of good luck that we were in the vicinity of this proposed new force on its first operation.

Guerilla resisters to imperialism must continually be on guard and ready to act without delay against such instruments of terror as those outlined in this and the preceding chapters. Sentiment has no place in stopping terror tactics, and only a ruthless counteraction can ever effectively halt it. This is true with regard to all exploiting nations, but particularly so of Britain, which so easily holds the lead in having exploited and destroyed the freedom of more peoples than all other nations combined. For several centuries the British have ravaged the world. They have spilled the blood of Americans and Europeans, Asiatics and Africans in their mad race for conquest and loot. This they achieved, not by military prowess, but by guile and terrorism, and by a careful selection of whom and when to attack. They are not a fighting race, and in all their history, never once have they won a war, when alone, against a first-class power. The only time they attempted this was against America, when Lord North and his British troops were ignominiously kicked into the sea by the young, half-armed and half-trained Americans. It is quite true that the British have always been one of a winning combination, as when at different periods they fought against Spain, France, Russia, Germany and Italy, but one looks in vain through the pages of history for a single instance of success when challenging alone a country of even half Britain's strength. Britain's proud boast is that she has fought seventy-seven wars in the last four hundred and fifty years, but her jingoes always omit to mention that ninety per cent of those victories were the slaughters and massacres of unarmed tribesmen from the jungles of West Africa to the rice-fields of China. When I was a schoolboy our geography told us that the British possessions were coloured red, and the large map of the world on the school wall and the globe were patched deeply with that colour. It was only later in life that I could appreciate how appropriate this colour was.

This is not a condemnation of all the British people, for there certainly has been in all generations a stratum of fine and humane people amongst them who passionately loved justice and hated British imperialism. The British have some splendid qualities, and through the ages many of them have championed and led emancipatory movements. Yet the puzzle remains as to why this large section could never prevail on any of its governments to act with human decency towards the weaker peoples they were attempting to destroy. The years 1920 and 1921 also saw the best of the British people championing decency and attacking British outrages in Ireland. Many Labour politicians and trade unionists spearheaded a campaign for a fair deal for Ireland, and Commander Kenworthy, RN, now Lord Strabolgi, deserves special mention for his unceasing efforts in this connection. The rank and file Liberals were almost equally friendly to the Irish people in their hour of need, and even some Conservatives were compelled, by reason of the outrages of the British forces, to raise their voices in protest. British daily newspapers of that period published hundreds of protests of responsible British personages. The following two excerpts are fair examples.

Sir John Simon, MP, one-time British Home Secretary and later Chancellor of Britain, now Lord Simon, in the *Cork Examiner* of January 21st, 1921:

> Sir John Simon, speaking at Streatham on yesterday, said the present conditions in Ireland are poisoning the relations between this country and America; it is holding up their name to contempt throughout the world and it made their protestation that they would go to all lengths to protect the interests of a small country like Belgium seem futile. History would mark them down as nothing less than a set of humbugs. There was no justification for treating the present Irish race as though they were a lot of cut-throats and assassins.

The *Daily News*, a leading British daily, of January 4th, 1921, carried a signed article by one of the most prominent editors of Great Britain, Robert Lynd:

> England is now ruling Ireland in the spirit of the torturer. How many Englishmen realise that the bloodhound and the thong are in use in Ireland as they were in the Slave States of America? I was taught that under the Union Jack all men were free and that the deliberate infliction of physical and mental torture on men, women and children was under that sign impossible. But human nature is much the same everywhere and the Irishman 'on the run' to-day is in some respects in a worse plight than the negro slave.
>
> There is no borderland to which he can fly. Were he not sustained by an invincible faith in God and a love of his country that counts life well lost for her, he would be a man without hope. He can be no more defeated by persecution than the Scottish Covenanters would be defeated by persecution. The most tragic figure in Ireland to-day is not that of the persecuted but that of the persecutor.

The Irish people should never forget those British champions who fought so hard to stop outrages and to force the British government to negotiate a just peace with Ireland. They contributed greatly to the signing of the Truce and without their efforts it is certain that many more Irishmen and Britishers would have died before the war was ended. In this sad tale of terror and counter-terror, two lights shine out of the darkness: the courage and tenacity of our own people who did not flinch or fail the Irish Republican Army and the decency and humanity of a not inconsiderable section of the British people who worked tirelessly for a peace with Ireland.

# 18

# VICTORY AT CROSSBARRY

BY the middle of March 1921, the British invariably operated in West Cork in units of not less than three hundred. Consequently the brigade flying column was brought to its greatest possible strength by the addition of every available rifle in the area and it now totalled one hundred and four officers and men. Unfortunately we had only forty rounds of ammunition for each rifle and there were no reserves. It was with the greatest reluctance we departed from our fixed policy of not putting all our eggs in one basket, and risking practically all our best officers and all our armament in one flying column. It was also no easy matter to manoeuvre, conceal, billet and feed a flying column of that strength over a long period, in an area that was then holding down at least five thousand British troops. But where was the alternative? We could not hope to engage the strong British forces with a smaller force, and in addition wanted men, who, if captured, would be killed by the British, had a far better chance of survival in a flying column, than if left to evade capture and death in small groups in the various battalion areas. The officers with the column then were Liam Deasy, Adjutant, Tadhg O'Sullivan, Quartermaster, Dr Con Lucey, Medical Officer, and Eugene Callanan, Assistant Medical Officer. The MO and his assistant did not wear the Red Cross insignia as the British would not recognise our rights to use it, so Lucey and Callanan were active fighting soldiers who carried first aid equipment in addition to their rifles. There were seven sections of fourteen riflemen in each, including the section commander. Those numbering one to seven were commanded respectively by Seán Hales, John Lordan, Mick Crowley, Denis Lordan, Tom Kelleher, Peter Kearney and Christy O'Connell. The strength of sections in other armies usually varies between seven and ten riflemen, but ours was organised to a strength of fourteen, mainly because as we were completely unsupported, the column had always to be ready to stem a flank or rear attack or both at one time, and a section of a lesser strength would be ineffective for that purpose. We could not model our fighting unit on other armies or according to textbooks, but only in the manner which the prevailing circumstances demanded. A piper now accompanied our flying column. He was Florence Begley, an assistant to the brigade adjutant, a well-known player of the bagpipes. This was an innovation and we were soon to test an opinion I had formed, that the best of soldiers will fight even better still to the strains of their traditional war songs, and that the harsh wild music of the bagpipes would have a demoralising effect on the Sassenach foes.

On the morning of March 16th, information reached us that three hundred enemy troops were being sent on the following day from Kinsale to Bandon as reinforcements. That night the flying column marched to intercept them at Shippool, half-way between Kinsale and Bandon. An hour before dawn on St Patrick's Day we occupied ambush positions on the roadside which ran close by and parallel to the railway line and Bandon River in the lovely wooded valley of Shippool. We lay all day, vainly waiting until four o'clock when our scouts, who had been sent to Kinsale to watch the enemy movements, returned. They reported that the enemy had set out as scheduled, travelled over a mile, were then halted and later returned to barracks. Obviously they were recalled because of information received that our brigade column had moved across their line of march. Incidentally, we were never able to trace their source of information. Immediately I received this news, the column was withdrawn to retire on to Skough, east of Innishannon. Twenty minutes later a British reconnaissance plane, flying low, zoomed along the valley, searching for us as we lay flat and still in extended order, hidden in the dykes, pressed close to the ditches.

The following day we remained in billets waiting for an

enemy move which I knew was now inevitable. The British would surely attempt a large-scale operation against the column, but we could only attempt to anticipate the tactics they would employ. It was an uneasy day and the most stringent security measures were adopted by the flying column. Reports from some of the garrison towns around us, including one brought by Seán MacCarthy, Upton, Chairman GAA, regarding Cork city, that all was exceptionally quiet, did not ease the tension, for such a lull in their activities was unusual and even ominous. It was easy to imagine General Strickland's divisional headquarters staff in the city, twelve miles away, feverishly at work preparing the troop movements which would eventually encircle, compress and destroy our flying column. In an inky darkness the column moved again northwards to cross the two Cork–Bandon main roads into Ballyhandle, six miles away. Kelleher's section was detailed as the advance guard, with instructions that half of the section was to travel inside both ditches of the road to prevent surprise by British ambushing units. At 1 a.m. the column arrived at John O'Leary's, Ballyhandle, and this house became column headquarters. The son of the house, Paddy, was a member of the column and captain of the Upton Company, and the daughter was a member of the Cumann na mBan. The column moved off to billet at the surrounding houses. Crowley and Kelleher left to mobilise the local company as an outer ring of unarmed scouts, while Deasy, a few others and I went into John O'Leary's. I felt so sure action was imminent that I refused to go to bed and lay down fully dressed on a sofa in a room off the kitchen. Just before 2.30 a.m. Crowley and Kelleher returned hurriedly to report seeing the lights and hearing the noises of lorries some miles to the west. I immediately ordered the assembly of the flying column. Ten minutes later a similar report was received of enemy movements to the east, and at 2.50 a third report came in of occasional glares of lorry lights and of dogs barking excitedly away to the south. By then there was no doubt that an extensive operation against the column was in full swing, but it was not until later, of course, that the details were confirmed.

At 1 a.m. on the morning of March 19th, four hundred troops left Cork, two hundred Ballincollig, three hundred Kinsale and three hundred and fifty Bandon. Later one hundred and twenty Auxiliaries left Macroom. Still later, troops left Clonakilty and more left Cork. They proceeded by lorries to four points, approximately four miles north-north-east, south-south-east and west of Crossbarry. There they dismounted and formed up in columns. About half of each column then moved on foot as they raided the countryside and converged on Crossbarry. The remainder again mounted the lorries and were moved slowly onwards after the raiding columns. Their tactics were apparently those of motorised infantry who could be rushed to any point where the IRA were contacted. This arrangement also allowed for the changing over of raiding troops on foot for the fresh men on the lorries.

They raided and closely searched every house and out-house

in the countryside. Each column took many civilians and some unarmed Volunteers prisoners. One of the eastern columns came to the house three miles north of Crossbarry, where Commandant Charles Hurley was recuperating from a bullet wound. They killed him, but he died fighting as he tried to break through. Two unarmed scouts had been sent on earlier to bring Charlie Hurley down to the column, but had been intercepted on the way and had been taken prisoner. The column clearly heard the shots that killed him at about 6.30 a.m. Thus the British made very slow progress as they moved on to where the column was waiting.

When the column mobilised at 2.30 a.m. it had full knowledge of the fact that the enemy was moving to attack it from several sides. Although the numbers of the enemy were not then known, the IRA had no doubt that they were outnumbered by ten to one at least. I had to decide without delay whether to fight or to retire and attempt to evade action. The decision to fight was made immediately. Each and all of the following factors governed the decision:

(a) It was extremely doubtful if the IRA column could retire in any direction without being met by numerically superior forces. The only direction from which the British were not known to be advancing was north to northwest. But there was no guarantee that they were not coming that way also. Had the column retired that way and met an enemy force they would have been in a serious position. The enemy would have held the high ground and their tactics need only have been to man the ditches in a 'holding' operation, while the other British columns closed in on the IRA.

(b) The IRA column had only forty rounds per rifle. This shortage demanded initially a swift and intensive fight at close quarters, which, if not in itself decisive, would have the effect of upsetting the carefully planned enemy deployment. If the column retired, this objective could not have been achieved, and the best the column could hope for would be an all-day series of skirmishes with the British, who would harass it continuously, even if it did not corner it. The IRA ammunition would not last several hours of this warfare, much less a full day.

(c) A heavy and successful attack on those large British round-ups was an overdue strategic necessity. Hitherto they had not been attacked and there was a grave danger that by their wholesale arrests of Volunteers, captures of dumped arms, and intimidation of the civilian population, they would seriously interfere with the Volunteer organisation and damage the morale of the people.

(d) From observations of enemy movements it was clear that the British force from the west would reach Crossbarry some time before the other British columns. That would even up the opening fight and the column was supremely confident of being able to defeat it and thus smash one side of the encircling wall of troops. This would leave the IRA column free to pass on to the west where it could, according to circumstances, turn either north or south with the practical certainty of avoiding for that day further contact with the British. In addition there was the expectation of the column increasing its armament, particularly its ammunition, from such an attack.

At 3 a.m. I spoke to the flying column giving them an outline of the situation and our plan of attack. The following action orders were stressed:

(1) No section was to retire from its position without orders, no matter how great the pressure. Arrangements for rapid reinforcement of any point had been made. Even though sections saw no enemy they were not to move to the aid of other sections, as the enemy were operating on various sides.

(2) No Volunteer was in any circumstances to show himself until the action started, for the plan entailed allowing the British forces to move right through the ambush position until the leaders were over the eastern mine, when it was to be set off. The order was then to attack the nearest enemy, whilst the second mine was to be set off if any of the enemy came near it.

(3) Communication between the column commander and the various sections was to be made by runners. The command post was movable between the centre sections.

(4) The direction of retirement would not be given until the move-off, but whatever sections were engaged on advance, rear and flank guards were to keep moving in extended order not nearer than three hundred yards to the main column.

The column marched off to Crossbarry at 3.30 a.m., and positions were occupied by 4.30. Crossbarry is situated twelve miles south-west of Cork city. It is about nine miles from Ballincollig, twelve from Kinsale and eight from Bandon. The old road from Bandon to Cork, which was and is quite a good road, passes through Crossbarry. Here it is met by two roads from the north and two from the south, and they form a double crossroads only thirty yards apart. It was west of those crossroads that all our sections were posted. Hales' section was placed at the western entrance to the ambuscade inside the northern ditch of the road. An old boreen ran up on this flank, and this was now blocked with a small stone wall to prevent armoured cars from entering and enfilading the column. As well as being able to fire on the enemy immediately in front, this section could also enfilade the approach road. Stretched along east from Hales' section for several hundred yards inside this northern ditch, and in the two roadside farmhouses, Beasley's and Harold's, were the riflemen of the section commanded by John Lordan, Mick Crowley, Peter Kearney and Denis Lordan. This last section on the extreme left was capable of enfilading the approaches to Crossbarry Cross in addition to frontal fire. Just beyond it, around the bend, another stone wall was erected to prevent any enemy lorries from racing through. Between Crowley's and Kearney's, and between Kearney's and Denis Lordan's sections, two observation mines were embedded in the road. The piper was in the centre of the attacking sections in Harold's yard, with instructions to play Irish war songs from the first crack of the rifles. Tom Kelleher's section was placed in the 'Castlefield' six hundred yards directly to the rear of Denis Lordan's section, to cover the left flank and the left rear approaches. Christy O'Connell's section was posted about two hundred yards north of the approach road, and six hundred yards to the west of Hales' section to cover our right

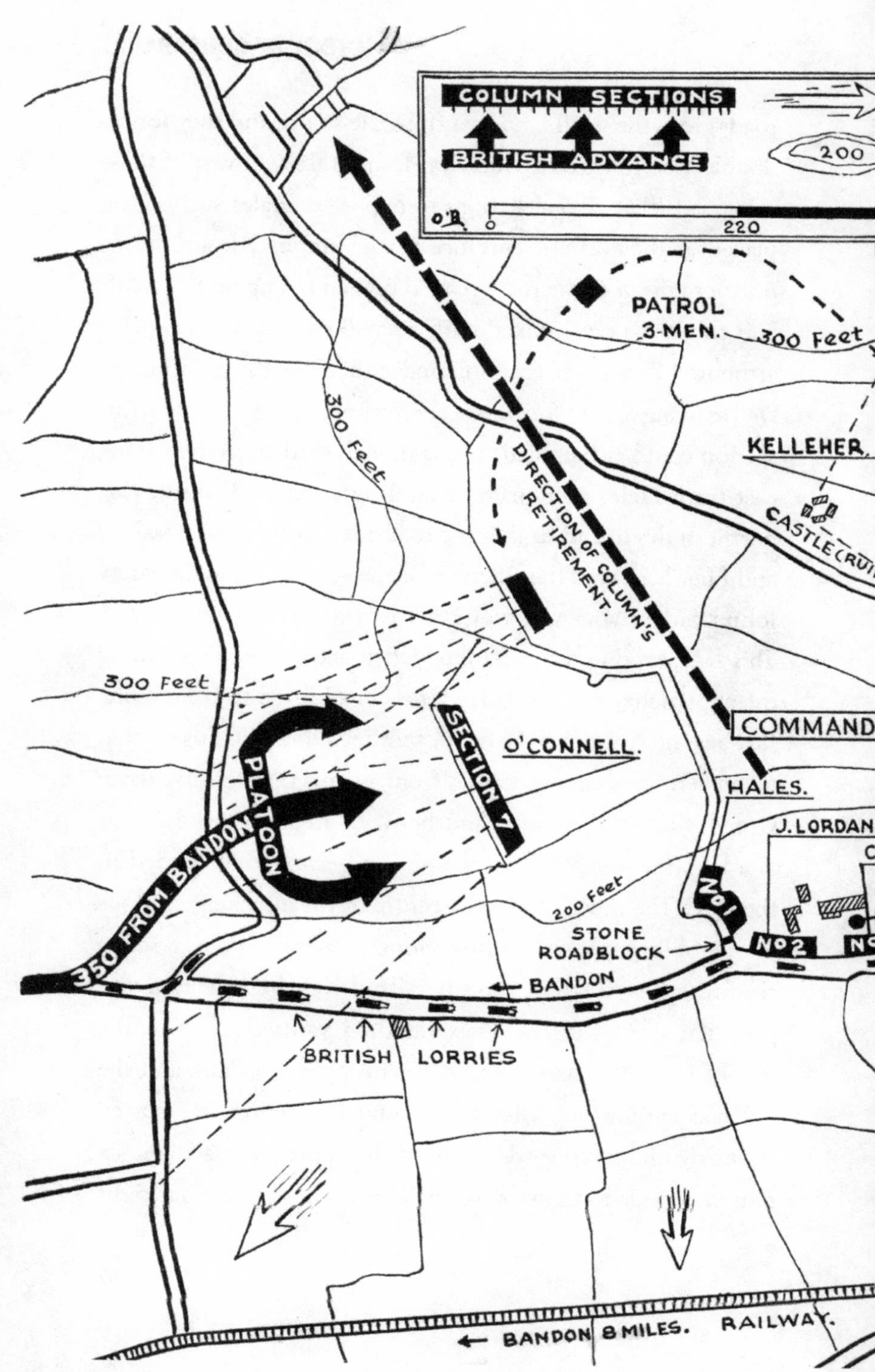
COLUMN SECTIONS
BRITISH ADVANCE
200
O'B
0
220
PATROL
3-MEN.
300 Feet
300 Feet
KELLEHER.
DIRECTION OF COLUMN'S RETIREMENT.
CASTLE (RUI
300 Feet
COMMAND
SECTION 7
O'CONNELL.
PLATOON
HALES.
J. LORDAN
350 FROM BANDON
200 Feet
No 1
STONE
ROADBLOCK
No 2
BANDON
BRITISH LORRIES
BANDON 8 MILES.
RAILWAY.

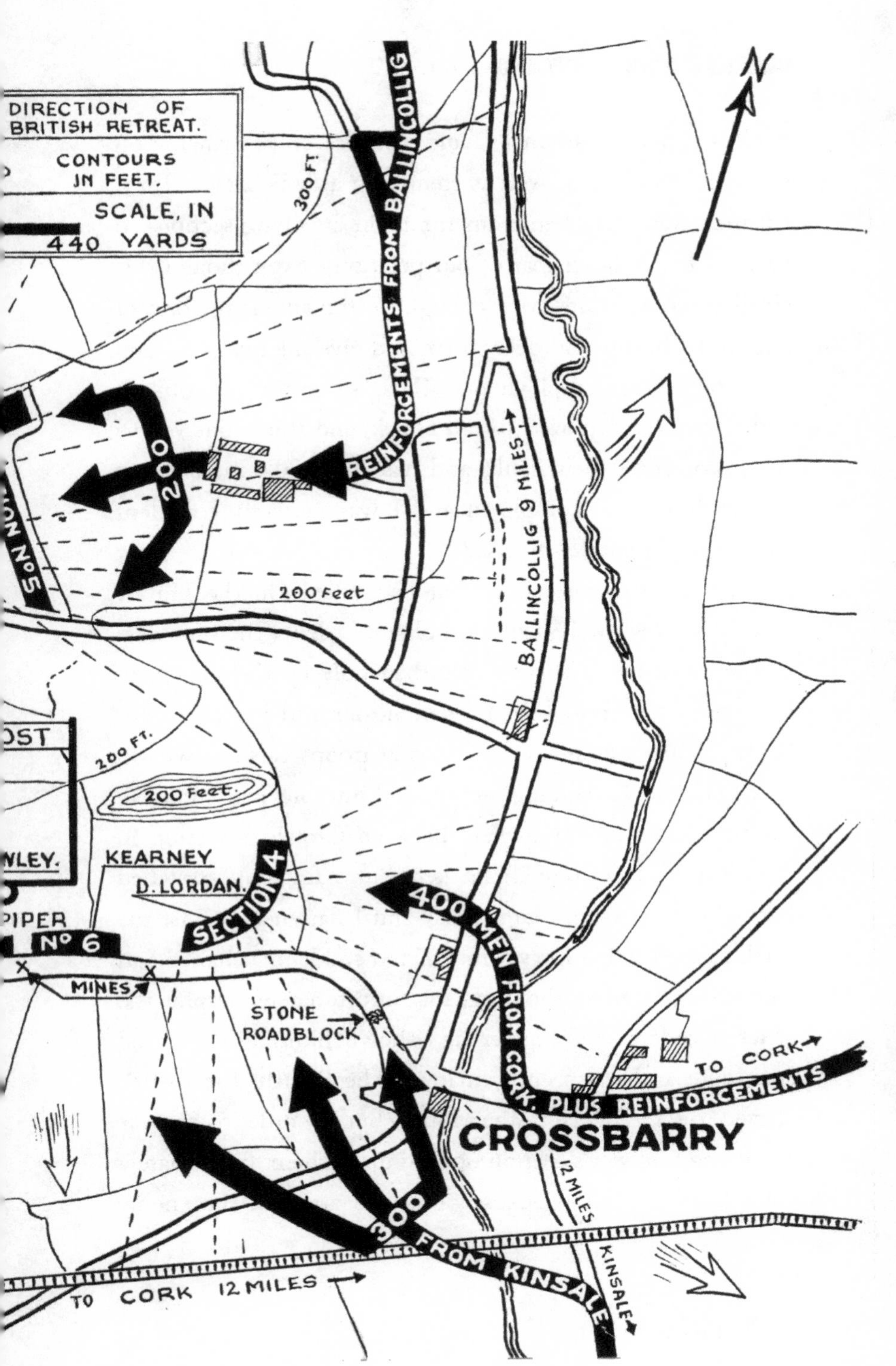

DIRECTION OF BRITISH RETREAT.
CONTOURS IN FEET.
SCALE, IN
440 YARDS
300 FT
REINFORCEMENTS FROM BALLINCOLLIG
200
SECTION No 5
BALLINCOLLIG 9 MILES
200 Feet
200 FT.
200 Feet.
KEARNEY
D. LORDAN.
SECTION 4
400 MEN FROM CORK. PLUS REINFORCEMENTS
PIPER
No 6
MINES
STONE ROADBLOCK
TO CORK
CROSSBARRY
12 MILES
300 FROM KINSALE
KINSALE
TO CORK 12 MILES

flank. From its position it could also fire on any enemy on the approach road as well as stemming a flank attack. Three riflemen were detached from the main attacking sections to patrol a half-mile in rear of our positions. Even though this small group was not strong enough to stop an enemy force of any strength, it would delay them and give the flying column time to change deployment. Thus, seventy-three officers and men were deployed for an attack, and thirty-one others were protecting their flanks and rear. By 5.30 a.m. all these preparations were completed and I was perfectly confident that we could not be surprised.

After hearing the shots that had killed Charlie Hurley at 6.30 a.m. we waited immovable and silent. The quietness of the breaking dawn was disturbed only by the sounds of the enemy transport, which crept nearer and nearer. About 8 a.m. a long line of lorries carrying troops came slowly on past O'Connell's flanking section and into our main ambush positions. Twelve lorries were between Crowley's section in the centre and O'Connell's flankers, but many more stretched back along the road. Liam Deasy and I flattened against the ditch as the leading lorry came on, but suddenly it halted and the soldiers started shouting, for unfortunately, despite the strictest orders, a Volunteer had shown himself at a raised barn door and was seen by many of the British. The British started to scramble from their lorries but the order to fire was given and Crowley's section opened up at them. Immediately John Lordan's and Hales' sections also attacked the enemy nearest them and away on our flank Christy O'Connell's men blazed at the enemy on the road below. Begley played martial airs on his war pipes as four of our sections attacked. Volley after volley was fired, mostly at ranges from five to ten yards, at those British, and they broke and scattered, leaving their dead, a fair amount of arms and their lorries behind them. The survivors had scrambled over the southern ditch of the road and were running panic-stricken towards the south. Three of our sections were ordered out on the road to follow them up. Using rapid fire they chased the enemy who lost many men. These British troops did not stop running until they reached the main Cork–Bandon road, a mile and a half away. Even then they did not attempt to re-form but straggled back in disorganised groups to Bandon, nearly seven miles away.

Within ten minutes of the opening of our attack we had smashed the British encircling lines wide open. We could have marched away to the south without fear of interference had I wished to do so. But now confidence in ourselves to meet the attacks we knew were coming from other British units was mixed with contempt for our enemy's fighting ability. The three sections were ordered back to collect the arms of the British dead. Helping them now was a man named White of Newcestown, who, although not a Volunteer, had been arrested that morning and carried as a hostage in the leading lorry. He had a doubly lucky escape from death as after escaping our first volley, he was nearly shot dead when I came on the road, before he shouted that he was an Irishman and a prisoner of the British. Now he was staggering under the load of a new British Lewis gun and eight fully loaded pans, which the enemy machine-gunners, dead on the road, never had a chance of using. The captured rifles were slung across the backs of Volunteers and the captured ammunition was distributed immediately amongst all our riflemen. It was a welcome addition to half-empty bandoliers. Then the lorries were prepared for burning and the British dead pulled away from their vicinity. The first three were burning when heavy rifle fire broke out on our left flank and all Volunteers were ordered back to their original action stations. Another British column of about two hundred had advanced from the south-east. They were attacked by Denis Lordan's section. Kearney's men were moved up to reinforce Lordan's and after heavy fighting the enemy retreated leaving a number of dead. This unit was not again seen on that day. Those troops too, like those on the lorries, had evidently had enough.

We had not long to await the third phase of the engagement, for shortly afterwards the sounds of rifle fire came from our right flank. Here about a platoon of British tried to come in across country but were met by O'Connell's section. This party had apparently been left behind the main British column to complete the raids. O'Connell's riflemen surprised them and the British hurriedly withdrew. The firing had died down so quickly that our reinforcing section which had started out was recalled.

Ten minutes later the fourth development of the action

opened. Still another British column came in on our left rear. Numbering about two hundred they had entered an old boreen about a mile back, and keeping close to the ditch as they crept in, they were unobserved for some time. Their manoeuvre did not, as they had hoped, bring them in on the rear of an unsuspecting flying column, as when they emerged onto the Castlefield, Kelleher's riflemen were waiting for them. Kelleher's section allowed them to come to within fifty yards of its position before opening fire and knocking over a number of them. The remainder hurriedly retired to cover from where they continued to engage our men. Immediately this action started I sent Jim (Spud) Murphy and eleven riflemen to reinforce Kelleher. Spud had his arm in a sling, the result of a bullet wound received a few weeks previously in a fight with the British, but he was such a fine fighter and section commander that I had no hesitation in detailing him for the job. There were now twenty-six officers and men facing this British column and our line was extended northwards to counter an anticipated enemy flanking movement. This soon came and again the enemy was met with such heavy fire that they hurriedly retreated once more. The fighting had gone on here for about ten minutes and as there were no British in sight anywhere but those being attacked by Kelleher and Murphy, I moved the whole flying column back, except O'Connell's section, to strike at this enemy unit with our full strength. But when I reached Kelleher's position all the British had gone and we saw no more of those either.

British corpses were strewn on the Crossbarry road, in the fields south of it, in front of Denis Lordan's section, near Christy O'Connell's section, and now here were several more of them lying around Kelleher's position. But we, too, had not escaped unscathed. Three of our soldiers lay dead and several others were wounded. Volunteer Peter Monahan, Volunteer Jeremiah O'Leary, Leap, and Volunteer Con Daly, Ballinascarthy, had died fighting for Ireland that morning. We laid our three dead comrades close together in a field, and placing the most seriously wounded, Dan Corcoran of Newcestown and Jim Crowley of Kilneatig, Kilbrittain, in our midst, moved back to the old boreen which flanked Hales' section, and Christy O'Connell's flankers were drawn in. About two hours had elapsed since the opening of the fight; we were in possession of the countryside, no British were visible and our task was completed. The whole column was drawn up in line of sections and told they had done well. Those British units were finished, but other fresh troops might be encountered as we retired to billets at Gurranereigh. These were fourteen miles due west of Crossbarry, but twenty miles as we would have to travel. Flankers would have to travel cross-country for at least twelve miles, where we would halt to look for breakfast. Strict march discipline would have to be observed, but the column would move at an easy pace so that it would be fresh and fit to fight again at any stage of our retirement. Shortly after the order to march was given we spied a gathering of British away in the distance; evidently groups of disorganised units. They appeared to be leaderless, as they were standing around in the centre of a small field on the sloping hillside east of Crossbarry. Through field glasses I could see them gesticulating as if they were arguing as to what to do next. We helped them to make up their minds, for although the distance was a bit far, the column was halted and deployed along a ditch. The range was given and three volleys from nearly a hundred rifles were fired at them. A few staggered and fell, others broke in all directions, and soon the west Cork hillside was clear of the khaki-clad troops. Crossbarry was over.

# 19

# MARCH TO THE WEST

THE flying column moved first north-north-west through Crosspound, on to Raheen, where it turned west through Crowhill on to Rearour. For five miles it then sloped west-south-west, and then turning due west again it continued on to cross the Bantry–Crookstown road near Béal na Bláth and so on to Gurranereigh, which was reached as darkness fell. The column had marched nearly the whole way through fields and boreens and had touched roads only to cross them. The first minor engagement of our retirement took place at Crowhill. Our right flanking section, observing a number of lorries of Auxiliaries travelling along a few hundred yards below, lined a ditch and fired a few volleys at them. Some of the lorries speeded through, but others halted and those Auxiliaries returned the fire, but strangely enough made no attempt to advance and follow up our flankers. A few miles further west at Rearour the same flanking section were themselves fired at from long range of over half a mile by a party of British soldiers. They suffered no casualties, although two goats grazing nearby were killed. Because the British were practically out of range our flankers did not reply but slipped on. Here again there was no attempt made to follow up the column. Perhaps the explanation is that the enemy was only a small unit with definite instructions to hold a certain line of country.

A few hours after this incident one could cease to worry as we had marched about twelve miles, and it was evening, with the promise of darkness and safety from further attack. As we marched along my mind went back over the incidents of the night and morning. A long chapter could be written about individual officers and men of the column, of the gallant and uncomplaining Peter Monahan, Con Daly and Jer O'Leary, who in the minutes after being fatally wounded and before their deaths, joked and smiled, dying as proudly as they had lived courageously; of the coolness and competence of Liam Deasy, Tadhg O'Sullivan, Con Lucey and the other officers who were such towers of strength throughout the long night and morning; the efficiency and courage of the section commanders; the prowess of the riflemen like Captain Denis Mehigan and Captain Con Lehane; of the heroism of Dick Spencer, who in full view of the British forty yards away, leaped out in the open to lift in, under heavy fire, badly wounded Dan Corcoran; of the coolness of Eugene Callanan when a British bomb landed near him; of Flor Begley marching up and down playing his warpipes as the British bullets sang past; and of all the unmentioned riflemen whose behaviour surpassed even my high expectation of such a smashing body of West Cork fighters. None of those won the triumph of Crossbarry, for it was, in truth, a composite victory of one hundred and four officers and men banded together as disciplined comrades. No genius of leadership or no prowess of any officer or man was responsible, for all shared in the effort that shocked the confidence of the British authorities in the power of their armed forces.

Now before reaching Kibolane in the evening, where we were to breakfast, I stood on the ditch of a boreen to watch the flying column pass. Flankers had been called in and the column marched in a long line of sections in extended order, about thirty yards between sections. Although they had neither food nor rest since the previous evening they were a cocky lot. Their faces were unshaven, unwashed and greying with fatigue, but their steps were still springy, and as they came in to pass where I stood, their shoulders jerked back so that no one would assume they were tiring. Their boots and leggings were muddy, their trench coats hung open, no collars adorned their necks, and their caps, when not stuck in their belts, were worn with the peak to the back or over their shoulders. Their rifles were at the trail, and some carried captured rifles slung across their backs and sets of enemy equipment as well as their own. The centre section lugged along with evident pride the captured Lewis gun and ammunition drums; the first machine gun we ever possessed. They not only looked tough but were tough. Yet I knew them to be light-hearted youths who would normally have been happy working on their farms, or in the towns or back at their schools, had they not volunteered to fight the savage British aggression that stalked the land.

The greatness of those men of the flying column had a double-edged effect on me. One knew they could be relied on to the last, but on the other hand, I grew to have such an affectionate regard for them that I worried continually in case I failed them through negligence or inefficiency. I dreaded to lose a single one of them through some fault of mine. Their confidence in me was even disturbing. No matter where they were marched, billeted or put in action, they never murmured or doubted the correctness of my decisions, and I shall always cherish the fact that never once during all the Anglo-Irish struggle did any officer or man question any of my decisions or show to me anything but the greatest loyalty and comradeship. I was a severe and impatient commander with many faults. On the parade ground, the march and in action I was the commandant, saluted and addressed as such. In the billets I was 'Tom', one of themselves and entitled to no more favourable treatment. Yet, somehow, these fine fellows would ensure that I had the best bed. After I had been hurt and when long marches with the column were something of an effort, during a halt some of those men would come up with a saddled horse and say casually, 'Commandant, this horse is idle and you might as well ride him the rest of the way.' In action against the enemy it was the same; men would keep closer than was necessary and would take unnecessary risks in protecting me. Their thoughtfulness and generosity were unbounded. I had no parent, brother or sister living in West Cork, and unlike the others never received parcels of shirts and socks. Still those column officers and men, with a fine delicacy, saw I had more changes than they themselves enjoyed. I often wondered at the great luck which had cast my lot amongst such comrades, and their fineness only made my responsibility the greater. So after each fight I examined my conscience to find out if there was anything I had left undone, or if I had ordered some movement which might have been better left unexecuted. Coming on to Gurranereigh on that evening of March 19th, I decided I had nothing to regret and I was as happy and carefree as the remainder. There was nothing to feel sad about, except those three we had left behind at Crossbarry, lying in a green field with their faces turned to the sky.

Gurranereigh was outside the West Cork Brigade area, but we were not respecters of borders and had crossed on many occasions. Toureen and Kilmichael fights were fought by the West Cork Brigade column inside the boundaries of Cork No. 1 Brigade, and we had dived for food and security so often into this area that my friend, Seán O'Hegarty, the OC Cork 1, had often acidly asked if we had any food or houses in West Cork, instead of trespassing all over his brigade. However, Seán's Volunteers at Gurranereigh gave us a great welcome. The news of our fight had preceded us, and in a short time they had arranged food and billets for the tired flying column. The headquarters billet was at Joe Sullivan's large farmhouse where, as on many other visits, we had received such a hospitable reception. Joe was over seventy years of age, a dignified and patriarchal old gentleman. He always received us with an old-fashioned courtesy, but never sought to hide his opinion that our generation was only a poor second to the one which peopled the land in the days of his youth. For Joe was a Fenian, and in 1867 he waited with his gun for the call, that never reached him, to rise against the British. In spite of the failure of the 1867 revolt, he held rigidly to the opinion that if the leadership had been different, the Fenians would have beaten the English into the sea. His sons were active Volunteers and his daughters members of Cumann na mBan. The family would sit around the fireside listening to the old man, and signalling me to contradict their father and so draw his ire on my own head. But I refused to play, and one of the sons would have to make an unfavourable comparison of the Fenians to the Volunteers. Then the old gentleman would lash out and the offending son would be squelched in a torrent of praise for the Fenians and of belittlement of their present-day successors, particularly that son of his who dared to question the superiority of the Fenians over all other generations of Irishmen. All the rest of us would support the old man and join with him in condemning his offending and misguided son. But sometimes out of respect for his West Cork guests, Joe would make a concession. The West Cork flying column was the best of the present poor lot. It had done fairly well, but only fairly well, around Rosscarbery, Ballinhassig, Bandon and Kilmichael, and by all accounts it had done middling at Crossbarry. But how much better the Fenians would have done all this fighting had they been alive that day. I always enthusiastically agreed with him and so we remained firm friends to the end.

It was in this old Fenian's house the details reached us that night of Charlie Hurley's death. Charlie was sleeping at Humphrey Forde's, Ballymurphy, and just before we heard the shots at 6.30 that morning, he was awakened by the noise of British soldiers battering in the front door with their rifle butts. As ever, thoughtful of the safety of others, he told the people of the house to remain upstairs in safety, and down the stairs he walked, clad only in his shirt and trousers, with his gun in his hand, to meet his death like the great Irishman he was. The enemy were in the kitchen when Charlie walked into view, firing as he rushed them. They fired and retreated through the front door, so Charlie made for the back door. He rushed out into the yard to be met immediately by a dozen rifles, and he fell dead in the farmyard with several bullets in him, chiefly through his head. He had died in the manner which we expected. He had foretold it himself. One day, as I was chaffing him, he turned to me and said quite gravely, 'When I am killed by them I shall be alone. I shall die fighting them, but none of you will be with me.' And so it was. The stormy life of one of the greatest patriot soldiers of Ireland of any generation had ended.

The same messenger brought the news of the escape of Seán Buckley. When Seán parted from Charlie the previous night, he went to sleep at the house of Mrs O'Connell, Ballinphellic, about a mile across country from Humphrey Forde's. About the same time as Charlie was killed, another column of soldiers arrived to arrest everyone in O'Connell's. Luckily for Seán these were men of the Hampshire Regiment from Cork, who did not recognise him. Had the Essex come to that house instead, they would immediately have known him, and Seán's death would not have been as merciful as that of Charlie. Seán posed as a farm labourer and was held for several hours. Miss Baby Forde, who gave such unstinted national service, pleaded so hard with the officer in charge to leave her the old farm labourer to milk the cows, that the officer who was about to take Seán away hesitated. He went back to have another look at Seán's spare figure, grey hair and gaunt face. The grey hairs won and the officer sent Seán off to milk the cows and get on with his work.

Arrangements had already been made for the burials of Con Daly, Peter Monahan and Jer O'Leary. Now Liam and I talked of how we would bury Charlie. Owing to the war it was not possible to have the fighting men of West Cork at a public funeral. We had to choose between giving him a public funeral or one where only armed Volunteers would be present. We chose the latter as we knew he would wish it to be so. The British had brought his body back into Bandon and had vainly tried to have it identified. Afterwards they photographed it and threw it into the workhouse morgue. Word was sent to the Kilbrittain Cumann na mBan and they went into Bandon to spirit Charlie's body away secretly to the church near his burial place at Clogagh. So on the day after Crossbarry, the flying column was again on the move. In the evening and through the night we marched twenty-four miles to reach Clogagh at 2 o'clock in the morning of March 21st. Armed sentries were thrown out, the priest was called, the men of the flying column filed into the church to pray that their dead comrade would have eternal peace. After a short time the column again formed up outside the church and, with rifles reversed, slow marched to the graveyard with Charlie in our midst. Perhaps it was because Charlie was such a lovable comrade that the scene was seared into my memory. It is still fresh and clear; the dirge of Flor Begley's war pipes caoining a lament, the slow march of the brigade flying column, the small group of only six other mourners, the rain-soaked sky and earth, and the wintry moon that shone, vanished and shone again as we followed him to his grave. The grief-stricken faces of the riflemen as I gave the order, 'Present Arms', for their last salute to a gallant patriot leader, the three volleys and the 'Last Post' ringing clearly in the night air are all still vivid. Then I spoke the tribute we all felt and pledged the fighting men of West Cork to carry on the work of liberation for which Charlie and so many others had already died. At 3.30 a.m. we again faced to the better fighting country in the west and without delay marched off to cross the dangerous Clonakilty–Bandon main road before dawn.

We reached Ahiohill, eight miles away, at 7.30 in the morning, after a nearly continuous march of thirty-two miles. We hoped we would not have to fight that day as we were exhausted, but we were content. We had striven to give a soldier's burial to the man whose memory will be forever enshrined in all our hearts.

That night in Ahiohill we received many reports to the reactions to Crossbarry. We scanned the daily newspapers to learn from the official communiqué of the British military headquarters in Dublin their version of the action. It gave a short, garbled account amounting to an apologia for their operating troops, which it announced as the Essex Regiment, the Hampshire Regiment and the RIC (including Auxiliaries and Black and Tans). The only mention of their casualties was that in our first onslaught eight of them were killed; five, including two officers, wounded, and their transport burned. For the first and only time up to the end of hostilities the British had not issued a casualty list. Nine days later, when we were to attack them again, they officially issued the names and ranks of their two killed and nine wounded. That was a reasonable casualty list and so could be published. But not a single name appeared of any of their Crossbarry dead. They would find it difficult to explain away the loss of so many killed and wounded, in an action against a group termed by them officially as civilians and rebels. Besides, the publication of such a large British casualty list would be as detrimental to British morale as it would be beneficial to that of the Irish. Hence their casualty list had to be suppressed. This communiqué also announced that six of our men were killed, seven wounded and that a quantity of arms, ammunition and bombs was captured from us. Our casualties were, as already stated, three killed and two wounded, and not a single firearm, bomb or round of ammunition lost by us. There was no mention, of course, of the arms and ammunition we had captured from them.

However, the news hawks of the British and Irish daily newspapers, who hurried to the scene, soon gleaned some of the facts, probably from individual soldiers who participated in the attack. Despite the stiff British censorship, they conveyed in their editions of March 21st that something out of the ordinary had occurred and that the rebels had come out on top. The British *Daily Mail,* hostile to Ireland, featured Crossbarry and announced in glaring headlines the strength of the fighting rebels, the seriousness of the engagement and, with amazement, our effrontery in playing the bagpipes. Other British dailies followed suit. Our own were less cautious than usual, and although they were compelled to publish the British version, here and there they slipped in sentences so as to give their readers a fairer account of the fight. The following are some excerpts from the daily *Cork Examiner* of March 21st:

> About two or three o'c. on Saturday morning a large party of military left Bandon in several lorries going towards Cork. Parties of military also left Cork, Kinsale and Ballincollig at the same time. The expedition was carried out on a most extensive scale and a large part of the country between Cork, Ballincollig and Bandon was surrounded. The military appeared to have received

word that an ambush was being prepared. The lorries halted at various points.

From about three o'clock the whole countryside was patrolled by military and houses in the Waterfall district and around were searched, while military patrolled the roads near Upton and Crossbarry. It was in the latter place shooting occurred about 7 a.m., when the Essex Regiment was ambushed. The party travelled in eight lorries, three in front and the remaining five some distance behind. Three lorries were in front, two large and a Crossley tender, travelling rapidly and close together, proceeded to where the ambush party lay and when they approached a small bridge near the place there were several loud explosions. These went off with terrific force and part of the bridge collapsed. Three lorries, now in the centre of the attack, were blown up. Fire was opened immediately and seven military and one policeman, Constable Kenward, were killed, whilst several others, including a policeman, were wounded.

Reliable sources stated that the actual scene was one hundred yards from Crossbarry and that two farmhouses, Beasley's and Harold's, were used as cover by the ambushers. The other lorries retreated towards Innishannon, Ballinhassig and three others to Bandon. Reinforcements were then dispatched quickly to Crossbarry.

Remaining members of the ambush party remained under cover and replied to the attackers' fire, which lasted half-an-hour. Reinforcements of the Hampshire Regiment arrived to find all the first party killed or wounded. The reinforcements engaged the attackers, these retreating towards Begley's Fort and a running fight was kept up for a considerable time. The civilians succeeded in escaping over the hills, it is claimed suffering many casualties. Following the ambush there was extensive military activity in the whole district. Houses, straw, hay, were all burned to the ground.

> The attackers arrived after midnight and took forcible possession of the Harolds and Beasleys. They imprisoned the householders, made themselves comfortable, cooked meals and played the piano. By five o'clock all arrangements were completed for the ambush. Bedroom windows were barricaded and a cowshed loopholed as were the ditch walls outside. A section of the ditch here commanded the road and this was strongly fortified. Trees and a thick hedge afforded good cover. At 8 a.m. the fight began and firing lasted fifteen minutes.
>
> When the firing ceased the attackers made their escape without casualties in a northerly direction over the hills and the occupants of the houses ventured out to find the road strewn with dead and wounded. Two of the soldiers died immediately after being wounded. Miss Beasley was prominent in her helping of the wounded.

The last sentence gives an indication as to where the *Cork Examiner* representative got at least some of his copy. Both Harolds and Beasleys were opposed to the IRA. Even though this report contained many enemy-inspired inaccuracies, the *Cork Examiner* had slipped in some pungent sentences containing facts. How the censor had allowed the *Examiner* statement to pass that the British retreated at three points and did not stop until they reached Ballinhassig, Innishannon and Bandon must remain a mystery; as also the fact that the censor did not insist on the deletion of the lines reporting that 'the occupants of Harolds and Beasleys ventured out to find the road strewn with dead and wounded.'

The British garrisons in West Cork reacted to Crossbarry

by lengthening the curfew period in many towns. It was now fixed at 7 p.m. in the town of Bandon. This, as already stated, did not hamper us, as the enemy were not keen on emerging from their fortresses to enforce it. Actually a few days after they had ordered curfew at 7 p.m. the IRA entered the town at 10 p.m. and shot dead a Bandon traitor on his own doorstep. The British held such a high opinion of this agent that they compulsorily closed all businesses in Bandon on the day of his funeral. Another reaction of theirs was to burn four Republican farmhouses in the neighbourhood of the action. On the following night we 'raised the ante' and burned eight loyalists' homes, including Beasley's and Harold's. This halted the British burnings for the time being, at least. Yet another was the arrival of more British reinforcements for the West Cork garrisons. Space to house them in their military and Black and Tan barracks became an acute problem. But all those reactions were of little consequence as compared to that of our own people who, whenever we met them, openly rejoiced at the victory of their own soldiers over the centuries-old foe.

# 20

# ATTACK ON ROSSCARBERY

NOW that Charlie was no more, some brigade officer had to leave the column to look after matters at headquarters. Liam Deasy was the obvious choice. He had been adjutant for many years, knew every company in the unit, had a lengthy experience of the numerous reports and communications continually passing between the brigade, GHQ and the battalions, and had played a major part in the building up of the brigade. Dick Barrett and he were to travel to Dublin about the appointment of Charlie's successor. This had to be made, as was the rule, by General Headquarters, though, indeed, this body was not likely to appoint anyone unacceptable to the brigade officers, and Dick undertook to convey the view that Liam should be appointed. When some time later I announced at the next brigade council meeting this appointment, there was general satisfaction. We had great difficulty in persuading Liam to leave the column, even temporarily. He did not want the vacant post, and sought to remain with us, but eventually he agreed to go back to our brigade headquarters. Many others were also disbanded for duties with their own battalions, while other officers and men were mobilised. It was practically a new flying column that left Ahiohill on the night of March 22nd. Its strength was seventy riflemen.

Jim Hurley was back with us again. He had been severely hurt destroying a bridge near Clonakilty in the first week of March so had missed the Crossbarry fight. Now he hobbled painfully on sticks, but short of a direct order, which I was reluctant to give, he would not leave. With him was Tim O'Donoghue, the Vice-OC, a big strapping man and a splendid officer. Others from Hurley's battalion also joined us, but we sorely missed Stephen O'Neill and Flyer Nyhan, captured some time previously. Con Connolly (Neilus), that veteran Volunteer and fine soldier, the Commandant of the Skibbereen Battalion, and some of his officers also came on, as did Ted O'Sullivan and others from the western end of the area. On the morning of Wednesday 23rd, we arrived at positions on the railway line, five miles from Clonakilty, to attack a train scheduled to carry enemy troops from Clonakilty to Skibbereen. This was one of the few occasions on which the enemy was able to deceive us as instead they travelled by road. Some days before they had reserved a number of carriages on that train, knowing well that we would hear of their arrangements. When the news reached me that they had left Clonakilty by road, we grinned, conceded them a point for being able to fool us and immediately withdrew.

Later that night when billeted in the Kilmeen Company area, Jim Hurley and Tim O'Donoghue informed me that my search for a man capable of making an effective mine was ended. On the following morning they brought over Captain McCarthy of that district, who had served as an officer in the Royal Engineers throughout the 1914–18 war and was an expert on explosives. He was most sympathetic to the IRA and readily agreed to help in any possible manner. After talking for more than an hour and realising McCarthy's suitability, I asked him to make a mine containing fifty pounds of explosives capable of breaching a wall, four charges with about seven pounds of explosives in each, and thirty canister bombs of about one pound each. Tim O'Donoghue was detailed to procure the materials from Dan Holland, Quartermaster of the Bandon Battalion, and from the quartermaster of the Castletownbere unit. That night we moved again and for five days zigzagged around evading contact with strong British rounding-up forces. In the early hours of March 30th we reached Benduff, three miles west of Rosscarbery. It was snowing heavily. That evening at seven Tim O'Donoghue arrived with the mine, the seven-pound charges and about thirty of the canister bombs. The mine had two fuses hanging from it so that if one detonator failed, the other would explode.

From the charges and home-made canister bombs fuses also hung. The fuses of the large mine were cut to a length tested to explode it seventy seconds after the fuse was lighted. The fuses of the seven-pound charges were of fifteen-second duration and those of the canister bombs only seven seconds. Accuracy in the length of all the fuses was vital, especially for the men carrying the mine or throwing the bombs.

The flying column paraded at 9 p.m. and the men were told for the first time they were to move at midnight to attack Rosscarbery Barracks. I outlined the plan of attack and repeated several times the detailed duties of each section, so that there would be no misunderstanding the responsibilities of every man. Three groups of five riflemen in each were detailed to cut telegraph wires and block roads, chiefly by felling trees, between Rosscarbery and the garrison towns of Skibbereen thirteen miles, Dunmanway thirteen miles and Clonakilty eight miles distant. The obstructions and wire cuttings were to be made at designated places and were to commence precisely at 1 a.m., ten minutes before the opening of the attack. Those groups moved off at 11 p.m. The remaining fifty-five members of the column were then reorganised into action groups. Ten specially selected officers and men were formed into a storming party. Each of these was given two automatics or revolvers and their rifles were to be carried slung across their backs. They were to lay the mine and rush the breach after the explosion. The second group of ten riflemen was to follow up with improvised torches, made by wrapping pieces of paraffin-soaked sacking thickly around one end of a stick. As soon as the storming party had breached an entry into the barracks, these were to be lighted and thrown in to expose the targets. The third group of twelve riflemen was to occupy positions north and east of the barracks and prevent the garrison emerging from the back or side. The fourth group of twelve riflemen was subdivided into three of four each to hold the roads in the immediate vicinity of the town. These would prevent our attacking party from being surprised by enemy reinforcements who might have sneaked past our more distant obstruction parties, and would also prevent any messenger or informer from leaving the town. The fifth group of the remaining eleven riflemen was to act as a reserve party and immediately the attack commenced they were to open up all the shops which sold petrol and paraffin and fill the fuel into a dozen buckets and half-pint bottles. Tom Moloney and James Hayes of the local company were given revolvers and were to act as guides.

Our actual attacking force comprised twenty-one officers and men. Defending this barracks were a head constable, two sergeants and nineteen constables, who were nearly all Black and Tans with European war active service. It was not the numbers of the enemy that mattered most. This large, strongly fortified barracks stood alone, back from the footpath, at the eastern end of the town. The nearest house to it was O'Mahony's, thirty yards across the street. The building was an exceptionally strong one of stone, and the walls of the ruins, which still stand, give some indication of its formidable constructional strength.

Moloney, our company IO, had informed me that an outlet had been made in the roof, and that in defensive exercises the garrison usually brought a machine gun through it. As usual, there were rolls of barbed wire all around the building, except on the narrow path from the front gate. This gate was even a problem, as Moloney had also noted that on some nights it was locked, and on others it was simply latched. A good IO was Tom Moloney, now in Boston, USA. We had to destroy this post, if at all possible. It was a thorn in our side and its destruction would mean that we would have an area of roughly two hundred and seventy square miles free of the enemy, to use as a base. That night I was prepared, if necessary, to lose several men to destroy it. The enemy had boasted many times that Rosscarbery was their one impregnable police post in Ireland.

I remained alone, as was usual before a major attack, trying to foresee and plan against any eventuality, from the accidental meeting of an enemy patrol to the assaulting of a warned and waiting garrison. Should the latter disaster occur, the warned garrison would wait until we arrived in front of the barracks, then light up the surroundings, open fire with machine guns and rifles, and the climax would be the explosion, in the midst of our dead and wounded, of our mine, the fuses of which would already be lighted. But such thoughts had to be put aside, for in guerilla warfare chances must be continually taken and one would never accomplish anything by always expecting the worst. So I turned my thoughts to my boyhood associations with the places in and around this town that I knew so well.

The road by which we would enter was not remembered by its official name, 'The New Line'. For me it was the road where, when I was thirteen years of age, a playmate had on a summer's evening bet me a penny I would not ride, without falling off, a cow of ours as far as the entrance of the town, a few hundred yards away. The old milch cow had ambled along steadily with me on her back to the entrance and, having won the penny, I was about to dismount when a mongrel, undoubtedly amazed at the unusual spectacle, decided to intervene. Before I could jump off he yapped at the cow's heels and off she went at a gallop. Every other dog in the town joined in the chase and the adult townspeople standing around roared encouragement as the cow and rider, pursued by a pack of snarling and excited dogs, galloped through the town. The cow made for the protection of the stalls, which had a low entrance door, but luckily I had enough sense to throw myself on a soft heap of manure outside. Later the reckoning at home was painful for 'disgracing the family with your hooliganism and damaging the poor cow, which is in calf again'. I could never make out which was the bigger crime.

Likewise, the footpath the column would walk in a short time was not on the North Square. This would be remembered for Bateman's bakery and sweet shop, which for a few glorious days had a broken window pane. There was a round hole of less than an inch in diameter, and by great luck it was directly in front of a large box of soft jujubes. With a bent pin on the top of a thin stick the sweets were cleared. When one of the gang got remorse of conscience and said it was a mortal sin to steal the sweets, that we would have to tell it in confession and make restitution, he was silenced immediately by the irrefutable pronouncement that as Batemans were Protestants, it was no sin at all for us Catholics to take their sweets. Taking from a Protestant was not stealing; as a matter of fact, it was the bounden duty of all small Catholic boys to relieve Protestants of their goods, especially their sweets. The road behind North Square was recalled as the place the farmers tied their saddle horses on fair and market days. Anxiously we would await the return of our young scouts from public houses to report: 'They are well on and arguing away. It is quite safe to take them.' We would then untie the horses and cautiously walk them to the outskirts. An hour or so later they would be returned covered with sweat having run several races on the nearby roads or strand.

The top of the hill leading to the school, where the kindly master, John McCarthy, ruled, was not the Caim Hill, but the venue for after-school fights. It mattered not that one had no quarrel with the boy one had to fight that evening. The older boys had decided it and that was all, for they were the law. Furtively during the day opponents would weigh each other up and work up a hate. But this was no good, as hate would not come until one or other landed a punch on the nose, the favourite opening blow of the time. Further east was the church where many of us, in obedience to a mother with the fantastic notion that her son would surely make a good priest, had served as altar boys. There never lived an Irish mother without that secret hope, even though her neighbours, without exception, were equally certain that 'mother's boy' gave more promise of dying the death of a gangster. The road outside the church was part of the mile and a half circuit we regularly ran barefooted at the age of fourteen, in preparation for the day when we would wrest the crown from the reigning monarch, Tom Longboat, the world's long-distance champion. South of this circuit was the sea and 'Sweeney's Hole', where before one was eleven years old, one learned to swim by being thrown into twelve feet of water by the elder boys. The Abbey graveyard, where five of our riflemen would soon be building a defensive position to protect our attack, was not remembered as the place where the bones of many generations of my forebears lay. Rather was it recalled as next to Jeff Wycherley's 'Abbey' field, where without his permission we used to play football, until a warning shout, often from one of Jeff's own sons, that Jeff was approaching, scattered us in all directions. These and other flashbacks coursed through my mind and eased the strain of waiting.

At midnight the flying column moved off. A mile from Rosscarbery it halted and the men were ordered to remove their boots and tie them on to the back equipment. The mine and bombs were taken from the farm cart by the riflemen. Then the bootless flying column padded silently into Rosscarbery and took up their allotted positions at 1.10 in the morning. The column had made its approach so efficiently that we afterwards learned not a single person in the town knew of our passing through until the action opened. The main attacking groups halted around a corner near the post office, thirty yards from the barracks. The first task was to ascertain if there was any sign of the enemy's awareness of an attack, and to find out if the entrance gate was locked. To do this equipment had to be removed as one had to wriggle up the path on one's stomach to the barrack gate and in the darkness feel around cautiously for the lock. It was latched but not locked and there was no sign of life from the barracks, except the tiny gleams of light shining through the loopholes of the steel window shutters. Immediately after I returned from the gate, the mine with its heavy encasement, weighing in all about eighty pounds, was raised coffin-like onto the shoulders of Jack Corkery, Peter Kearney, Tom Kelleher and Christy O'Connell. In one hand each held a revolver and steadied the mine with the other. Denis Lordan applied a lighted candle to both fuses simultaneously and we started off at a half run to the barrack door, the mine bobbing up and down as its fuses spluttered and burned, but being kept fairly steady by Tim O'Donoghue and Ted O'Sullivan who trotted alongside the bearers. As I snapped the latch, opened the gate and covered the few yards to the door, I was flanked by Mick Crowley and Jim Hurley. The bearers lowered the mine noiselessly and Mick and I each placed a brick under its outer edge to tilt it against the barrack door. Then we sprinted back around the corner to lie flat on the footpath with our hands pressed hard against our ears.

The roar of the explosion came a few seconds afterwards. The storming party leaped to its feet and ran for the barracks, where a lighted torch showed us that no breach of the nature we had expected had been made. The vagaries of the blasts of explosive bombs are better known now than they were in 1921. The blast of our bomb had blown mainly backwards removing the roof of O'Mahony's house across the road. But part of it had also damaged the barracks to some extent. A hole had been made in the outer barrack door and the steel shutters of two of the windows had been blown skywards. None of the garrison had been hurt and, before we had completed the examination of the door, in a matter of seconds some of them were firing out through it. Rushing it was out of the question, but we had at last, in the hole in the door and the two unprotected windows, at least a sporting chance of fighting them for the barracks. So the column settled down to a struggle that I knew would be a grim and lengthy one.

We let them have some volleys through the broken windows and the door, but we were handicapped because of our cramped surroundings and only a few of us could get fire positions. Con Connolly and four riflemen were ordered across the street to occupy the upstairs windows of O'Mahony's. They were to fire at the upper windows of the barracks and particularly to watch the roof. Four other members of the column had already entered the post office to destroy the telegraphic and telephone apparatus. The volume of fire from the barracks increased and the garrison had far more rifles in action than we could bring effectively into play when our first bomb was thrown. This Mills, lobbed through the hole in the door, exploded in the hallway, and there was at once some reduction in the volume of enemy fire, but before long it again increased. It was now necessary to keep one of our improvised torches continually burning at the barrack door so that we could see our way to the targets, but unfortunately this also showed us up to the enemy. Our second Mills bomb had hardly exploded inside the barracks, when the enemy launched their first at where we were standing ten yards from the barrack door. By the light of our torch we saw it coming, dropped flat with our arms protecting our heads and waited for it to explode harmlessly over us. Then our home-made canister bombs were called for and a bombing duel commenced. The canister bombs had to be lighted from a candle before being thrown in through windows and doors, and in the intervals we were lying flat outside the building dodging their returning Mills and egg-shaped bombs. The British were making a very bad mistake and I fervently hoped they would continue to do so. Their bombs were timed to explode five seconds after the pin was pulled out and the spring released. They launched them immediately they released the springs, and as we were only ten yards away the bombs reached us in under three seconds giving us an invaluable two seconds to flatten out. Had they counted two as we did after releasing the springs before launching the bombs, they would have exploded as they reached us and undoubtedly caused us severe losses.

The fight continued as a ding-dong affair, both sides using rifles, revolvers and bombs. It took us nearly two hours to clear the enemy from the front ground-floor rooms, but some of them fought on from those in the back. Eventually we drove them from their last ground-floor position. When the garrison retreated upstairs they left two dead comrades, Sergeant Shea and Constable Bowles, below and maintained their sturdy defence from the top storey. As well as firing from the front top-storey windows, they were now pouring heavy rifle fire down the stairs and dropping an occasional bomb. Then we exploded two of our seven-pound charges in the ground-floor rooms in an endeavour to bring down the ceilings, but the upper-storey floors still held. This having failed, bottles of paraffin and petrol were fired at the smouldering stairs and soon it was on fire. We continued to rain bullets through the ceilings at this stubborn defence and they were at last driven into one back top-storey room. Then the end came after four and a half hours of fighting. We could not get up the stairs through a sea of flames, but neither could they come down to surrender. So they threw all their arms and ammunition on to the burning stairway, lowered their wounded through the back window and climbed down after them. They huddled together, a disarmed, defenceless and shocked group of men in various stages of undress. Nine were wounded, some very badly: Head Constable Neary, Constables Brady, Woodford, Sullivan, O'Keefe, Roberts, Doyle, Kinsella and Harken. The bodies of Sergeant Shea and Constable Bowles could not be reached as they lay on their funeral pyre in the now fiercely burning barracks.

The RIC and Black and Tans, as a force, were detested by the masses of the people and had committed many atrocities in West Cork. This garrison, however, had not killed or wounded a single citizen, nor had they burned houses, or effected any arrests. They were unique in this respect. When the Auxiliary and military forces operated around Rosscarbery this garrison had, on numerous occasions, saved the lives of some of our people, and intervened when the terrorists were clubbing and beating defenceless men. Their behaviour was all the more praiseworthy because of the several previous attacks made on them. Charlie Hurley and I had fired shots at their barracks in 1920 when we failed to contact any patrol. Seán Lehane and I had later searched the town for them, but finding none, had watched the barrack door from a lane across the way. A man dressed as a civilian passed and it was only when he turned into the barrack gate we realised he was a policeman. We were only able to get a snap shot at him as he dived in the door. Only a short time before Jim Hurley, Jim Murphy and one or two others opened fire on a patrol, killing Constable Brock. Yet no members of this garrison had ever run amok. Therefore we sought no revenge. The enemy survivors found shelter and were given first aid in some houses in the town and in the nearby Convent of Mercy. This garrison had fought exceptionally well and had defended their barracks to the end. But good as those men were, they were far excelled by the men of the flying column. Of the twenty-one officers and men detailed for the actual attack, not more than ten could be used to fire a shot or throw a bomb because of the difficulties of approach. These had to breach the fortress and root out room by room twenty-two experienced and better-armed opponents who were entrenched behind the solid walls of a prepared defence. The smashed garrison and the destroyed barracks tell the story of how well the men of the flying column had carried out that task.

By some extraordinary good luck none of the column were killed or wounded, but were a tired, dishevelled group with scorched clothes and blackened faces when the fight had ended. As we had no report of the approach of enemy reinforcements, we dallied in the town until daybreak to clean up and rest a little. When we paraded in the town square before moving off, the barracks was only a smouldering ruin. The men of the column, in high spirits, commenced to sing the old fighting songs of our race as we left and marched first to the west to mislead any informer who might contact the British reinforcements. Then the column turned north for a few miles, wheeled again to the east and after an eleven-mile march reached breakfast and billets in the parish of Rossmore.

After midday, reports reached us of the British reinforcements converging on Rosscarbery. Several columns, including the terrorist Essex and Auxiliaries, were moving from Bandon, Clonakilty and Dunmanway. Because of our obstructions they did not reach Rosscarbery until the afternoon. None of the enemy passed within four miles of our billets and it was clear from their tactics that they accepted our deceptive short march to the west as an indication that we had retired in that direction. We continued to rest until darkness eight miles east-north-east of Rosscarbery, while they swept on to the west of that town. Then the flying column marched a further twenty-two miles, across the Bandon River at Baxter's Bridge, to reach before dawn that stronghold of the IRA, the Newcestown Company area.

That day's daily press, April 1st, 1921, carried the British official communiqué and the British-inspired press stories of the fight. With all their untruths and inconsistencies, they are given verbatim hereunder as another good example of the British authorities' apologia for a defeat they could not quite suppress, but which they minimised by misleading statements:

> Official Report: 'A telegram received at Dublin Castle on Thursday evening states that the garrison consisted of one Head Constable, two sergeants and nineteen constables. They put up a most sturdy defence. Sergeant Shea and Constable Bowles were killed and buried in the debris. After the explosion, which blew out the barrack front, Head Constable Neary, Constables Bradley, Woodford, Sullivan, O'Keefe, Roberts, Doyle, Kinsella and Harkins were wounded.
>
> 'The rebels captured no arms or ammunition, all the stores being left behind in the flames, while the police jumped for their lives from an upper window of the barracks at 7 a.m. after beating off the rebels.
>
> 'The attackers carried away their dead and wounded. The bodies of Constables [*sic*] Shea and Bowles remained in the

burning building. They could not be reached, as the police bombs left behind were exploding.'

*Cork Examiner* report, Friday, April 1, 1921: 'Owing to telegraph lines being cut, reports at first are not complete of alarming attack on R.I.C. barracks at Rosscarbery and of heavy loss to the garrison. Definite information states the attackers numbered two hundred, and stole up to the barracks at 2 a.m. and with the aid of a huge explosive, blew in the front portion of the building and immediately opened a terrific fire with rifles and bombs.

'The garrison of nineteen took up all defensive positions. The front portion of the building was soon burning and the garrison were obliged to abandon successive positions, fighting all the way, until only the top storey was intact. Here all the police, wounded and unwounded, continued their resistance for five hours from 2 till 7 a.m., when enveloping flames compelled them to abandon the building.

'To do this they were obliged to jump from the top window to the ground. A few escaped to Clonakilty about 9 a.m. and reinforcements arrived to find the attackers gone and most of the small garrison dead or wounded. The killed were Sergeant Shea and Constable Bowles; seriously wounded: Constables Doyle, Kinsella and Harken [*sic*]; wounded: Head Constable Neary, Constables Bradley, Woodford, Sullivan, O'Keefe and Roberts. The remainder were unhurt. No arms or guns were lost. It being fair day in Rosscarbery, numbers of people were about in the early morning. The roads to Skibbereen were trenched and trees were felled near Shepperton.'

The following letter from Michael Collins shows the reactions of our General Headquarters:

# ATTACK ON ROSSCARBERY

Oglaigh na hEireann,
April 7, 1921.

To: The Brigade Adjutant,
Cork 3 Brigade.

I have just received report of the Rosscarbery fight. It was a splendid performance and, as I know the position of the place so well, I appreciate it all the more. I hope some time shortly to make the acquaintance of the officer who arranged this encounter and carried it out with such gallantry and efficiency.

D/I.

# 21

# FIRST SOUTHERN DIVISION FORMED

DURING the first half of April we tried on three occasions and failed to contact the enemy. The British were now only emerging from their bases to conduct large-scale round-up operations. They would sally forth from three or four towns simultaneously, converge on particular districts, comb them and return to their fortresses. To meet this new situation our tactics were to evade encirclement, to destroy bridges and roads before and behind those rounding-up units, and to snipe their patrols and barracks whenever possible. These sweeps by the British caused us no casualties. Indeed, it is a remarkable fact that not a single member of the West Cork IRA was killed or wounded or an active service IRA man captured during the whole of April.

As man does not live by bread alone, so too the IRA could not continue to exist only by flying column manoeuvres and fighting. Side by side with those operations marched the work of organisation and allied activities, and April 1921 is a good example of those efforts. During that month I recollect attending a brigade council, a battalion council, several meetings in connection with a proposed large-scale landing of arms in West Cork, and towards its close, a meeting in North Cork of representatives of nine southern brigades at which the First Southern Division was formally established.

In mid-April we received a message from our GHQ causing us to drop all other activities and to hurry to the district round Union Hall. This concerned the proposed landing in West Cork of twenty thousand rifles, five hundred machine guns and several million rounds of ammunition from an Italian steamer. Earlier in the year officers from the three Cork brigades and South Tipperary had met to urge GHQ to import arms and to spread the fight to non-fighting areas. Liam Deasy and I had represented West Cork at one of those meetings. These were quite informal and not sanctioned by GHQ. To me the discussions were indicative of the lack of control which GHQ exercised or could exercise over the brigades, and it was quite evident also that some officers were of the opinion that our headquarters needed pressure to intensify and develop the fight for freedom. I was not then in a position to judge the zeal and efficiency of our GHQ, but could not help thinking that any of the brigade officers at those meetings would have taken it very much amiss if a few of their battalion officers arranged a meeting to bring pressure on their brigade staff. If brigade officers could meet without the authority of GHQ to press for a certain policy, then battalions, companies and even sections should logically be entitled to similar action. That, of course, could easily lead to the demoralisation of the whole army, for surely in a very short time the confidence in and the authority of the controlling officers would be completely undermined. But there were no ill results of those unauthorised meetings, mainly because, perhaps, the officers attending were sincere, sensible and intelligent men, and as far as I know GHQ never expressed disapproval of those discussions. At the first meeting it was stated that GHQ had asked Cork 1 Brigade to send them a reliable officer with seafaring experience to go to Italy in connection with the transport to Ireland of twenty thousand rifles, five hundred machine guns and five million rounds of ammunition. Michael Leahy, Vice-OC of Cork 1 Brigade, had been selected for this task.

The decision to entrust the landing of all those arms to the West Cork Brigade may have been a flattering tribute, but its wisdom was open to question, as our area was being steamrolled by the enemy, and a less active area might have been chosen. On the other hand, quiet areas were invariably inefficient and not capable of defending such a landing. The other two Cork brigades had offered us every rifle and man at their disposal to ensure the safety of the landing and distribution of the arms. The united strength of the Cork brigades was then easily as great as that of any other six counties combined.

We had given much thought during the early months of the year to this landing of arms, and the responsibility weighed heavily on the few of us who knew of it. The landing of such a large cargo during the early period of the national struggle, when enemy activity was relatively small, would have been in itself a big undertaking, but now, in April 1921, when the Anglo-Irish War was at its height, it was a grim and colossal task. Our brigade did not shirk it, but one felt at times that the success or failure of Ireland's fight for freedom might well depend on the manner in which the brigade planned the landing and distribution of this invaluable cargo. So we sweated and slaved around Union Hall for nearly a week. We had many headaches, and because of the absolute necessity for complete secrecy, we could not delegate inquiries or any part of the work to any but a few specially selected officers. Charts had to be procured and examined as to how far into Union Hall harbour the Italian ship could ride; the trawlers and small boats to which the cargo was to be transferred had to be listed; arrangements had to be made for the commandeering of all motor transport in West Cork to distribute the arms to the dumps already waiting in Cork and Kerry; the reliability of motor drivers had to be ensured; crews arranged for the trawlers; personnel selected for the various tasks; routes chosen for the transport, while other roads and bridges over a large area had to be noted for destruction. Positions had to be examined near Clonakilty, Bandon, Macroom, Dunmanway, Skibbereen and Bantry, where small parties of IRA riflemen would protect our obstructions and delay any enemy attempt to reach Union Hall. A main defensive line had to be chosen near Union Hall at which the brigade column would cover the landing, and countless other details had to be arranged. From the message we received from Dublin, we judged that we were working against time and that the arms were due in the immediate future.

To make matters more difficult, there was large-scale enemy activity round the Union Hall area. Deasy, Buckley, Tadhg O'Sullivan, Denis Lordan and I were sleeping near Mouletreahane when, at four o'clock one morning, a scout alarmed us with the news that the whole district was surrounded and that the British were approaching within a hundred yards of the house. We had only time to partly dress, grab our arms and equipment and get out the back way before the enemy arrived. Hanging on to each other's equipment so that we could keep together in the dark, we edged cautiously towards a little hill half a mile away. On top of the hill was a very small field about forty yards square. All around us were the sounds of the enemy, and as we could not move further in any direction without running into them, we took up defensive positions and waited. Liam manned one ditch, Seán another, Tadhg a third and Denis the fourth, while I moved around between them. All of us except Seán Buckley had left some clothes behind. I had left my socks, leggings, pullover, cap and trench coat, and we were nearly frozen when the British withdrew about seven o'clock. Later we heard it was part of a combined round-up by the Skibbereen, Clonakilty, Macroom and Bandon garrisons. Those in our vicinity were the King's Regiment from Skibbereen. They found our beds warm, our abandoned clothes, and arrested the owner of the house. They severely interrogated our good friend, who admitted that five armed men had slept in his house, but asked how he could have refused shelter to armed men without risking being shot by them. Eventually the British released him, but brought their spoils of war, our clothes, with them to Skibbereen. Later Colonel Hudson was to return them to me under amusing circumstances.

We completed our plans and left the Union Hall district quite satisfied that nothing had been overlooked. We reached our headquarters at Belrose on the 21st, and on the following day Liam Deasy and I set out on our two-day journey to the North Cork Brigade area where the formative meeting of the 1st Southern Division was to be held on the 24th. On the evening of our first day's march we met Seán O'Hegarty, Brigade OC of Cork 1, and Florrie O'Donoghue, the Brigade Adjutant, and billeted with them that night. On the following morning we moved off early on our sixteen-mile walk to the venue of the meeting, travelling cross-country and on by-roads. Liam and I compared notes with Seán and Florrie as we travelled along. I already knew those Cork 1 officers and liked them well, although there was some friction previously because we had 'invaded' their territory on several occasions. O'Hegarty was a veteran of the movement and as early as 1915 had been ordered out of Cork by the enemy and forced to live in County Wexford. He was an implacable enemy of the British and had faith only in armed action as the way to his country's freedom. His prestige with the Irish Republican Army was exceptionally high, not only as a result of his long years of national service, but because of his fine character, keen brain and personality. Honest, outspoken even to a fault, hating sham and pretence, he had commanded the Cork 1 Brigade tirelessly and efficiently through the most difficult period of its existence. Seán became brigade commander after the arrest of Terence MacSwiney in August 1920, and was responsible more than any other individual for the aggressive and militant activities which placed Cork 1 Brigade amongst the leading brigades in Ireland. O'Donoghue, though younger than O'Hegarty, was also a Volunteer since 1916. He had filled many offices in his brigade at different periods. Shrewd, calm and capable, I rated him as one of the ten best officers I met during my membership of the IRA. An 'all round' officer, his speciality was intelligence, and he can be bracketed justly with Michael Collins, the Director of Intelligence, as the outstanding IO in Ireland. I was to get to know Florrie well, for he was to be the first-appointed adjutant of the 1st Southern Division, while I was to be later the first-appointed deputy divisional commander of that unit, so for some time we worked closely together. Not the least of his good qualities were his pleasant easy ways and his loyalty to brother officers.

Waiting for us at Lynch's, Kippagh, North Cork, were Liam Lynch and Seán Moylan, Cork 2 Brigade, Humphrey

Murphy and Andy Cooney (Tipperary), Kerry 2 Brigade, and John Joe Rice (Kenmare), Kerry 1 Brigade. There were no representatives from Kerry 3 (Cahirciveen); Waterford 1, Waterford 2 or the West Limerick Brigades. Ernest O'Malley, a staff captain who carried the document from the chief of staff setting up the division and appointing Liam Lynch as its OC, had also arrived. Talking to Liam Lynch was that splendid fighting officer Dan Breen, who, although from outside our divisional area, had come along to meet the group who were to establish the first divisional unit of the IRA.

The meeting opened shortly after our arrival on a rather depressed note, for we were all acutely conscious that representatives were present from only five brigades instead of nine. This augured badly for the success of the division, as we knew that every brigade had received fourteen days' notice of the time and venue of the meeting. O'Malley read the rather long and involved headquarters document setting up the division and then proceeded to expound on it. His language during his exposition of the document and his constant use of long military words and phrases left no doubt in the minds of his listeners that he had read a military book of some sort. Soon O'Hegarty started to shuffle and when in the next sentence O'Malley again used the words 'terrain and topography' O'Hegarty interrupted. O'Malley stopped nonplussed and then Seán went into action. Stating that the meeting had had enough rameis, he asked why Collins, Mulcahy or some senior GHQ officer had not come along to the meeting instead of sending a messenger, why no GHQ officer had ever visited the southern fighting units during all the period of the fighting, why GHQ had done nothing towards extending the fight to the inactive areas and why GHQ had not yet imported the arms and ammunition so badly needed. Seán then criticised the GHQ communication in detail, and after ten minutes of a telling and hard hitting talk sat down. In the lull that followed Liam Lynch formally took over the divisional command. Almost immediately it was announced that our food was ready and the meeting adjourned for an hour. We had still the sweat and grime of travel on us and Seán had located a canvas bucket, soap and towel. He now invited me down to a nearby stream where, he said, we could get a decent wash. Seán scooped up buckets of water from the shallow stream and, judging by the violent manner with which he splashed them over my soaped head and body, he was still thinking of 'terrain and topography'.

On the resumption of the meeting I was the first speaker, and O'Malley's description in his *On Another Man's Wound* of my contribution as 'assertive, almost aggressive' is probably correct. The headquarters document was so divorced from the realities of the situation in the south that most of us were in an angry mood. Nearly all the officers present expressed their disappointment with the Dublin communication, which might have been suitable for issue from the headquarters of an established, regular army, such as the British, French or American forces, with reserves of men, munitions, equipment and money. Not one of us was opposed to the setting up of the unit of a division as such, but we were all at a loss to understand how its establishment on paper would help the brigades at the most critical period of their existence. Seán Moylan, who was to succeed Lynch as OC Cork 2 Brigade, rounded off his comments: 'We started this war with hurleys, but, by Heavens, it seems to me we will all finish it off with fountain pens.' The GHQ document, written so obviously without any idea whatever of the day-to-day struggle of the active brigades striving to keep up the pressure and to escape annihilation by vastly greater forces, could not by ornate language and meaningless military phrases alone be expected to be readily accepted by the southern officers. We wanted action or the promise of action without undue delay to meet the publicly expressed threat by the British to bring over a further two hundred and fifty thousand troops to blockade the active areas and smother with men and munitions the fighting IRA units. So that at least some of the already incoming British reinforcements would be contained and held, we looked for some sign from GHQ that the fight would be extended to the east, the north, the midlands and the dormant western seaboard, where in many counties not an enemy had yet been killed. We sought proof that every effort was being made to procure .303 ammunition to enable the already scantily supplied flying columns to defend themselves and fight back during the long, bright days of the many summer months just ahead. The GHQ document gave no indication of its concern over those realities, and I, amongst others, felt that in all the circumstances the setting up of a division would not help.

The limitations of a divisional unit of a guerilla force of unpaid Volunteers, badly armed, without rapid means of communication, without transport, money or barracks, as an effective instrument of control, were very apparent. Indeed, the divisional unit and the guerilla army of the Irish Republic were, in times of war, a contradiction in terms. The functions of a divisional staff, if it were to be an instrument of control and direction, should be to make new appointments, replacing useless officers who had failed to fight their units, to move brigade columns as the situation demanded, to ensure a sufficient supply of arms and ammunition, to issue operation orders, to co-ordinate the attacks of several or all its brigades, to reinforce weak units and generally to direct the fight. The very nature of the Irish Republican Army of volunteer guerillas was directly opposed to those functions. Although it was highly disciplined, its members would resent the removal of officers by an authority outside the brigade, unless very good cause existed, and a brigade might easily be disrupted by such action. The movements of a brigade flying column could not be decided by anyone outside the area, as these were mainly governed by the changing positions and activities of the vastly greater British forces. In fact, a headquarters of a division of three and a half counties, such as the 1st Southern, could not expect to even contact any brigade flying column in less than three days, because the IRA had neither wireless, telephonic or telegraphic means of communication. For that reason too, a divisional operation order could not be acted on by flying columns as all operation orders must be based on the most up-to-date information, and as this might not reach the divisional headquarters for several days it might very probably be no longer correct and if acted on might well lead to disaster. The division could not supply the brigade with arms, ammunition, equipment or money, for it possessed nothing itself, and it would not be capable of enforcing an order to transfer material from a strong unit to a weaker one unless the brigade officers agreed to the suggestion.

Despite the Herculean work of the few officers of the staff of the 1st Southern Division, the establishment of this unit did not affect at any time the military situation in the south. During its two months of existence up to the end of hostilities with the British, it did not and could not effect the replacement of even one of the several useless officers who encumbered many units; it did not and could not add a man, a rifle, a bomb, a round of ammunition or a shilling to the strength of any brigade, nor did it organise any action or issue a single operation order to any unit. It may be claimed that if the war continued for another six months the division would have justified its formation as a unit of control, but that is pure conjecture. My own opinion remains that in guerilla warfare no unit larger than a brigade could ever be effective as a striking force, and it could not be directed in its activities by a higher authority from outside the brigade area, until the final phase of the war, when the guerillas had built up their own strength and had whittled down that of the enemy to something like equality. And no one will suggest that the Irish Republican Army had even approached the stage of semi-equality in men, armament or equipment, up to the end of its hostilities against the British.

It should be clearly understood that the limitations of the division were those inherent in the Irish Republican Army itself, and not in any way due to the personnel who were eventually to compose the staff. Liam Lynch, the Divisional OC, was one of the outstanding Irishmen of that period. He was the senior brigade officer in the south, having been in command of the North Cork Brigade since its formation. The standard of organisation and the record of activities of this brigade made it clear to me, before that meeting where I first met him, that Lynch was a highly efficient brigade OC and that he had been amongst the foremost in pushing the armed attack on the occupying forces. Now I studied him closely as I already knew that I was to be asked by him to go on the divisional staff for the organisation, training and the eventual operating of the divisional fighting forces, the flying columns of the nine brigades. That meeting and my later associations with Liam Lynch have built in my memory a picture of a man whose honesty and single-mindedness of purpose struck one as a bright light. Lynch could not lie nor could he quibble. He was a terrific worker and never seemed to relax, day or night, from his military duties. His faith in a military victory over the British forces in the not too distant future appeared to be over-optimistic to me, who, whilst believing in the ability of the IRA to force eventually a British evacuation, did not then or at any time during the struggle consider that the IRA were even within striking distance of attaining the strength and armament necessary to gain a decisive military victory in battle. Yet Lynch's faith was an asset and there can be no doubt that he inspired and encouraged the officers of all the brigades he visited in his tour of the divisional area. Liam Lynch was not very receptive to ideas, he was stubborn, a fault, if such it is, he shared with many of those present at the meeting, notably myself. He was not very fluent in discussion, and when angry or excited would stutter slightly, but that did not prevent us from realising that this man of the highest personal standards was an ideal choice for the post of divisional OC. It had not been my lot to witness his physical courage, so well testified to by those he had led in North Cork actions, but two years afterwards almost to a day, I was to observe his coolness and bravery when the IRA Executive Council, of which we were both members, was surrounded on the slopes of the Knockmealdown Mountains, where a short time later Liam was to die by Free State bullets at the age of thirty.

In justice to Lynch's memory, and in the interest of historical truth, it is necessary here to refer to a statement by Piaras Béaslaí in his book, *Michael Collins and the Making of a New Ireland*, that:

> It was about this time that Liam Lynch and other Southern I.R.A. Officers went on a deputation to G.H.Q. in Dublin to state that owing to the shortage of arms and ammunition and enemy pressure they were unable to continue the fight.

Unquestionably this statement is not true. No deputation of southern officers ever visited GHQ during the Anglo-Irish hostilities for any purpose whatever, much less for that stated by Mr Béaslaí. The date referred to in Mr Béaslaí's previous paragraph is May 12th, 1921, so it must be presumed that the mythical visit took place between April 1st and the Truce in July 1921. But it is a fact that Lynch never left the 1st Southern Divisional area in all those months. Furthermore, no brigade or battalion officer from the Kerry, Cork or Waterford Brigades visited Dublin or GHQ between the end of March and the Truce except myself towards the end of May and Seán Buckley in mid-June. Mr Béaslaí quoted no authority for his unfounded statement, which is a sad libel on Liam Lynch. It is not suggested that Piaras Béaslaí deliberately lied, but he wrote this book immediately after the Civil War, when passions were inflamed and propaganda slanders on both sides were still flying thickly around. I have no doubt that Mr Béaslaí heard some such canard, which he subsequently published in good faith. On Mr Béaslaí's own side in the Civil War and against that of the dead Lynch were the pre-Truce chief of staff, the adjutant-general, the director and assistant directors of organisation and many other GHQ officers. All those who would surely know if Lynch ever stated that he was unable to continue the fight are still alive and can testify that Mr Béaslaí's allegation is without foundation. It need hardly be added that every divisional and brigade officer in the south rejects completely Mr Béaslaí's statement about Liam Lynch.

As the divisional meeting progressed it became clear that Lynch would have difficulty in getting together a full and efficient staff. No one present would leave his own brigade or transfer his best officers to the division. After a long struggle O'Hegarty agreed that O'Donoghue should be released as divisional adjutant and for over a month Liam and Florrie were to carry on alone. A long discussion then took place on the plans for the safe landing of the Italian arms in West Cork and their primary distribution to the dumps already completed throughout the divisional area. At the final stage the meeting was galvanised by a suggestion that we should agree on a concerted action against the British forces in an attempt to halt their executions of IRA men following farcical court-martial trials. This was something concrete and there was unanimity that the troops of every British garrison in the divisional area should be shot up on May 14th, if the executions pending in Cork Jail were carried out. O'Malley informed us that the Limerick City, East Limerick, South Tipperary, Mid-Tipperary and Kilkenny Brigades were in a few days to be grouped as the 2nd Southern Division and he undertook to ensure that those units would carry out similar attacks on the appointed day. On this decision for joint action the meeting closed.

On our way home to West Cork we rested one night in Cork 1 Brigade area where we were well looked after by officers and men of the local unit who were armed with rifles. The only one of those on duty that night that I can now remember was

Seamus Fitzgerald of Cobh. Indeed it should be recorded that whenever West Cork officers had to travel through other Cork Brigade areas during hostilities, they were always received with the greatest kindness and special precautions were invariably taken for their protection.

# 22

# COUNTER-TERROR

WHILE the men of the brigade flying column, in conjunction with the local companies, were pursuing, in early May, harassing tactics against the British, three more Volunteers were to die for the Ireland they loved so well. On May 9th, the enemy were carrying out one of their large-scale sweeps from several garrisons, when Captain Frank Hurley of Laragh was trapped alone in his own district by the Essex Regiment. Recognising him they marched him towards Bandon, but Frank was never to reach that town again, for true to form the Essex butchered him on the roadside about a mile and a half from their barracks. Frank, a veteran Volunteer, Captain of the Laragh Company, was a fine soldier and comrade, and had fought conspicuously with the brigade flying column in many of its engagements.

On that same day another company of the Essex Regiment

operating near Newcestown, a few miles from Laragh, fired on Volunteer Geoffrey Canty of Scrahane, as he sought to escape their net. Wounding him, they brought him down. There was no witness as to what happened after the Essex came up to their victim, but when local civilians came on the scene after the departure of the British, they found the dead body of the young patriot, who, not being armed, never had a fighting chance to escape.

Two days later, on May 11th, the same battalion of the Essex operating further to the south at Cloundreen, Kilbrittain, fired on Lieutenant Con Murphy of Clashfluck, Timoleague. In this instance the Essex were not able to indulge their sadistic tastes, for their first volleys ended the life of a good flying column soldier and a first-class company officer.

The merciless murders of those men would have called for immediate counteraction, but we knew, since April 29th, that the divisional 'shoot up' of the British scheduled for May 14th was almost due. General Strickland, Cork, the British GOC of the martial law area, had chosen to ignore the written warnings that if the executions of the IRA men planned for April 28th were carried out IRA counteraction would be taken against his forces. The press of April 29th stated that British firing squads had executed in Cork on the previous day Maurice Moore, Ticknock, Cobh, County Cork; Thomas Mulcahy, The Island, Burnfort, Mallow, County Cork; Paddy O'Sullivan, Thomas Street, Cobh, County Cork; and Patrick Ronayne, Burnfort, Mallow, County Cork.

Already after similar farcical courts martial they had executed on February 1st Con Murphy, Ballydavid, Millstreet, County Cork, and on February 28th six others: Seán Allen, Tipperary; John Lyons, Aghabullogue, County Cork; Timothy McCarthy, Fornaught, Donoghmore, County Cork; Thomas O'Brien, Dripsey, County Cork; Daniel O'Callaghan, Dripsey, County Cork; and Patrick O'Mahony, Derry, Donoughmore, County Cork. And on May 4th the enemy was to drive home his contempt for our declaration of counteraction by executing in Cork another patriot, Patrick Casey, Caherally, Grange, County Limerick.

None of those executed men were from West Cork and none of our Volunteers were ever to be judicially executed, since the British officers in our brigade area invariably acted as judge, jury and executioner, without bothering about the formality of a trial for suspected IRA men. Yet the executions of those Irish soldiers stirred us all deeply, and although the British prisons where those men had been confined were in Cork 1 area, all other brigades in the south were greatly concerned as to the possibility of the rescue of those doomed to death. We knew that Cork 1 had been untiring in their efforts, but we also knew that since they had rescued Donncadh MacNeilus, a prisoner awaiting execution, from Cork Jail on November 11th, 1918, the British defences of their prisons had been made well-nigh impregnable. In April I had discussed the defences of Cork prisons with a very good friend of the IRA who had the entrée to them. He was Reverend T. F. Duggan (now Very Reverend

Canon Duggan, President, St Finbarr's Seminary, Farranferris, Cork), and he was prepared to take any risk to save the lives of the Irish soldiers condemned to die. Father Duggan had been a military chaplain in World War I and had a good grasp of technical military matters. Not being suspected by the British of IRA sympathies, he had many opportunities of making a study of the jail defences, and his information only confirmed the view of Cork 1 Brigade of the impossibility of rescuing the prisoners, although Father Duggan personally thought it could be effected.

The West Cork arrangements for the attack on the British on May 14th were completed in good time. At 3 p.m. on Saturday, May 14th, every one of the ten garrisons in the area was to be attacked. All the arms were to be at the disposal of the hundred and twelve officers and men detailed for the attacks over an area extending about eighty miles, from Innishannon to Castletownbere. Precisely at the appointed hour the following assaults took place and the casualties given here are those as issued by the British themselves and published in the daily press of May 16th and 17th. In this listing it will be noted that some British units gave the names of their casualties whilst others only gave the numbers, and it must be remembered also that the IRA attacking parties claimed to have inflicted many more casualties than those admitted by the British.

When approaching Castletownbere, a quarter of a mile from the town, Battalion OC Liam O'Dwyer, Peter O'Neill and Christy O'Connell, with other riflemen, had a skirmish with an enemy patrol. The British retired into the town, but as the remainder of the garrison were then on the alert owing to the exchange of fire, the IRA party could not close with them. No British casualties were announced. Three miles away, at Furious Pier, Rossmacowen, another IRA party of riflemen under Micheal Óg O'Sullivan attacked a party of the KOSB Regiment. The British in this instance announced that four of their troops were killed and two wounded. The press gave the names of the dead as Privates Hunter, McCullen, Chalmers and Edwards; the names of the wounded were not given. As Battalion Commandant Tom Ward's riflemen were proceeding towards the town of Bantry, they were observed by eight Black and Tan riflemen who opened fire and then retired rapidly to their barracks. Ward's men exchanged the fire and pursued the Black and Tans, but the British did not announce any casualties. Near Skibbereen, Battalion Commandant Con Connolly's men shot dead a Constable McLean and seriously wounded Constable Cooper of the Black and Tans. At Drimoleague, Company Captain Daniel O'Driscoll's men attacked Black and Tans close to their barracks, but no British casualties were announced. Liam Deasy was to have taken charge of the Dunmanway attack, but had been injured ten days previously and was unable to do so. Instead, Ted O'Sullivan was brought up and he, with Paddy O'Brien, Girlough, converged with two sections of riflemen on the Square of Dunmanway to attack a lorry of enemy reported to have been at the Square on the several preceding Saturday afternoons. Finding no enemy at the Square, the IRA proceeded towards the Black and Tan barracks, but on the way there was an exchange of shots with two Black and Tans, who gained cover in a nearby house. No British casualties were announced. A party of riflemen under Battalion Commandant Jim Hurley and Vice-Commandant Tim O'Donoghue entered the town of Clonakilty and searched the streets and public houses for enemy forces. Failing to find any they moved on to the Black and Tan barracks at MacCurtain Hill, where they exchanged fire with the Black and Tans, but failed to draw them or the British soldiers from their fortresses. Hurley's men remained for over an hour in the town before withdrawing. No British casualties were announced. At Kilbrittain, Company Captain Jackie O'Neill's riflemen fired at Black and Tans. The British announced two Black and Tans wounded. At Innishannon, Battalion Adjutant Jim O'Mahony, Captain Jack Corkery and two other riflemen shot dead a Black and Tan named Kenna a few hundred yards from his barrack door.

As I did not participate in any of the foregoing I cannot give further particulars, but as I commanded the Bandon assault on that afternoon, I can give a more detailed account of it. Bandon, the military and Black and Tan headquarters of West Cork, had a garrison of over three times the strength of that situated in any other West Cork town. Because of the zeal of their officers and the many attacks on it, this garrison was expected to be the most alert and ready. The enemy precautions against attack were so elaborate that it would be difficult to get within shooting distance of the barracks in daytime without being observed. This made it necessary to approach Bandon by the least expected route of attack, and in such a manner as to enable us to close rapidly to within shooting range before they took up defensive positions. These circumstances indicated that the attacking party should travel to the town by motor and on a main road.

A month previously an old Ford motor car had been taken from the Essex Regiment and hidden in a field under a haystack. On May 11th, it was taken from its hiding place, its hood stripped off and its windscreen removed. Six outstanding West Cork Volunteer officers, Mick Crowley, John Lordan, Seán Lehane, Tom Kelleher, Peter Kearney and Billy O'Sullivan had been selected for the Bandon assault. Lehane was to act as driver of the car and Billy O'Sullivan to use the Lewis machine gun. The others were armed with rifles and automatics and we had also two Mills bombs. For two days before the attack, Lehane practised driving to orders, cruise, slow, fast, turn, ditch her left or ditch her right. On the last order Seán would rush the Ford close up and parallel to the ditch indicated and halt with jammed brakes, when we would all tumble over the ditch, so gaining cover. This was our only hope should we meet enemy armoured cars on the road or in Bandon.

At noon on the 14th we arrived at Anna Hurley's of Laragh. This lady, the leader of the Cumann na mBan of the Bandon district, was a sister of Frank Hurley, who had been murdered by the Essex Regiment during the previous week. She was asked to leave immediately for Bandon and to remain there until two o'clock to observe the movements of the murderers of her brother. In particular, she was to note if the enemy were strengthening any of their defences and to report back at 2.30 p.m. When Anna returned punctually she reported in detail various enemy troop movements and that the Black and Tans were very busy adding to the sandbag defences outside their barracks at the Devonshire Arms. This last news was most unwelcome, as it could be considered as indicative of the awareness of the enemy of a coming attack. Since the meeting on April 24th, when those attacks were agreed on, it must have worried many that fourteen brigade staffs and their subordinate officers had foreknowledge of the assaults. There was always a distinct possibility that one out of the hundreds who were aware of the date and time of attack would be captured and, under torture, inform. Or it could happen that some irresponsible Volunteer would mention that matter in the presence of an enemy agent. General Strickland and his officers knew the attacks were coming, because he had been officially informed that if the executions took place the IRA would take counteraction against his forces, but if the enemy knew of the date and time, disaster would overtake the IRA in the south, as all our attacking parties would be mown down by a waiting, properly disposed enemy. On that Saturday I was of the opinion that the British knew of our coming that day, but the Bandon assault had to be attempted.

Informing the others of my suspicion that the enemy had some inkling of the proposed attack, and that it would not be wise or justifiable to risk all seven officers cramped in a small car, I asked for two to volunteer to stay behind. There was a stony silence and none of those men would drop out. Eventually an order had to be issued that the two heftiest were not to travel as they would cramp the movements of the others as well as present the easiest targets. These two were John Lordan and Tom Kelleher, but as we were moving off they made a final appeal to be permitted to travel to within half a mile of Bandon, when they would go into the fields and take their chance at finding a target. The assault party in the Ford car hit the Dunmanway–Cork main road about two miles west of Bandon. Three-quarters of a mile from Bandon we halted to drop John Lordan and Tom Kelleher to scramble over the northern ditch of the road and set off across the fields for the town. Lehane drove on at about fifteen miles an hour. Billy O'Sullivan's Lewis gun rested where the hood had formerly been and he was flanked by Mick Crowley and Peter Kearney with their loaded rifles at the ready. In order that I could see better over the ditches and so detect any lurking British, I sat up on the back rest of the front seat with my feet on the cushion on which Lehane sat. A quarter of a mile from the military barracks we spied an armed sentry at the turn of the road fifty yards ahead. He was standing up on the roadside ditch looking towards us, with his rifle and bayonet fixed at the 'At Ease' position. He was as unexpected as he was unwelcome but I had time to whisper to drive on at the same speed and to take no notice. I do not know who the sentry thought we were, but immediately he saw us he jerked his rifle to the 'On Guard', then as we came to within twenty yards of him he must have accepted us as either Auxiliaries or Black and Tans as I was wearing an IRA officer's tunic, the others trench coats, and all of us equipment. To my great relief as we came on to him he brought his rifle to the 'Slope' and as we passed he saluted smartly. I returned his salute casually and we passed on.

Our plan of attack was to drive slowly between the Essex military barracks and the Black and Tan barracks, which stood about sixty yards across an open space from it. At a signal, fire was to be opened on anything in the uniform of the British armed forces standing around the two barracks. The car party was then to drive down North Main Street, across the bridge, up South Main Street, firing at any enemy in sight. It was to retreat out the Kilbrittain road, where a mile from the town men of the Bandon Company were waiting to draw spiked harrows across the road, as soon as the Ford passed, to delay any armoured cars in pursuit. Two hundred yards after passing the unexpected sentry, all this had to be changed, as within a few hundred yards of the military barracks we saw about one hundred of the Essex and a sprinkling of the Black and Tans in a field south of the road. Armed groups of troops in steel helmets stood about, with full equipment, leaning on their rifles, talking and laughing, as some others, unarmed, kicked a football around. Lehane got the order 'Slow', and as we came abreast of the enemy, 'Stop'. Seán obeyed like an automaton, and then: 'Pick out the armed gangs first. Let them have it.' The machine gun captured at Crossbarry spluttered a drum full of ammunition at its former owners, the rifles cracked a half dozen times, and the surprised enemy let out a few yells as some dived for cover and others flattened out on the ground. As the rifles were being reloaded, Seán got the order: 'Forward and turn her.' He shot the Ford forward some distance and turned it in view of the barracks, at the windows of which some volleys were fired in an effort to delay pursuit. The car raced back past the place where we had opened fire, and out beyond the point where the sentry had been standing, but who had now vanished completely. When we had turned off the main road to the comparative safety of the byroad, Lehane broke the silence, which, except for the issuing of orders, had remained unbroken since we had dropped Lordan and Kelleher. In his fine voice he started to sing:

> We will pay them back woe for woe,
> Give them back blow for blow
> Out and make way for the bold Fenian Men.

Four miles from Bandon we sprinkled a tin of petrol over our reliable Ford and soon it was a blazing mass. This was necessary, as it would have meant certain death for the man on whose property it might be found. Then we set out across country for Newcestown.

The British officially announced that we had killed an Essex soldier, and wounded several, including a Black and Tan. Later we were to hear that several meant seven. We thought we had hit more than eight of them, but even accepting their figures we were satisfied that we had once again shaken them up badly. The fact that five IRA men could close with them in their strongest garrisoned town at three o'clock on a May day and retire unharmed, must, apart from the casualties inflicted, have had a detrimental effect on the enemy morale. The reply of the British was a poor show, but judging by the report in the *Cork Examiner* of May 16th they must have become very warlike after our departure, as it stated 'the terrific machine gun and rifle fire, lasting for over half and hour, which broke out in Bandon on Saturday afternoon was in the general opinion an attack on the military barracks.' There was little shooting by the enemy during our attack, but apparently they must have fired wildly for over half an hour after we had retired. It was in this firing that the enemy wounded the two civilians, as most certainly there was no civilian with the unit we attacked. The manner in which Crowley, Kearney, O'Sullivan and Lehane adapted themselves, without warning, to the changed plans, and their exemplary discipline, coolness and courage, were beyond praise. Seán Lehane has since died, but this fine fellow will long be remembered by those who knew him. Commandant of the Schull Battalion, a fine fighter and a grand soldier, Seán was a merry comrade with the drollest of sayings. His ready wit and fine singing voice relieved the gloom and eased the tension for many of us when the world appeared a most dreary and difficult place.

The results from other brigades were keenly awaited as it was felt they would give a fairly good indication of the state of the organisation over two divisional areas. It must be recorded that they were in general disappointing. In his book, *On Another Man's Wound*, Ernest O'Malley complained that although orders were issued nothing was done in the Second Southern Divisional area. No casualties were caused to the British and as far as was known no skirmishes took place in the whole of County Waterford, North Cork, West Kerry or South Kerry Brigades. The West Limerick unit killed a Constable Bridges and wounded another Black and Tan at Drumcollogher. Kerry 1 inflicted the only casualty in the county by killing Head Constable Benson at Tralee. Cork 1 Brigade did very well. The city battalions shot up many of the enemy posts and succeeded in killing Constables Creighton and Ryle and wounding Constables Hayes and Brackwell in Cork city. That good band of East Cork fighters killed Sergeant Coleman, Constable Comyn and Constable Thomas, wounding Constable McDonald, all of the Black and Tans, and killed one Royal Horse Artillery Gunner at East Ferry. There may have been good reasons for the failures of some of those units to effect casualties. Because events crowded in on us for the concluding six or seven weeks of the fight with the British, there were more important things to attend to than to inquire from the brigades which had failed, and as far as I know nothing was done after the Truce to clarify matters. It should be remembered in fairness to those units that some may not have received their orders or on that day may have been forestalled by heavy enemy offensive activity or may, indeed, have failed to contact enemy targets. One such unit was the North Cork Brigade. We had been greatly surprised that there were no reports of attacks in Liam Lynch's old area. Afterwards we learned that there was good reason for this. On the morning of May 10th, extraordinary enemy activity commenced in North Cork and this was to continue for six days, during which time the North Cork IRA were so hard pressed that the attacks could not be undertaken. I had a personal reason for remembering the commencement of this enemy offensive in North Cork. On the morning of May 10th, two cousins of mine, Paddy O'Brien, the column leader in that area and his brother, Dan, of Knockarbane, Liscarroll, and John O'Regan, Liscarroll, were surrounded by British troops at O'Donnell's, Aughrim, Liscarroll. By some miracle, Paddy, who was the most wanted man by the British in North Cork, fought his way through to safety and it was only two hours later he learned that John O'Regan was dangerously wounded and that Dan had been captured trying to help John. Dan stood before a drumhead court martial on the morning of 14th, and faced the enemy firing squad on May 16th, the last of the patriot soldiers to be judicially executed in Cork by the British.

The total casualties inflicted by the West Cork Brigade were considered, in all the circumstances, as very satisfactory. The British had paid for their official and unofficial executions.

The question arises as to what effect they, together with those inflicted in Cork 1, Kerry 1 and West Limerick Brigades, had on the British policy of executions. Except for the usual British imperialist yells of 'Outrage', no official comment was made by them as to their future behaviour, but it is significant that no other IRA man was executed in Cork after May 14th, except Dan O'Brien, already sentenced to death before our counter-attacks took place.

# 23

# CALLED TO GHQ

I HAD received two messages from the adjutant general that President de Valera had asked to see me to get a detailed first-hand account of the military position in the south, and that I was expected at General Headquarters on May 19th. I did not relish the idea of this journey, although I welcomed the opportunity of meeting, for the first time, the President and the members of GHQ staff. There was a note of urgency in the second message from the adjutant-general so there was no time to walk the long journey from Cork to Dublin. Travelling by motor car was out of the question, as any motor would have been halted and searched many times on such a journey. Therefore, the train had to be my mode of travel, and that meant travelling unarmed, as one armed man had no chance of getting through the usual military searchers at the various railway stations occupied by the enemy. I had no experience of travelling this way and doubted my ability to bluff my way through as a neutral civilian, but the journey had to be undertaken. At first I considered travelling as an engineering student of University College Cork, as Mick Crowley and Jack Buttimer, Dunmanway, another good flying column man, were both engineering students and available to coach me in that role. However, I switched to travelling as a medical student, and there was no dearth of coaches for that role either as there was a number of medical students on active service with our brigade: Eugene Callanan, Conor J. McCarthy, Denis A. Murphy (Beara), Pat Murphy, Peter Kearney and that dashing flying column soldier, Jeremiah McCarthy of Dreeny, Skibbereen, now in the United States. My preparations for the journey were extremely thorough as I had the incentive of being well aware that, should I be captured and recognised, the British had more than ample evidence against me to enable one of their drumhead courts martial to rapidly arrange my exit at the end of a rope or before one of their firing squads. So the medicals coached me and supplied notes on medicine, textbooks, forceps and other paraphernalia usually found in the possession of a second-year medical student. Ted Ryder of near Crookstown lent me his name and a number of his letters in their used envelopes. The O'Mahonys of Belrose bought for me a hat, shoes, shirts, socks and pyjamas. Miss Kathleen O'Connell of the Ballydehob Cumann na mBan, who had stored my only civilian suit, was to have it at our headquarters at Caheragh, Skibbereen, on May 16th.

Arriving at headquarters on the morning of the 16th, after travelling all night, I immediately went to bed, or to be more correct, to sleep on the ground rolled in a few army blankets under a small makeshift bivouac of two rubber groundsheets. This was erected about two hundred and fifty yards from a friendly farmhouse in the corner of a field, and it was effectively camouflaged by a heavy growth of briars. The farmhouse was too dangerous to sleep in as it was known to be a resort of the Volunteers, but we usually had our meals there. After a few hours' sleep I was rudely pulled out of my blankets with the news that a big column of British soldiers on foot was halted a few hundred yards down the road and that they were inquiring for me by name. Rapidly dressing, I did not wait to make further inquiries, but grabbing my arms and equipment, set out as fast as I could run in the direction away from the enemy. That evening I learned how they had got on the track. Three miles from Caheragh, they had held up the scout carrying my clothes. Unfortunately, after the parcel had been taken from Miss O'Connell's house, someone, fearing it would be lost, had written my name and rank very clearly on the brown paper cover. The troops, the King's Regiment, from Skibbereen, grilled the scout as to his destination, but as he would not answer, they placed him inside the ditch, stripped him of his outer clothes and left him under a small guard. An officer then put on the labourer's clothes and set out in the direction in which the scout had been travelling. A few hundred yards behind him came the British troops. The disguised officer called at numerous houses, produced the parcel with my name on it and asked where I was staying. He was passed along to Caheragh and eventually was shown the farmhouse near where the bivouac was situated. The officer in charge must have assumed I had some of the flying column with me for then he made his first mistake. Instead of surrounding the farm immediately, he waited for the reinforcements he had already requested from Skibbereen. Meanwhile, one of the men from a house where the officer had made inquiries, noticing the soldiers following up the messenger and suspecting the trick that he had been playing, set out cross country to relay the message which I was to receive in time. Father John Crowley, CC, of Caheragh, now at Blackrock, Cork, was one of those who passed on the warning. This is only one instance out of many hundreds which could be given to show the great help friendly people can give their guerilla army and how they can effectively hamper an enemy.

The loss of my only suit so close to the day of travelling was upsetting, but a friendly tailor, near Crookstown, working through the night, made a new one which reached me at O'Mahony's, Belrose, on the morning of the 19th. On that evening the O'Mahony girls delivered me safely outside the Cork railway station, handed me my first-class return ticket and a number of pro-British newspapers and periodicals. Thanking those fine girls for their many kindnesses, I walked nervously past some enemy soldiers and Black and Tans to the waiting train. Travelling by train was then unpopular and there were several empty first-class compartments, but deciding that I would be far less noticeable with others, I entered one where three men were already seated. Two of these appeared to be middle-aged staid businessmen, but the third looked like a British military officer in mufti. I sat directly opposite this man. Within a few minutes we were engaged in friendly conversation and soon he told me he was in the army and as he put it 'going on a spot of leave and not sorry to leave this damned country'. In turn he learned that I was a medical student going to Dublin to be examined by a specialist for suspected lung trouble. At the first military examination of the passengers at Mallow my companion, producing his own identity card, immediately informed the sergeant in charge of the search party that I was all right and travelling with him. He was to repeat this on two further train inspections so that I had not to answer a single question throughout the journey. I parted with this amiable travelling companion outside the Kingsbridge check barrier; he to report at a military barracks before crossing to Britain in the morning and I to locate Jim Kirwan's public house in Parnell Street, where General Headquarters had arranged to contact me.

Jim Kirwan was a Volunteer of long standing and all his assistants were members of the IRA. When I asked one of them to tell 'George' I had arrived, he returned with Jim, who, after looking me over, brought me to a private room to meet Gearóid O'Sullivan, the Adjutant-General. Gearóid and I left immediately for Liam Devlin's home, nearby in the same street, where in the sitting-room upstairs Michael Collins, Diarmuid O'Hegarty and Seán Ó Muirthile were waiting for me. Soon afterwards Collins, O'Sullivan and Ó Muirthile and I set out for the suburbs to the house of Mrs O'Donovan, an aunt of Gearóid. Here, with the other three, I was to stay during my six nights in Dublin. Each morning, with one or more of the others, I left for the IRA offices, which were in the centre of the city and being conducted under the guise of harmless businesses. Those six busy days were full of interest for me. I was never alone, spending most of the time with Collins and O'Sullivan and I must have met some thirty officers, including those of GHQ, the Squad and the Dublin Brigade, as well as President de Valera and Cathal Brugha, the Minister of Defence. The way of life of those GHQ officers was in great contrast to that of the West Cork IRA. Dressed like businessmen, carrying brief or attaché cases, with their pockets full of false papers to support their disguise, they travelled freely to their 'business' offices and to keep their various appointments. To a great extent those GHQ men kept regular business hours at those offices, but after closing hours often worked late into the night at some other venue. They seemed to have no fear of arrest or, if they had, they did not show it, but that might be because Collins and his associates by the time of my visit had practically wiped out the informers and 'G' men of Dublin Castle, who alone were in a position to identify them. Their lack of precautions was amazing and even made one angry.

One night at about nine o'clock, Mick, Gearóid, Seán and I were returning to the suburbs on a jarvey car when, a few hundred yards from Mrs O'Donovan's, we ran into a hold-up by about fifty Auxiliaries. Collins had time to say, 'Act drunk', before we were ordered off the car to be minutely searched. I was next to Collins and he put up such a fine act, joking and blasting in turn, that he had the whole search party of terrorists in good humour in a short time. Collins and the others appeared to be quite unperturbed, but I, being searched for the first time and never having seen Auxiliaries before, except to fire at them, felt anything but happy. When we reached Mrs O'Donovan's and spoke about our escape, I asked why, in the name of Heaven, they did not use a scout on a bicycle on those journeys to signal any hold-up in front. Mick as usual guffawed and chaffed me about being a windy West Cork beggar. Failing to see the joke, I told him crossly that it was quite true, I was a windy beggar as I had a wholesome regard for my neck; that it was all very well for himself and Gearóid who were TDs, since the British had an unexplainable idea that Members of Parliament should not be executed and that anyway they would find it hard to sustain charges of murder against GHQ officers, whereas they had no difficulty in that respect about officers from the country units. Mick then became serious and before long convinced me that their only hope of survival was to act as they were doing. That he was right is proved by the fact that during all the Anglo-Irish War not a single senior GHQ officer was captured, recognised and detained.

I had several lengthy interviews with the Chief of Staff, Richard Mulcahy. This calm, unhurried man was meticulous in seeking out details, and probed me on questions affecting the organisation, discipline, training and tactics of the IRA in the south. An instance of his thoroughness is shown by the subsidiary questions he asked when I told him of the number of trained riflemen we could put in the field if arms and ammunition were available. The chief of staff wanted to know the number of first-, second- and third-class shots amongst them. When I told him that no officer could answer that question, as there was never enough spare ammunition to enable each rifleman to fire a musketry course, he expressed surprise and asked how the flying column could then be taken into action with any degree of confidence. The answer was that each man had fired three rounds at a target, and that anyway, as the West Cork tactics were initially close-quarter attacks, no rifleman, no matter how poor a marksman, could miss a human target at ten or fifteen yards' range. Strangely enough, when discussing the divisional units then being formed, for these must have been mainly children of the chief of staff's own creation, I got the impression from him that he agreed with my views that the divisional units could have little or no effect on the armed struggle and that our largest effective military formation would continue to be the brigade. Throughout those talks the chief of staff was courteous, friendly and interested.

Gearóid O'Sullivan, the Adjutant-General, and I talked much during my Dublin visit. In contrast to some others,

Gearóid freely expressed his opinions on men and matters. Although one did not agree with all his views, it was quickly apparent that he was a man of high intelligence and a capable staff officer. It was generally accepted by all who were in close touch with him that he did a splendid job as adjutant-general of the IRA during the Anglo-Irish struggle.

Diarmuid O'Hegarty was the Director of Organisation and also, at the time of my visit, secretary of the cabinet of the Irish Republic. He was a brilliant organiser with a first-class brain and, although he spoke little, he was obviously well thought of by the other members of General Headquarters. Diarmuid was assisted by Eamonn (Bob) Price, who extensively toured the country, organising and inspecting units of the army.

Seán MacMahon was Quartermaster-General. I had little contact with him except on two occasions when I had failed to beg, borrow or steal .303 or .450 ammunition from him. Seán's position was painfully clear. He could not give West Cork or any other unit the ammunition he had not got. Although sympathetic to our appeals, MacMahon was nearly distracted by the incessant calls that poured in from outside brigades for arms and ammunition, knowing only too well that his dumps were practically empty and his reserves exhausted.

With Piaras Béaslaí, the Director of Propaganda, I discussed *An t-Óglach,* the underground IRA weekly. This little paper, edited by Béaslaí, helped quite a lot to let the scattered IRA units throughout Ireland know the truth about the activities of the army, and undoubtedly was a factor of prime importance in maintaining the morale of our fighters. I was very anxious to meet the Director of Engineering, Rory O'Connor, to discuss engineering problems with him, but he was not in Dublin during my visit. Liam Mellows, the Director of Purchases, whom I had already met in the south, was also away, but I met many others prominent in IRA circles, including Liam Tobin, Tom Cullen and Tom Keogh.

But the outstanding figure in all GHQ was Michael Collins, Director of Intelligence. This man was, without a shadow of doubt, the effective driving force and the backbone at GHQ of the armed action of the nation against the enemy. A tireless, ruthless, dominating man of great capacity, he worked like a Trojan in innumerable capacities to defeat the enemy. Versatile to an amazing degree, Collins, who had fought through 1916, had after his release from prison become one of the chief organisers of the Volunteers. At the same time he was one of the secretaries of Sinn Féin, the political wing, and was largely instrumental in the victories of Sinn Féin in the 1918 elections. While maintaining his hold on the political machine and becoming Minister of Finance in the first Dáil cabinet of the Irish Republic, he was Adjutant-General of the IRA, feverishly pushing the organisation of the armed resistance movement. Quickly realising the importance of the army intelligence department, he took over that responsibility and built a splendid organisation from the ground upwards. Nineteen-twenty saw Michael Collins Acting President of the Republic, while Mr de Valera was in America and Mr Griffith was in jail. Yet with all these ministerial, political and administrative responsibilities, his army activities increased. There was no branch of the army headquarters into which he did not enter. Policy, training, organisation, arms, supplies, propaganda, all felt the impact of his personality and efforts. One day during my stay he left our lodgings to meet his intelligence assistants at his office at 9 a.m. He attended a cabinet meeting at 11 a.m. After lunch he was back at intelligence at 1.30 p.m., then in conference with the propaganda department for an hour, whence he travelled to meet some seamen who were smuggling in a small quantity of small arms. From there he travelled to another office to meet a number of people from the country who had large amounts of money for the Dáil Loan, which Collins had successfully launched. He reached us at Vaughan's Hotel at 6.30 p.m. and, after swallowing his tea, went upstairs to his private room to meet separately officers from five different country units.

I was present with him during those interviews, which continued until 10 p.m., when Collins seemed to be as fresh as when he breakfasted in the morning. At first I thought it was odd that all those men should have had interviews with an officer who nominally held the rank of D/I about matters which were no concern of the intelligence department. That was before I realised that Michael Collins was virtually commander-in-chief in fact, if not in name, of the Army of the Irish Republic. Before meeting Collins, I had often heard officers from the southern units remark that the only way to get GHQ to do things was to 'See Mick' about it. There was a unanimous feeling amongst the field officers that 'Mick' would back them to the hilt and that of all the people in Dublin he was the practical go-getter. He was an interesting study during those talks with the country officers. He delved deeply into all the details of their units, advising and encouraging, and in two instances reprimanding in a harsh and sneering manner. To one of the officers from a particularly inefficient unit who asked for arms, Mick, with a scowl on his face, his hands deep in his pockets, his right foot pawing the ground, shot back, 'What the Hell does a lot of lousers like you want arms for? You have rifles and revolvers galore but you have never yet used them. A single bousey, like X (a Black and Tan) is walking around your area alone for six months terrorising and shooting people and ye are afraid to tackle him. Get to Hell out of this and do not come back until ye have done some fighting.' Collins continued to swear as the officer hurriedly left the room.

Collins was attempting a difficult job. Prominent in his character was his great liking and regard for officers who were doing their best. Whether a man came from a successful fighting area or not, nothing was too good for him if Collins thought he was endeavouring with all his might to carry the fight to the British. This great son of West Cork had a vast pride in his race and to me it seemed that he exulted more in an Irish victory in a local engagement because it proved that Irishmen could fight better than the English, than for its contribution to the final victory of the nation. Big-hearted and generous, as I was personally to experience, this energetic and restless man seemed to be forever battling with something or someone, even with himself. Some nights he would come bouncing in to Liam Devlin's or Vaughan's and challenge someone to wrestle him as he wanted exercise. One night I declined his challenge, stating that as he was about sixteen stone and I about eleven he should take on Ó Muirthile or one of the others nearer his weight, but he would not take the refusal, so we swayed around and around the room many times. Somehow I prevented him from using his superior weight, but eventually we fell together and then we were fighting in real earnest on the ground. Gearóid O'Sullivan, Seán Ó Muirthile and some of the others pulled us apart and we rose angry, each denying we had started the fight and willing to go on with it. Yet in a few minutes the angry and scowling Collins was gone, and in his place the smiling and good-natured Mick was chatting as affably with me as if the incident had never occurred.

The respect with which Michael Collins was held by the IRA is best emphasised if I am permitted to go outside the period with which this book is properly concerned. In July 1922 I was a Republican prisoner in Mountjoy Jail and attempted to escape. Within sight of freedom, I was recaptured and for nearly three weeks I was held in solitary confinement in a basement punishment cell. Towards the end of my punishment period I was transferred at midnight in an armoured car to Kilmainham Jail, where I was again allowed to mix with other military prisoners. Here I made another unsuccessful attempt to escape, but because of the humanity of the governor, Seán

Ó Muirthile, there was no further punishment. I was talking with some other prisoners on the night of August 22nd, 1922, when the news came in that Michael Collins had been shot dead in West Cork. There was a heavy silence throughout the jail, and ten minutes later from the corridor outside the top tier of cells I looked down on the extraordinary spectacle of about a thousand kneeling Republican prisoners spontaneously reciting the Rosary aloud for the repose of the soul of the dead Michael Collins, President of the Free State Executive Council and Commander-in-Chief of the Free State forces. There was, of course, little logic in such an action, but I have yet to learn of a better tribute to the part played by any man in the struggle with the English for Irish independence. Through all the hates and bitternesses of civil war, those Republican prisoners remembered that the dead leader, latterly their enemy, was once an inspiration and driving force in their struggle with the alien army of occupation.

Here I may as well also kill the canard that the IRA plotted and planned Collins' death in 1922 and in fact assassinated him. About a week after his death we were transferred from Kilmainham to Gormanstown and on the very first day there I succeeded in escaping. Ten or eleven days later I walked into West Cork and interviewed the men who had fired the shots, one of which had ended the life of Michael Collins. The facts of his death were that a West Cork column was lying in ambush for several days on the Bandon–Macroom road to attack the Free State troops who periodically used that route. On August 22nd, 1922, this column waited for several hours at Béal na Bláth, but in the afternoon, having decided it was unlikely that the target would pass that day, the order to withdraw was given. The main body of the column had retired over a mile and the small rearguard over a quarter of a mile from the ambush position, when a Free State convoy appeared. The main column was out of sight and range, but the small rearguard turned and opened fire from nearly five hundred yards range at the passing convoy, which immediately stopped. The Free State party dismounted and lying on the road returned the fire, but the rearguard after firing less than a dozen rounds hurried on after the main body. One of those long range shots had killed Michael Collins, the only one of his party to be hit. It was almost five hours later when the IRA column first heard that Collins had been with the Free State convoy and that he had been killed in the skirmish with the column's rearguard.

The dominating position of Michael Collins at GHQ may have been in part due to his holding the portfolio of Minister of Finance, and that for a period he had been Acting President of the Irish Republic. A still greater factor was that he held the office of Chairman of the Supreme Council of the Irish Republican Brotherhood, and practically every GHQ brigade and battalion officer of the IRA was a member of this secret organisation. According to the constitution of the Irish Republican Brotherhood, the chairman of the Supreme Council (head centre) was automatically the president of the

Irish Republic and entitled to the complete allegiance of every member of the organisation. Yet the IRA, including its IRB members, had also taken an oath of allegiance to Dáil Éireann, the elected parliament of the Irish Republic. The inner cabinet appointed by this parliament was composed of de Valera, Griffith, Brugha and Stack, who were not then members of the IRB, and Collins, who was the Head Centre of that organisation. In this analogous position of dual allegiance by the army lay the seeds which soon sprouted the differences that arose between Collins and his ministerial colleagues. But the paramount reason for Collins' power at GHQ and his prestige with the IRA must be sought for within the personality and the character of the man himself. It was mainly the recognition by all others of Collins as a tireless worker for Ireland and a realistic and capable leader that placed him in his unchallenged position at General Headquarters.

This appreciation of Collins should not in any way suggest that the other GHQ officers were a mediocre group and that Collins was a giant amongst pygmies. A fair test as to their individual and collective capacities is to ask oneself as to what other officers in the IRA could be nominated to occupy more effectively their posts. Could the IRA have thrown up a more competent chief of staff than Mulcahy, a better adjutant-general than O'Sullivan, a more successful quartermaster-general than MacMahon, a more efficient director of engineering than Rory O'Connor or a more capable director of purchases than Liam Mellows? I confess that I, at least, met none who could have worked harder and more efficiently than our GHQ personnel, although I could name brigade officers who were quite capable of holding any post at General Headquarters.

It became fashionable after the Truce with the British for inefficient units to throw the onus for their lack of action on the shoulders of GHQ. The truth demands that this should be faced up squarely. Never throughout 1920 and 1921 did GHQ repudiate or reprimand any unit for its aggressiveness or its activities. On the contrary, headquarters encouraged and urged the army to fight and to keep on fighting.

It is true that the headquarters of a guerilla army can give little active help to the fighting units because of the inherent limitations of such a force. To an even greater extent than a divisional headquarters, it is handicapped by lack of an efficient and rapid communication system and this alone prevents contact with or effective control of brigade units. GHQ was never even aware of the movements or intentions of flying columns outside Dublin until it read accounts of engagements, often garbled, in the daily press. GHQ had no secret bank from which it could supply brigades with money; on the contrary, it lived itself penuriously, mainly on moneys collected by the units. GHQ had no means of making ammunition, although it had established a crude factory for making bomb cases. We all dutifully groused because it did not send us ammunition and arms, but after seeing for myself the frantic efforts being made by GHQ officers concerned to get supplies, in the face of what appeared to be insurmountable obstacles, one critic was satisfied. One GHQ department which was of real value to the brigades was that of intelligence, for Collins passed on punctually and regularly every scrap of information his superb department collected to the unit concerned.

There is only one criticism of GHQ which, in my opinion, could stand investigation. It is that during 1920 and 1921 Collins, Mulcahy, O'Sullivan, MacMahon and other senior GHQ officers should have visited country units. Apart from the good effect such visits would have had on the morale of a hard-pressed fighting brigade, they were the only means by which headquarters could accurately learn of the trials and difficulties and the actual conditions prevailing in the units outside Dublin. It is true that Price, Mellows, O'Connor, Andy Cooney, O'Malley and others did tour some areas during that period but, nevertheless, visits of the more publicised senior officers to all areas would undoubtedly have greatly heartened those units. It may be argued that the risk of losing men like Collins on such journeys would not be justified and that those GHQ officers could not be spared for even a day from their work in Dublin. There is no doubt that those were the governing motives which kept the GHQ leaders in Dublin, and no one who knew them would suggest that it was either indifference or lack of willingness to take a personal risk that prevented them from visiting the country areas. Yet one must adhere to the view that it would have been wiser had those members of GHQ travelled around to hearten and sustain hard-pressed units and galvanise into action the lagging and inactive ones. For over and above all other considerations is the fact that wars are not won at GHQs or defeats avoided there but on the field of battle. An intact and fully manned general headquarters is of no use to a nation if its field army is smashed and disorganised.

# 24

# REPORT TO PRESIDENT DE VALERA

ON the third day of my visit to Dublin, Collins told me that Cathal Brugha, the Minister for Defence, had made an appointment for me to meet him that evening. Collins brought me along and, having introduced us, left almost immediately. I did not then know of the coolness which existed between those ministers, but could not help noticing the air of formality and even curtness which permeated their meeting. Cathal, with a minimum of words, asked me some questions and used only monosyllables to comment on my replies. He neither criticised, approved nor suggested anything in connection with the armed struggle in the south. He appeared to be unduly taciturn and walled off by an impenetrable reserve. Puzzled at his manner, after about twenty minutes I reacted by adopting his own style, answering tersely or only in monosyllables and soon there were awkward silences. On several occasions I was tempted to ask why he had arranged the meeting as it was not of my seeking, but refrained. Eventually, forty minutes after our introduction, I said I had another appointment and we wished each other goodbye. This was the only time I met Cathal Brugha and during this unsatisfactory interview I completely failed to elicit a single one of his views on the policy and tactics of the IRA or on defence, of which he was the responsible minister. Later, during my visit, when I learned of the differences prevailing between Collins and Brugha, I came to the conclusion that the extreme reserve of the Minister for Defence at the interview was due to his natural suspicions that I was one of the Collins party.

This factual account of our meeting should not give the impression that Brugha was a difficult or suspicious individual. Those who knew him better in the Irish revolutionary movements, and did not meet him under the circumstances in which I did, found him an amiable and likeable comrade. For long prior to 1916 this sphinx-like, quiet-spoken, determined man had laboured in the IRB, the Gaelic League and kindred bodies, preparing for the testing years which were still to come. During the 1916 Rising, Cathal Brugha was riddled with British bullets. Elected as a Deputy for Waterford in the 1918 general election, he was appointed Minister for Defence in President de Valera's first cabinet of the Irish Republic and he held this office until the Treaty split in 1922. He had not the charm of manner of de Valera, nor the good fellowship of Collins, and as he was not a ready mixer had little contact with the IRA officers outside Dublin. I have never heard it suggested that Cathal Brugha was an outstanding leader of capacity and initiative, but it should be remembered that his post as Minister for Defence of a guerilla army gave little opportunity of displaying traits of first-class leadership. It could not be otherwise when even his GHQ and divisional staffs found such difficulty in contacting the brigades.

Although few of the country officers or men ever met Cathal Brugha, his name and fame had reached the most distant companies of the IRA. He was universally respected and admired for his integrity, his unselfishness and the great services he had rendered the nation through the long and weary years of his labours for Ireland. But Brugha's place in Irish history, high amongst our great patriots, will of a certainty be determined, not by those virtues, but because of his incredible courage. He appeared to be the very reincarnation of one of those Irish warriors of yore, the story of whose bravery in battle has been handed down to us in song and in story. Cathal Brugha's courage in 1916 and the calmness with which he then faced the British when riddled with their bullets is only surpassed by the epic of his own passing in 1922. Then, alone of all a garrison, he refused to surrender, walked towards his enemies with his revolver blazing until he fell, mortally wounded.

On the morning of May 23rd, Michael Collins drove me to a very large house in the Dublin suburbs to meet President de Valera. Although this appointment was the main object of my journey from West Cork, I did not feel too happy about the coming interview. Conflicting pictures from different individuals of the President and his policies had disturbed me, and the confusion in my mind was all the greater because Éamon de Valera was the idol of all those I had met in the independence movement in the south. One Dublin informant had told me that de Valera was a cold, austere puritan, who never smiled and who stood aloof from the masses for whom he had a deep contempt; another, that de Valera was anxious to stop the war against the British, that he was only with difficulty restrained from repudiating the Cork brigades, particularly the West Cork Brigade, for their aggressiveness and ruthlessness, and that he was about to accept an offer of Dominion Home Rule, which, as my informant put it, 'he had in his pocket since he returned from America last December'. It was even hinted to me that I should paint a rosy picture of the military position in the south so that he would not have an excuse for slowing down or even stopping the fight for freedom. I did not like this de Valera at all, and had already made up my mind to give him as little information as possible, so the interview was likely to be a short and stormy one. Because of my youth and inexperience, I did not then realise that cliques, the great curse of every national and revolutionary movement, were already formed and active in the capital of our country.

After Collins had introduced us he chatted cordially with de

Valera. Those two leaders, later to become opponents, appeared to be close friends as they discussed some matters about the National Loan. After five minutes Collins left and the President talked to me of the struggle in the south. Within ten minutes of our meeting I knew that the portrait of this man as a cold, austere, contemptuous leader was false, for indeed, he was quite the opposite – smiling, courteous, affable and interested. For two and a half hours the President talked, questioned and listened. His charm of manner made me perfectly at ease, and I have yet to meet anyone who ever had a private interview with Mr de Valera who did not come away impressed with his courteousness and good manners. I soon realised also that, far from wanting to stop or slow down the war against the British, he was enthusiastic about developing it. He questioned me closely about our struggle, armament and tactics. He wanted to know the details of our fights at Kilmichael, Rosscarbery, Crossbarry and other places, and listened carefully as I replied to his questions about the executions of spies and informers. He was generous in his praises, and he looked unhappy and troubled only when told of those members of IRA who had already died fighting for Ireland in West Cork. Early in this two and a half hours' meeting it seemed to me that I was having an intimate talk with a brother officer rather than being questioned by the President of the Irish Republic. So I opened my mind to this man who had so greatly impressed me. He talked of the difficulties of the summer campaign and asked about the tactics we should adopt to defeat the proposed blockade which, he said, would probably be started in Cork. The ammunition shortage worried him, but he was hopeful that 'Mick' would get some through in time.

The President reverted several times to the opinions of the people and seemed concerned as to what their attitude would be under increased British terrorism and greater economic pressure. To my immature mind it appeared that he was giving undue importance to this factor. The people could do nothing about it while the Irish Republican Army was holding its own, although I was careful to point out that our West Cork supporters, who were the finest of our race, would not falter or break under any pressure. Towards the end of our talk President de Valera asked the all-important question, 'How long can the Cork flying columns keep the field against the British?' I replied that no one could answer such a question as so much depended on the decisions of the enemy and on our ammunition supplies. If, for instance, the enemy drafted a further thirty thousand into County Cork from Britain and the inactive areas and were allowed to concentrate on us, and if GHQ still failed to supply .303 ammunition, then the position would be difficult but not hopeless. The Cork flying columns might evade the blockade or break through it to operate through Waterford, Tipperary, Wexford, or up the Midlands, or in the west of Ireland, forcing the British to follow and so withdraw their extra troops from Cork. Then we could return again. President de Valera understood that position but pressed for a reply to his question. The unworthy suspicion, already planted in my mind, that de Valera was about to end the struggle, and that I, amongst others, was being used to cover that action, returned sharply to my mind. Because of this I was guilty of the only exaggerated statement during the whole of my talk. After a long pause I replied that if large-scale British reinforcements were not sent to Cork we would last at least another five years. At this reply the President sat bolt upright and said he thought I was rather optimistic, which in truth I knew only too well myself. As we continued to talk he appeared so pleased at the prospects of our survival for another five years that I knew immediately my suspicions were wrong, but I have never since regretted my over-optimistic estimate of our powers of resistance.

The task of impartial writers in every land must be rendered exceedingly difficult because of the existence of biased records of leaders, written or uttered in moments of partisan bitterness. Our nation has more than its quota of those who scarify and libel past and present leaders, often for some single act with which the partisans did not agree, while they completely omit the great good those leaders accomplished. According to the daily press of 1934, Bishop O'Doherty of Galway, addressing a Confirmation class of Irish children, could only refer to the two patriots, Tone and Emmet, as 'Cut Throat Tone' and 'Emmet who led the rabble', making no mention of the ideals, sacrifices and deaths of those two for Ireland. Daniel O'Connell is violently attacked because of some differences with the Young Irelanders towards the end of his days, the Great Liberator's traducers, having nothing to record of his previous forty years' leadership, when he raised a people near serfdom from their knees to stand upright and assert their rights as men. Parnell hounded to his death by jackal politicians of his own party thirsting for his place, aided by a not inconsiderable section of the Irish people, is held up to public scorn for one act of his private life, and nothing is mentioned of his lifelong services to the people and his incomparable leadership throughout the many weary years. So, too, have the later-day leaders suffered because party bitternesses have obscured the truth, which in political strife, as in war, is always the first casualty. The Treaty and anti-Treaty propagandists depicted the leaders on both sides as monsters without a redeeming feature, and of all the leaders to suffer by slander and misrepresentation, bedevilment and belittlement, Mr de Valera is easily to the fore.

Luckily the stature of de Valera's greatness throughout those years is not dependent on any individual's opinion, but on established facts. His integrity and steadfastness have never been questioned and his capacity may best be judged by the trust which his comrades of the Republican movement placed in him. Clarke, Pearse, Connolly and the other Easter Week heroes allotted Commandant de Valera the command of the all-important Boland's Mills section of the insurgent army in 1916. How well he carried out this trust is shown not only by the sentence of death passed on him by the British after the surrender, but by his election to leadership of the 1916 survivors in Lewes Jail. Mr Griffith's tribute to Mr de Valera was to resign in 1917 the presidency of Sinn Féin which he had held since its formation and to propose de Valera as leader. In that year also, Collins, Brugha, Stack and all the others unanimously urged on him the leadership of the reorganising Republican organisations – military and political. Early in 1918 the Catholic Bishops of Ireland, the Irish Parliamentary Party, Irish Labour and other organisations accepted his leadership in the fight against conscription, although de Valera had then only a party of two members of parliament. As President of Sinn Féin he led the nation in December 1918 to elect the Republican parliament. In January 1919, at the first meeting of Dáil Éireann when the Declaration of Independence was enacted, it was de Valera who was unanimously selected as the first elected President of the Irish Republic. It was he who demanded a hearing of Ireland's claims at the Versailles Peace Conference, who later toured the United States of America to organise the Irish race and to address the Congress of that mighty nation in support of the Irish Republic. And it was President de Valera who returned to Ireland during the height of British terrorism to sustain the people and to encourage with all his strength the Irish Republican Army.

How in the face of those few of his many accomplishments anyone can cast a doubt on his greatness during those years is beyond comprehension. His leadership was then unchallenged; he was not simply the spokesman of the people but the main architect and inspiration of victory against the British. If the finest years of our long and chequered struggle for freedom were those from 1916 to 1921, when the unity, self-respect, intelligence and courage of the Irish people reached the heights, then too was the nation blessed with this man's leadership, which was worthy of a risen people. No subsequent disagreements should make us forget the debt we owe to him or to the persistence, ability and courage of men like Collins, Brugha, Griffith, Stack and the others who laboured with him in those critical years when the Irish people faced the full blast of the oppressor's violence.

I had arranged to leave Dublin for West Cork on May 24th, but Michael Collins asked me to stay over for another day to see a demonstration of a new sub-machine gun, the Thompson. Two ex-Irish-American army officers, Mr Cronin and Mr Dineen, had smuggled in two of those guns and if the test proved satisfactory, five hundred more were to be purchased in the United States and brought over to Ireland without delay. On the morning of the 24th, Mick Collins, Dick Mulcahy and I drove to a large, unoccupied house in the suburbs. There the two Americans and some of the Dublin armed Squad were waiting in the basement and soon the lecture on the gun was in progress. After about twenty minutes the Thompson gun was assembled, loaded, and some bricks placed apart against the wall about twenty yards distant as targets. Cronin invited Collins or Mulcahy to fire the first shot of this new gun in Ireland, but both urged me to take the honour. Fearing that I would miss with this newfangled gun and so let down West Cork in front of those GHQ and Dublin Squad officers I declined, but eventually took the gun, aimed, and with great luck smashed all the bricks into smithereens.

The smashing of the targets by the first shots from a Thompson gun in Ireland was taken as a good omen by all who were present, but my interest in the efficiency of the gun was far less than my concern not to miss in front of the party who would rag me unmercifully and probably offer to teach me to shoot. Before we left the building Collins and Mulcahy had decided to purchase five hundred of the Thompsons. Because of statements made later that GHQ knew early in 1921 that peace was on the way, it is of interest to note that this decision, made less than six weeks before the Truce with the British, clearly indicated that neither Michael Collins nor Richard Mulcahy had any idea that the end of the struggle with the enemy was at hand.

That night Michael Collins talked at length of the many abortive peace feelers sent out by the British since the commencement of hostilities. He had a great distrust of the motives behind those enemy moves and considered them in the main as attempts to seduce the support of the people from the Irish Republican Army. Of chief interest to me was the peace move of December 1920, when Archbishop Clune of Perth, Australia, acted as intermediary between Mr Lloyd George, British Prime Minister and Michael Collins, Acting President of the Irish Republic. During the first week of December the Archbishop had discussions with the British Premier and then contacted Michael Collins in Dublin. He returned to London and had further discussions with Lloyd George, after which he reported progress to Mr Art O'Brien, Irish Republican representative in London. O'Brien sent a courier immediately to Collins with a full account of the Archbishop's statements. This dispatch, published in full in Piaras Béaslaí's *Michael Collins and the Making of a New Ireland*, shows how easily hostilities could have been ended except for one stipulation made by Lloyd George, which vitally affected the West Cork Brigade. After stating that Lloyd George expressed himself strongly in favour of a Truce, the Archbishop went on to quote the Prime Minister as saying on December 9th, 1920:

> Regarding the cessation of hostilities on their side, he (Lloyd George) wants Macroom (Kilmichael) to be exempted. Military say that the perpetrators are on the hills in Cork. They are insisting on being allowed to pursue and capture them. He does not know if this is true.

This stipulation ended the negotiations. When the British Prime Minister spoke those words, eleven days had already elapsed since the Kilmichael fight, and his troops had been both hesitant and extremely wary in seeking out the West Cork Brigade flying column. The word 'capture' was certainly a peculiar one for the Prime Minister to use in describing the intentions of his troops should they ever corner and overwhelm the flying column. Collins, so proud of his native West Cork, was in great form at this British attempt to isolate it, and felt that the Prime Minister had conferred a signal honour on the brigade. In his teasing way he tried to make me angry, saying that they were fools not to accept the terms and leave the West Cork crowd to stew in their own juice, as the British could then concentrate on knocking the stuffing out of them, and that the West Cork Brigade would not stand up to them for three days. When informed that his estimate of the West Cork men's survival if left on their own was a gross understatement, and that anyway they would last long enough to dispatch sufficient of their numbers to Dublin to exterminate the cabinet which concluded such a Truce, Mick laughed heartily and expressed approval.

# 25

# ESCAPE FROM ENCIRCLEMENT

THE journey from Dublin on the morning of the 25th was uneventful, except for a casual inspection of the train by enemy military. One had some anxiety as to how the Dublin Brigade had fared that day in their attempt, timed for one o'clock, to destroy one of the strongholds of British civil administration: the Dublin Custom House. Nearing Cork, there was a return of nervousness and the hope that the arrangements made for the previous day by the Cork 1 Brigade would be repeated. I guessed that Mick Murphy, Dan O'Donovan, Dom O'Sullivan, Tom Crofts, Connie Neenan, Jerome Donovan, or some other city officer had been waiting to get me clear of the city. Sure enough, there was that fine fighting officer, Dan O'Donovan, and two others across the road from the station exit. All four of us walked rapidly a hundred yards towards the east to a waiting horse and trap, in care of a Fianna boy of fourteen, Dick Casey of Blackpool. Taking the reins from him and thanking Dan and the others, we set off at a good pace towards Tivoli, swinging north and then west to circle the city without interference. Nearly two hours later, we sighted our old headquarters, O'Mahony's of Belrose. In that beautiful late May afternoon, we chatted lazily as the horse ambled up the slight incline to the entrance of the home of the O'Mahonys. There was a stillness all around, and for miles we had not met a living soul. Reaching the entrance gate, I was in the act of pulling on the left rein to turn the horse in the avenue, when forty steel-helmeted British soldiers rose over the ditches at both sides of us and, with levelled guns, roared at us to halt and put our hands up. Automatically the horse was pulled back on his haunches, for one sensed without conscious thought that had the enemy noticed the horse turning into this known IRA headquarters, nothing would have saved us from the consequences.

About thirty of the soldiers crowded around as we stepped from the trap with our hands reaching stiffly for the sky. Glancing at their identification numerals my heart sank as I saw they were the dreaded merciless Essex. Realising that very stupidly Dick had not been coached as to the story we were to tell if held up, I called out loudly for his benefit, without waiting for questions, that I was Ted Ryder, a medical student from Cork College, going to my mother's farm near

Crookstown, and that the boy was Dick Casey, son of one of our farm labourers, who had driven the horse and trap into Cork for me. The British then searched me, turning each pocket inside out, opening my clothes and nearly stripping me, before they had every scrap of paper, loose match and copper in my possession in a neat heap on top of the contents of my attaché case. The officer handled the medical paraphernalia, read some of the medical notes copied in my own handwriting, shook out the worn medical textbook and glanced over the British magazines and the two anti-Republican daily papers, *The Irish Times* and the *Daily Mail.* Then he questioned me closely for nearly ten minutes about my family, the college, my political views and my knowledge of and attitude to the IRA. His manner remained hard and suspicious until in answer to his question as to why any medical student should be travelling home from college just before the annual examinations, he was told that my doctor had ordered me to stop studying for a year, as one of my lungs was affected with tuberculosis. He appeared more friendly when he learned that the doctor had also ordered me to bed for a week's rest before travelling to Dublin to a tuberculosis specialist, but said he would have to detain me until the Major arrived. My pallor, mainly due to my fear, and my thin body, must have helped this officer to accept me as a sick man. He ushered me in O'Mahony's gate and told me to join a group of about a dozen local male adult prisoners who were herded together. All of these knew me, and as I anxiously watched their faces for the tell-tale look of recognition which would inadvertently betray me, I thought desperately hard of how to avoid being kept with them, for almost certainly all of them would be brought as prisoners at least as far as Bandon Barracks. My only chance of release or escape was to remain apart from those suspects, so I called the officer and asked if it were really necessary for me to stand around with such a mob. He grinned as he said it would be all right for me to return and wait on the road.

At intervals, in groups of sixty or seventy, other detachments of the Essex converged onto the road from different directions, until at least five hundred of the raiders were assembled. Many of them looked curiously as they passed, and several of their officers came over to question me. A captain tried to trap me by handing me a map and asking me to point out my home as he could not understand why a traveller from Cork to Crookstown should use this particular road we were on. Awkwardly fumbling with the map I told him that never having seen a map I was unable to point out my home, but that it was three miles nearer to where we stood than to Crookstown village. Before he could ask further questions a diversion came. Someone called that the Major was coming and my interrogator hurriedly joined the other officers who were bustling about lining up their companys and platoons. At that moment around the corner from the Crosspound direction came our arch enemy, Major Percival, strutting in front of yet another detachment of the Essex.

Nearly two hours had elapsed between the time of our

capture and Percival's arrival. During the first ten minutes, I was almost frozen with the fear of the death they would give me. While answering questions, thoughts kept intruding of the painful deaths suffered by so many of my comrades at the hands of those savages. The fear of death itself was overshadowed by the greater fear of torture and a lingering exit. Most hideous of all was the fear of my own doubts as to whether I could stand the racking and the tearing without showing weakness. And then mercifully, for no explainable reason, I was no longer afraid. Perhaps this change in morale was due to Providence having so ordained that, when man has reached the depths of fear and despair, an unnamed reserve force is released which enables him to rise above those horrors and regain his self-respect. But whatever the reason, after the first fifteen minutes I was calm and detached, and now I looked curiously at Percival as he approached. Dressed in a tunic and shorts, he gripped a Colt revolver in his right hand. The cruelty of his set face was accentuated by the two buck-teeth, which showed like small fangs at either side of his bitter mouth. His hard eyes, darting suspiciously from side to side, rested on me momentarily as he came up. Halting his detachment, he joined the group of waiting officers standing rigidly to attention about twenty-five yards down the road. After some minutes' conversation with them, he went in O'Mahony's gate, returning in a short time to shout the order to take all the prisoners down to the transports on the Crossbarry road. After glancing towards me, he spent some time examining my belongings and listening to the other officers, who were probably repeating the details of my interrogation.

He came slowly up the road, followed by four others, halted a few paces in front of me, folded his arms and stared into my eyes as if he would read into my mind. After a long time he stepped forward, removed my hat, stepped back, again folded his arms and again stared. I met his stare and held it with what I hoped was a slightly puzzled look until he turned away. He had gone only ten paces when he turned, walked back and again stared at me before speaking the only words he uttered in my presence, 'Release him.' Then he walked rapidly away. Hardly crediting my good fortune at being the only suspect released, and thanking the officer who told me to go, Dick and I resumed our journey. When the horse had walked around the bend out of sight of the enemy, the temptation to lash him to a gallop was almost unbearable, but an inner voice cautioned to keep him walking. He continued to walk until we were about four hundred yards from O'Mahony's gate when a lash of the whip startled him into a gallop. Through Crosspound he tore, up the hill west of the old road until he was pulled up panting and sweating after his mile and a half gallop at Tom Kelleher's home at Crowhill.

Tom's mother and sisters, Ellen and Julia, having heard the noise of the galloping horse, were waiting in the yard. One of them called out that the place was alive with enemy soldiers and that we should run. Asking one of them to saddle a horse, I ran to the nearby ditch where my guns were dumped.

Then a vow was taken as the guns were being loaded and the equipment buckled on that never again while hostilities were on would those guns be separated from me. The only occasion during all the Anglo-Irish War that this had happened was during the Dublin trip, and for me that had very nearly been the end. As I mounted the horse, Mrs Kelleher came running from the house with a jug of milk in one hand and a bottle of Holy Water in the other. I drank the milk while the good woman, praying audibly that God would protect us all from the Sassenach, shook half the contents of the bottle over me. Within seven minutes of arrival I was riding away to the west.

After changing horses twice during my all-night ride of about forty miles, I reached my destination without further contact with the enemy. Before leaving for Dublin it had been arranged that on the day following that of my scheduled return, the brigade flying column would reassemble west of Dunmanway and seek a fight with the Auxiliaries the next day. It was planned that a Drimoleague Squad under that first-class company captain, Daniel O'Driscoll, would as early as possible on that day shoot a Black and Tan, or failing that target, attack the Drimoleague enemy post with rifle fire. This was expected to draw out to Drimoleague O Company of the Auxiliaries as reinforcements from Dunmanway, nine miles distant. As all roads between Dunmanway and Drimoleague, except the main one, had been cut for some time past, the Auxiliaries would have to travel through a splendid ambushing position at Gloundaw, about halfway between the two towns. It was here that a full-strength brigade flying column of one hundred riflemen, supported by twenty shotgun men from the local companies, proposed to attack the terrorists who were expected to number about one hundred and fifty. Close to Gloundaw a waiting IRA scout took my horse and pointed out the direction in which the column had moved. After crossing a few fields I saw the column below me settling into their positions. Halting to examine their dispositions from the high ground, a wave of happiness came over me for I was back again where my affections lay. Weariness and misgivings fell away as Liam Deasy, Mick Crowley, Seán Lehane, Jim Hurley, Peter Kearney and others welcomed me home.

Before noon, word reached us that O'Driscoll and his men had succeeded in shooting a Black and Tan near his own barracks. Now it was almost certain that the Auxiliaries would come. Walking along the rough ground immediately overlooking the road where over a hundred of our fighters stretched out motionless, one sensed the increasing tension, for a tough fight was anticipated. But all day passed and no enemy appeared, so the disappointed column withdrew to billets seven miles away. On the following evening, information reached us that there were large troop movements away to the east, as well as marked activity by the garrisons at Bantry, Skibbereen, Clonakilty, Dunmanway and Bandon. Then we knew the reason the Auxiliaries had not attempted to reinforce Drimoleague. It was clear that a round-up was being launched and that the Dunmanway garrison, as well as the others, had detailed orders as to its task, which would not allow of an unscheduled sortie. It was the second evening after Gloundaw when I first comprehended the magnitude of the enemy effort, for as we probed to get around to the rear of the oncoming enemy from the east, it was clear there was no way out in that direction. On the third day, news came of thousands of the enemy sweeping in from North Cork, reaching in a line from west of Ballyvourney to Macroom. Pivoted on that town, another line had dotted the country south to the coast near Clonakilty, from which they had started to sweep. In the south the Atlantic Ocean was an effective barrier, not to mention the British Marines and naval sloops which patrolled the coast. Much later that night we heard that, away to the west, other British troops held the Kenmare, Kilgarvan and Headford line of escape to Kerry. Afterwards we were to learn that enemy troops from as far away as the Curragh and Templemore participated, and I was to read the Special Operation Order issued by General Strickland, commander of the martial law area, to his brigade commanders, in which he defined their mission as that of seeking out the IRA columns, bringing them to action and annihilating them.

The enemy advanced from the north and the east, their infantry supported by field artillery which, lately motorised, was again horse-drawn, to enable it to circumvent our road obstructions and to travel over boggy and mountain terrain. For a similar reason, their ammunition carts, field kitchens and water carts were drawn by mules. Thankfully one noted that they were working strictly according to an office plan that detailed the movements and timings by which every unit reached its day's objective. Obviously field commanders had no power to depart from the plan and no right to initiate any move not contained in it. This cumbersome plan, suffering from its thoroughness, appeared to be to blockade an area of over a thousand square miles by forming three lines of troops, the first reaching from the sea near Kenmare, north through Kilgarvan to Headford, the second from there east-south-east to Macroom, and the third due south from that town, to again meet the sea in the vicinity of Clonakilty. The plan must also have detailed the British units in Kerry to form a holding line along the Cork–Kerry border, and against this wall the IRA column was to be driven by the eastern and northern forces, and there annihilated. It is difficult to understand why the famous plan did not include the elementary tactic of using one thousand of their many troops as five mobile reconnaissance units darting forward simultaneously five or six miles apart in front of the slow-moving lines, to contact and engage the IRA column known to be within the blockaded area.

The fourth evening saw the brigade flying column manoeuvring and weaving in front of the oncoming British. Driven relentlessly towards the west and south, the column was being compressed into an ever-narrowing corner of the south-west of our brigade area, while the enemy lines had contracted to less than half their original lengths as they closed in.

That night the flying column, with rifles at the ready and a bullet in each breech, moved gingerly across country and noiselessly along the grass borders of the byroads. Cautiously it emerged at Ouvane Bridge on the main Bantry–Glengarriff road which skirts Bantry Bay. It marched rapidly along this route for about a mile and a half until it turned onto a byroad to the north and its destination for that night: the Valley of Coomhola. This lovely green oasis nestles in the contrasting beauty and majestic splendour of the harsh mountain land which overlooks Bantry Bay and stretches away to the north to meet its brother mountains in Kerry. Into this peaceful valley of the appropriately lovely name the flying column marched about midnight, and soon the men were resting in the homes of its hospitable people. That night sentries and scouts were doubled as the others rested without removing either boots or clothes.

On the following morning, scouts were sent out in all directions to seek information of the enemy approach, while the column stood to arms in billets. Those men were now grave and serious, as each realised, as I did, the closeness of the huge enemy forces seeking to destroy them. Gone were the merry quips, the laughter and the songs one usually heard in other days when approaching a billet, and the men now sat around, their rifles between their knees, silent and thoughtful. They showed no nervousness, but, as if to indicate their appreciation of the position, each man was freshly shaved, his boots and leggings shone with an extra polish, and his rifle gleamed with the signs of a special effort with oil and pull-through. Salutes were more formal, and the sentries paced with a more military tread, as if to proclaim to all that they were confident, alert and unafraid.

That evening four of us sat and smoked in the drawing-room of Marcella Hurley's home, our brigade column headquarters, while Marcella, famed singer of many Feiseanna, played the piano and sang for us the traditional love and battle songs of our people. News arrived that some British artillery guns had been shelling the slopes of Shehey Mountain with shrapnel, hoping to flush out a flying column. Ten minutes later we were informed that naval sloops were landing British marines and soldiers some distance away in Bantry Bay, and fifteen minutes afterwards the whole column was moving up the old hilly road to the Kerry border. Two miles on we halted to await darkness, after which the march was resumed.

Early that day we had consulted local officers as to the feasibility of bringing the flying column during darkness across the treacherous boggy land that formed the plateau of the mountain country between the old Kerry road and Gougane Barra. If this were practicable the column, when at Gougane Barra, would be outside any ring of troops based on the Kealkil Pass of the Keimineigh–Ballingeary road, and would have direct access to the southern slopes of the Kerry mountains. The local officer undertook to have the one man capable of guiding us across in such circumstances, waiting at the point where we were to leave the road for the mountain journey. When we reached him he had collected and tied into one a number of ropes, and after warning us not to step a yard from the path over which he would lead us, he set off in the lead, holding the front of the long rope. We trailed behind him, walking on each other's heels, hanging on to the rope and to the coat or equipment of the man in front. It was a nightmare march of many hours in the thick darkness, and at times we sank over knee deep into the boggy ground, although we never left our guide's path. Without this man's help men could have floundered to their deaths in the deep holes on either side, but eventually he led us all safely to the top of Deepvalley Desmond, beneath which lay lonely Gougane Barra. In our march from Coomhola we had crossed the line taken by O'Sullivan Beare's column of fighters when they too evaded the British enemy of their generation, while away to our left was the 'Priest's Leap', so named because a priest fleeing from the British terrorists of the Penal Days was reputed to have saved his life by spurring his horse to jump this seemingly impassable chasm. Now as we waited in the darkness to descend Deepvalley Desmond to another storied spot, Gougane Barra, the home of Saint Finbarr, memories of Calnan's appealing poem commencing 'There is an isle in lone Gougane Barra' must have returned to many as it was one of the poems in the readers of our schooldays. For over an hour man after man, with the aid of stretched-out rifles and that useful rope, swung and slithered down that rough passage to the level ground of Gougane Barra. Some were bruised and wrenched, but none seriously, and we quickly reached the hotel to be welcomed by hospitable Mrs Cronin, her daughter and two Volunteer sons.

After a short delay the column moved to rest billets in the nearby rocky countryside. Here we appeared to be comparatively safe, as we were now outside the ring of roads likely to be used by the enemy. It was probably the best defensive fighting country in all Ireland. Only one small, twisting, easily defended rough road lead into our billet area, while behind us stretched mile after mile of roadless mountain land, well covered with bracken and dotted with large rocks across the hills to the Kerry Valley. On this ground we would stand, and if the British came, fight, trusting to Providence that our ammunition would last until our ally, darkness, came, when we would steal or fight our way through their lines. During the day we fortified positions as the rumblings of British transports and rumours of enemy movements kept the column on the alert, but no enemy approached our lair. That night we stayed on still waiting in our stronghold. The following morning messages came that the British, having completed their operation, had commenced on the previous night to retire to their bases. For seven days they had been away from their barracks, combing the countryside, sleeping in bivouacs or in fields, fed by a large Army Service Corps, and they had not succeeded in capturing one active Volunteer, a rifle, revolver or a round of ammunition. Within two hours of hearing of their departure on that June morning, the flying column was trekking after them to the east, for now was the time to show friend and foe, that far from being destroyed or intimidated, the West Cork IRA was increasing its pressure in and around every enemy garrison town in the brigade area.

# 26

# THE SPLENDID PEOPLE

THIS account of guerilla days now enters the last month of Anglo-Irish hostilities – the month before the Truce. For the student of our armed struggle it is necessary to evaluate here the strengths and the weaknesses of the contending forces of British Imperialism and Irish Republicanism. The first consideration should be the field forces of both armies. For this purpose it is advisable to detail the strengths of all the British garrisons within the county of Cork, since those enemy units operated against any or all of the three Cork brigades of the Irish Republican Army, and were not confined to the locality in which they were stationed. Before me is a document dated May 17th, 1921, signed by Major General Strickland, General Officer Commanding the 6th Division, which stated *inter alia* that the following units of British infantry, Machine-Gun Corps, Royal Field Artillery, Royal Garrison Artillery,

Royal Engineers and of the Auxiliary Division were stationed within County Cork on that date. The strengths of units given hereunder are approximate as none are given in General Strickland's document:

INFANTRY:

The 1st Battalion, The Buffs Regiment; The 1st Battalion, The King's Regiment; The 2nd Battalion, The Hampshires; The 2nd Battalion, The King's Own Scottish Borderers; The 2nd Battalion, The South Stafford Regiment; The 1st Battalion, Essex Regiment; The 1st Battalion, The Manchester Regiment; The 2nd Battalion, The Queen's Own Cameron Highlanders; The 2nd Battalion, The East Lancashire Regiment; The 1st Battalion, The West Surrey Regiment; The 1st Battalion, The Gloucestershire Regiment.

As the numerals 1st and 2nd denote, all those eleven battalions were first-line units, and had each a battle strength of about nine hundred and fifty officers and men. However, British Army battalions are rarely at full strength, and it is more accurate to assume each unit was approximately one hundred and fifty under strength, about eight hundred officers and men. This gives a total of eight thousand, eight hundred first-line infantry troops.

MACHINE-GUN CORPS:

The 1st Battalion Machine-Gun Corps, strength four hundred and eighty officers and men.

ROYAL FIELD ARTILLERY:

The 2nd Brigade R.F.A., The 7th Brigade R.F.A. Six Batteries. Strength, seven hundred and twenty officers and men.

ROYAL GARRISON ARTILLERY:

The 31st Fire Command (Queenstown), The 32nd Fire Command (Bere Island). Strength, four hundred and forty officers and men.

ROYAL ENGINEERS:

The 33rd Company, Royal Engineers. Strength, two hundred and forty officers and men.

DIVISIONAL AND BRIGADE HEADQUARTERS' STAFFS, TRANSPORT AND SUPPLY UNITS:

Strength, two hundred officers and men.

AUXILIARY DIVISION:

'J' Company, Auxiliary Division (Macroom); 'L' Company, Auxiliary Division (Millstreet); 'O' Company, Auxiliary Division (Dunmanway). Strength, five hundred and forty officers and men.

In the British House of Commons on June 2nd, 1921, Sir Hamar Greenwood, British Chief Secretary for Ireland, stated that the total enlisted strength of the Auxiliary Division in Ireland was one thousand, four hundred and ninety-eight officers and men, therefore, the Cork area held over one-third of all this terrorist force.

This captured document, signed by General Strickland, records all the above-mentioned units under his command as being stationed in County Cork on May 17th, 1921. It makes no mention of the naval forces, Royal Marines or armed coastguards stationed at the County Cork bases, and lacking other authentic enemy records, no estimate of those naval forces will be attempted or included here. Neither does General Strickland's document deal with the twenty-three garrisons of Black and Tans within County Cork on that date, ranging in strengths between twenty and one hundred and fifty, and totalling in all one thousand, one hundred and fifty officers and men. Excluding naval personnel, approximately twelve thousand, six hundred armed British troops, Auxiliaries and Black and Tans occupied the county of Cork seven weeks before the Truce between Ireland and Britain.

Standing against this field force was that of the Irish Republican Army, never at any time exceeding three hundred and ten riflemen in the whole of the county of Cork, for the very excellent reason that this was the total of rifles held by the combined three Cork brigades. The only other IRA arms within the county were five machine guns and some three hundred and fifty automatics and revolvers. Even this small force could hardly be mobilised for a major operation likely to continue for a day, as its ammunition did not exceed fifty rounds a rifle, two fills per revolver and automatic, and a few full drums for each machine gun. Explosives, engineering supplies, signalling equipment and other army requirements were almost as nonexistent as our artillery or trench mortars. Those figures, showing the Irish Republican Army outnumbered by over forty to one in armed men and to a far greater ratio in firepower before the Truce, may justly cause one to wonder why the British did not succeed in exterminating the small Irish field force in 1920 and 1921. The answer, of course, is that in the last analysis the struggle was never one between the British Army and a small Irish force of flying columns and active service units. Had this been so, the few flying columns operating would not have existed for a month, no matter how bravely and skilfully they fought. This was a war between the British Army and the Irish people, and the problem before the British from mid-1920 was not how to smash the flying columns, but how to destroy the resistance of a people, for, as sure as day follows night, if a flying column was wiped out in any area, another would arise to continue the attacks on and the resistance to the alien rulers. The Irish people had many weapons which the British lacked: their belief in the righteousness of their cause, their determination to be free, their political structure as declared in the general election of December 1918, and a strong militant body of youth, who, though as yet unarmed, were a potential army of great possibilities.

With that small field force of flying columns stood ten thousand enrolled Volunteers in the twenty-three battalion areas of the city and county of Cork. Those had not the experience or training of the men of the flying columns, but by and large were of the same calibre, lacking only the arms to enable them to quickly take the field. Meanwhile they were a well-nigh inexhaustible source of replacements for flying columns. That was not all. They did not simply stand and wait until called on, but were actively engaged in harassing the enemy in their company areas. Some attacked and sniped enemy posts, arrested spies, burned so-called loyalist houses, trenched roads, scouted, guarded and arranged billets for the flying columns. They formed the battalions and companies, the structure on which the very existence of the flying column depended. Those units maintained brigade communications, collected money for the arms fund, supplied intelligence reports, and in short were the mainstay of the whole militant Republican movement. The importance of those battalion, company and section units of organisation in guerilla warfare cannot be overemphasised. Should a brigade flying column be wiped out, those units could continue activities and throw up another flying column, but if they collapsed, all was lost, as without their support an active service unit could not exist. Throughout hostilities the fighting brigades realised this and certain key officers were transferred periodically back from the flying column to ensure that their units were maintained at the highest possible level.

The Cumann na mBan, the women's auxiliary organisation, ranks high in this estimate of values. The members, organised in companies and districts corresponding to IRA units, were not in any sense women politicians, holding debating classes or propounding political theories. They were groups of women and girls from town and countryside, sisters, relatives or friends of the Volunteers, enrolled in their own organisation, for the sole purpose of helping the Irish Republican Army. They were indispensable to the army, nursing the wounded and sick, carrying dispatches, scouting, acting as intelligence agents, arranging billets, raising funds, knitting, washing, cooking for the active servicemen and burying our dead. Many sick and wounded Volunteers owe their lives to those girls, who cared and nursed them under great difficulties. On bicycles those members of the Cumann na mBan carried dispatches long distances, day or night, and on occasions the quick delivery of those saved the lives of Volunteers. Their work, particularly in government concerns, as intelligence agents, was vital to the well-being of the IRA. From post offices they abstracted copies of cipher messages passing from enemy headquarters to garrison commanders which the IRA quickly broke and acted on. At times, members of the Cumann na mBan scouted 'wanted' men on their journeys and ran many risks to ensure their safety. They raised large sums of money for the army, and without their hard work, amounting to drudgery, members of the IRA would often have lacked clean clothes or have gone hungry. They were a splendid body of young women and their value to the IRA was well appreciated by the enemy, who banned the Cumann na mBan as an illegal organisation.

As well as having to meet the organised opposition of the IRA and the Cumann na mBan, the British had also to contend with a hostile populace. By the end of 1920, except for a small minority of less than ten per cent, the people had boycotted or ostracised enemy garrisons, and the hate and contempt shown by our people must have had a very serious effect on the morale of the isolated British forces. Except for a very few, no one would speak to them, old men spat as they passed, old women looked through them with contemptuous stares, children jeered at them, no girl, except the unfortunates, would meet them, and some publicans and shopkeepers refused to serve them. Those British troops were enemies and were made to feel it by those sturdy people. It is true that the British did not take all this lying down and they made our people pay. The shops and public houses where service had been refused were looted, broken up and sometimes burned, old men felt the butts of rifles, and old women, girls and children were assaulted and insulted. But those reprisals did not stop the expressions of hate and contempt, and the isolation of the British grew as the boycott intensified. This was only part of the people's contribution to the fight for freedom. Nearing the Truce, unasked and unorganised, nine out of every ten of the adult civilian population were watching and reporting to us on the movements of the British troops or on the activities of any suspected British agent. A farmer ploughing up a field would stop in the middle of a furrow, abandon his horses and plough and run perhaps a mile to warn IRA men of an enemy approach. A woman driving to market in her donkey cart, detecting British troops in ambush, would pass through it, and at the next house root out a messenger to send back with the information. Schoolboys of twelve peeped over ditches and scanned the countryside with their sharp young eyes, looking for the khaki or dark-blue uniforms. A publican or barmaid hearing some half-drunken officer tell of a raid arranged for early the following morning would have the information to the threatened district that night. Railway employees carried dispatches, facilitated wanted men when passengers and obligingly delayed trains, so that IRA squads could seize and carry off the mails. Middle-aged men dropped their business and work to drive members of the IRA; wives and daughters scrubbed and cleaned their homes so that visiting column men would eat of their best in spotless surroundings. Men would leave their beds to watch all night while tired IRA men rested. Doctors travelled surreptitiously to treat our sick and wounded, and teachers warned children against mentioning the movements of the IRA while urging them to report those of the enemy.

All those contributions were important, but to me the greatest of all were the examples of courage, loyalty and self-sacrifice given to us in the IRA by some of the civilian population. We, the Irish, are not a master race, for there is no such breed in this scattered world, but neither are we of the material of a subject one. Like all peoples, we have our weaknesses and failings, our blackguards as well as good people, our cowards as well as our brave men, our mean souls as well as generous ones, but, surely, our proportion of men and women of high courage and great generosity is amongst the highest in the whole world. Not all of us in the IRA had the courage and tenacity of the Charlie Hurleys, the Pat Deasys, or the others who died so valiantly, but who, with any sense of decency, could betray by cowardice or by a dishonourable act, a people who were daily giving such examples of stoicism, courage and generosity? Owing to lack of space this book omits the names of hundreds of the IRA and Cumann na mBan whose names deserve to be recorded. For a similar reason, the names of hundreds of outstanding families cannot be included, and although it is invidious to mention only a few, no one will feel slighted if, to properly explain the part taken by the civilian population, mention is made of only a few.

Memories. Four of us sitting fully armed in an upstairs sitting-room in a house in Shannon Street, Bandon, waiting for news of some of the enemy it was hoped to attack. Underneath in the shop, the owners, Mrs Fitzsimons, a widow, and her sister, Miss Bannon who lived alone, were engaged serving customers. At intervals, those two gentle ladies, no longer young, came in to ply us with tea, food and cigarettes. I marvelled at their calmness and courage. Looking only to our comfort, those two did not seem a whit concerned that at any moment they might be in the line of fire and their home and business a shambles.

Another memory. People who shall be nameless, living in a small, thatched house on poor land in the Dunmanway district. They eked out a bare existence and were rearing a young family on a few acres of arable land that fed two cows.

At five o'clock one winter's morning, tired and weary, we knocked at their door and the woman of the house greeted the three of us. When she had raked up the fire and put on the kettle, she asked us to tend it as she had to go out for a while. Putting on her heavy working boots, she went away, and we sat silent for we guessed the reason for her early morning journey. She had gone a half-mile to knock up a luckier neighbour and to borrow butter and eggs, so that her visitors could have a hearty breakfast. Her family could not afford those luxuries very often, but never once would she fail to have them for those she called 'The Boys'. She would have to skimp, scrape and save to repay the borrowed luxuries later, but that did not matter. Although acutely uncomfortable at the trouble we were causing, we dared not attempt to stop her or to refuse the eggs or the butter, as had we done so we would have hurt that fine pride so pronounced amongst the grand peasantry that enriches West Cork.

Yet another. Barrett's, Kinsale Junction. Willie, an active IRA man, was absent, but his generous wife, who had so often catered for us, was there with her four young children, the eldest not yet eight years. Some of the flying column arrived about midday to attack a troop train, which we had been told was due to pass through the Junction a few hours later. Apologetically, I told Mrs Barrett that we would have to use her home as one of the firing positions to cover the railway station, a short distance away. Noticing my reluctance to endanger her family and her home, she angrily asked if I considered that the Barretts would worry should their home be burned out afterwards; that they were honoured it was to be used to fight from, and to allow her half an hour to remove the young children to the safety of a neighbour's home, when she would return in time to make tea for us before the fight began.

Just one more of the many memories of those splendid people whom British aggression failed to break. The Crowleys of Kilbrittain. On a February day four of us left the flying column to visit the parents of Lieutenant Patrick Crowley, who had been killed by the Essex Regiment. We came out from a wood at the back of the place where their home once stood, about five hundred yards from Kilbrittain Black and Tan post. Unseen we approached the destroyed house and saw Mrs Crowley sitting on a stool in the yard, gazing thoughtfully at the ruins of her blown-up and burned-out house, while Mr Crowley moved some rubble to strengthen the little henhouse, which alone had escaped the orgy of British destruction. Those two, near the close of their days, he, grey-bearded, thin and hardy, she ageing and frail-looking, neatly dressed in black, were alone. Paddy had been killed by the British a week previously, Denis lay badly hurt in a British jail after a merciless beating by his captors. Con, one of our best fighters, was also a prisoner under the name of Patrick Murphy, and the shadow of death hung over him too, for should he be recognised, another Crowley would die for Ireland. The fourth and remaining son, Mick, seriously wounded early in the struggle, was a leading flying column officer, and his chance of survival did not appear to be high as he, too, was a most active and daring officer. The two daughters, Ciss and Birdie, among the most excellent of our Cumann na mBan, were absent on IRA work and would not return until late that night. The sorrows and sufferings of this ageing couple must have weighed heavily on them, but there were no signs of weakness or complaints as they listened to our words of sympathy at the death of their fine son. They were indomitable, unbreakable and proud of the part all their children were playing in the battle for freedom. To them, Pat had died well for Ireland, and it was unthinkable that any of their other sons would not fight on equally well until the end. It was God's will that Pat had died, and perhaps He would see that the others would be spared. And one day when the British were driven out they would rebuild their home.

Who can fully estimate the value of men and women like those in a nation's fight against alien rule? Their spirit and their faith in the justice of their cause did not allow of defeat at the hands of imperialist mercenaries. British guns were not able to cow them, British money could not buy them, nor could British guile and duplicity wean them from their support of the Irish Republican Army, for indeed, they were as truly soldiers of the resistance movement as any Volunteer of the flying column.

# 27

# TRUCE

AFTER their last major effort to corner and destroy the Cork IRA flying columns, the British forces retired to their barracks in early June. They had hardly reached their bases when the West Cork IRA resumed their offensive activities. During this last month of hostilities, although we could not draw the enemy out for a major engagement, the number of our burnings, kidnappings, raids, road destructions and attacks on posts and enemy personnel reached the high level record for any single month. Some of those burnings were reprisals for the destruction of houses like O'Mahony's of Belrose, Tom Kelleher's of Crowhill, and others which the Essex destroyed a few hours after they had captured and released me. The value of those homes would total approximately three thousand pounds, but the IRA exacted a heavy price in return, and destroyed property of active British supporters to the value of at least one hundred thousand pounds. First we burned to the ground in that district all the British loyalists' houses, Colonel Peacock's home, Stephenson's of Cor Castle, Brigadier-General Caulfield's, Denneny's and Stennings', all in the Innishannon district.

As there were no other active loyalist homes in that area, we went further afield to teach the British a lesson, and once and for all end their fire terror. Poole's of Mayfield, Bandon, was burned; Dunboy Castle was gutted, and the Earl of Bandon's stately and massive home at Castle Bernard blazed for half a day before it crumbled in ruins. To those counter burnings the British did not reply; they evidently had had enough. In addition to those counter-reprisals, the IRA burned out the Allin Institute, a meeting place for British loyalists under the guise of a Freemason Hall, in the centre of Bandon. The Skibbereen Courthouse, a seat of British Law Administration, was also destroyed, and Whitley's and Hungerford's of Rosscarbery were added to our list.

During that last month of hostilities, many other buildings were destroyed in West Cork as they were about to be used to house the incoming British reinforcements. We were fully aware that British Army Maintenance Engineers, accompanying the rounding-up forces in their last operation, had inspected and measured many large buildings which they contemplated taking over as temporary barracks. Amongst those buildings were the coastguard stations – Howe's Strand, the Galley Head and Rosscarbery – and the IRA promptly burned them to the ground. But the main British hope for additional barracks lay in the commandeering of the workhouses. All those British-built institutions were planned and erected with a view to their suitability for conversion to military barracks in an emergency such as that which arose in 1920–1921. Already they were in occupation of those in Clonakilty and Dunmanway and now they proposed to take over those at Bandon, Skibbereen and Schull, which would accommodate a further two thousand troops. By the morning of June 24th, all three were smoking ruins, and the British were left to seek other barracks. The two most important were destroyed in the early hours of the morning of June 23rd. Some sections of the flying column under Liam Deasy, destroyed the Skibbereen building, while the remainder entered Bandon for a similar task. The Bandon Workhouse stood at the eastern end of the town, and at 1 a.m. the flying column occupied positions in South Main Street and Shannon Street, fifty yards from one and a few hundred yards from the other two enemy posts. At the same time, Battalion Adjutant Jim O'Mahony, with a number of his unit, arrived at the workhouse and proceeded to evacuate the inmates and the staff to nearby houses. At 1.30 we saw the flames from the burning buildings and the flying column barring the way, steeled to meet the British forces who were expected to come from their fortresses and try to save their burning buildings. They did not attempt it, but stayed securely behind their protecting walls. About 2.30 I came on to one of our sections covering Bandon Bridge, and saw several of the riflemen looking towards the burning workhouse with grins on their faces, instead of watching for an enemy approach. I spoke sharply to them, and thought that some of the flying column had grown dangerously contemptuous of their enemy and this overconfidence might easily lead to disaster. But, as I moved on to another section, I knew there was some excuse for their grins and their carelessness. Two nights before some of them had seen Lord Bandon's castle burned, and tonight they were witnessing another symbol of the conquest being destroyed: twin evils of British domination, the castle of the Lord of the British Ascendancy and the poorhouse of the native Irish who had been pauperised. Lord Bandon's castle, situated outside the western end of Bandon, was set on fire at 4.30 a.m., but the British did not venture out to save it until four and a half hours later. Now the workhouse had been burning for over an hour, and again the British garrisons, only a few hundred yards away, were evidently not prepared to risk a sortie, knowing that we held the way against them. We waited on until 3.30, and then, after firing a few rounds to express our derision, withdrew without interference.

During this last month of hostilities too, the West Cork IRA kidnapped a number of British armed forces and members of their civilian administration. Three coastguards were taken at Howe's Strand, three Royal Marines at Castletownshend, a British major at Reendesert, Bantry, and four Justices of the Peace at Bandon and Clonakilty. Those last mentioned, taken on June 21st, were the Earl of Bandon, Sealy King, JP, of Bandon, J. J. Fitzpatrick, JP, and J. St Leger Gillman, JP of Clonakilty. Seán Hales and Jim O'Mahony were in charge of the party arresting Lord Bandon; Denis Mehigan of that which took Sealy King, while Jim Hurley's men arrested Fitzpatrick and Gillman. All four were taken specifically as hostages and were to be executed should the British shoot or hang any IRA captive. All were informed of their fate if the British did not heed the warning they had received in writing after the hostages were taken, and not one of the four doubted that we would carry out our threat. They were held until the peace talks had made it obvious that a truce was imminent, when Sealy King, Fitzpatrick and Gillman were released, but Lord Bandon was held our prisoner until after the Truce became operative. One of their stories here must suffice. When Lord Bandon was taken from his burning castle, he was brought south to the Clogagh Company area, where he was left with a guard who had been instructed to shoot him should the British appear likely to recapture him, and then to fight their own way clear. Those instructions were given in Bandon's presence and he became a model prisoner, often advising his guard not to make so much noise as a British rounding-up party might hear them. He was given permission to write, under strict supervision and censorship, letters to the British Prime Minister and to General Strickland giving particulars of the fate that awaited him and appealing to them to ensure that no IRA prisoner would be killed. He lived under the same conditions as his guards and was in no way ill-treated, but he would certainly have died had one West Cork IRA prisoner been murdered subsequent to our ultimatum to the enemy.

Luckily for Lord Bandon such did not happen, although three of our patriot soldiers were brutally killed by the army of occupation during June. Volunteer Daniel Crowley, of Behegullane, Dunmanway, while attempting to evade the Auxiliaries was shot dead near his home on June 7th. The British official communiqué issued from Dublin Castle stated that he refused to halt when called on, was fired at and killed. Volunteer Matthew Donovan, Quarries' Cross, Bandon, was taken prisoner during a round-up on June 10th, near his home, by the Essex Regiment and executed on the roadside. The Essex officer who murdered him got hysterical and ran to a nearby labourer's cottage, shouting, 'Water, water. God forgive me I have just murdered an innocent prisoner.' He sat on a chair in the kitchen, crying out at intervals for God's forgiveness, until led away by some of his ruffian comrades. The savage Essex also murdered Volunteer John Murphy of Cloghane. He was a farm labourer and was working in a field when they arrested him on the morning of June 22nd. The Essex did not use a bullet but bayoneted him to death in the field, and his lacerated and badly torn body was found some hours later where he fell. When news came of this brutal outrage, Lord Bandon's life hung on a very slender thread. He had been a hostage for some hours, but the IRA ultimatum could not possibly have reached the British at the time of Volunteer Murphy's murder. That alone saved Lord Bandon. None of those Volunteers were armed when killed, each was alone, and not one of them had ever been called for flying column service.

The taking of those hostages was but a further step in our campaign, which was, frankly, a counter-terror aimed to stop the British terror murders of IRA prisoners. Lord Bandon, the descendant of Colonel Bernard, a British adventurer who for his military service in destroying the Irish had been given the lands of the dispossessed O'Mahonys, was the British King's lieutenant for Cork city and county. As such he was the chief representative of the British crown, on whose authority the British armed forces purported to rule, coerce, kill and terrorise the Irish people. The IRA policy of burning a few castles had proved very effective as a deterrent to the wholesale burnings of Irish homes. Our decision to execute men like Lord Bandon might or might not influence the British to stop killing IRA prisoners, but from mid-June 1921, while one British loyalist was available as a hostage in our area, we were well set to test them. The British issued periodical communiqués from Dublin Castle: 'There is still no news of the Earl of Bandon, kidnapped from Castle Bernard on June 21st.' Another pointer to his importance in British eyes was the arrival of Miss Leslie Price, Director of Organisation of the Cumann na mBan, on the night of July 7th. On several occasions previously she had been in our area organising the Cumann na mBan, and she located us in the early hours of the morning of the 8th. She brought a message from President de Valera, who asked to be informed immediately as to whether Lord Bandon was alive and in good health, as one of the British negotiators had specifically asked about him, and he (de Valera) had undertaken to let him have the information without delay. Immediately Miss Price received the required information she returned to Dublin.

In those last weeks of the struggle also, British military stores were seized at Aghadown railway station; telegraph and telephone apparatus were removed from post offices at Glandore, Union Hall, Leap, Castletownshend and other places, telegraph poles were hacked down, wires were cut and roads extensively trenched. Rounding-up forces were sniped at Gortaclone and Ballylickey, enemy garrisons were fired on at Bantry, Skibbereen, Drimoleague, Clonakilty, Bandon, Innishannon and Kilbrittain. During the final four weeks, Bandon was entered eight times by armed parties of the IRA, the Innishannon post was fired at on four occasions and Kilbrittain Barracks sniped at five times. British soldiers were wounded at Ballylickey, a Black and Tan sergeant and an enemy agent in Bandon. Yet another Essex soldier was shot dead within sight of his Bandon Barracks and one more Black and Tan was killed in Skibbereen. There was no slowing down of IRA activities in West Cork until the announcements in the daily press made it clear that the end was at hand.

The last engagement of the flying column was on June 26th. On that evening the column was six miles north of Rosscarbery. It had just paraded under my command for the last time, for I was no longer a West Cork officer, but one of the 1st Southern Division. The sections had been ordered to disperse to their battalions, and the majority of the men had already set out for their units, when a messenger arrived to inform us that between one hundred and twenty and one hundred and fifty Auxiliaries had entered Rosscarbery that evening. The messenger did not know if this was a re-occupation of that town, or a lightning raid to carry out arrests. Whatever the enemy aim, those terrorists had to be attacked before they had time to settle in or to carry out their mission. Unfortunately only thirty-three of the flying column were available, and there was no time to recall the remainder, because if the attack was to be successful, it had to be attempted at once. Within twenty minutes of the messenger's arrival, the thirty-three IRA men, regrouped into three sections of eleven, were on the march. In daylight we came down the Ardagh road and halted four hundred yards north of Rosscarbery. One section was sent off to the west to enter the town from the high ground on that side, while the other two sections moved cautiously down Caim Hill to enter the square from the east. It was planned that the stronger IRA party from the east would open the attack, when our western section would join in. But matters did not work out that way, as we were still over two hundred yards from the Square where the Auxiliaries were concentrated, when firing commenced to the west.

Our western section had met an enemy patrol on the outskirts, who after a skirmish retired rapidly to the town. This shooting gave warning to the main enemy body, and by the time our twenty-two riflemen could get into firing positions, our targets had dived into numerous houses for cover. However, we closed in while the Auxiliaries opened wild and erratic fire from some houses. We engaged them for some time by firing whenever we could locate an enemy-occupied house, and succeeded in wounding several of them, which fact was admitted in the communiqués from British headquarters published in the daily press of June 28th. Not knowing exactly all the houses the enemy had occupied, I decided not to risk in daylight our score of riflemen up an approach street, without cover, against a force seven times their number fighting from the protection of houses. Within fifteen minutes our small party was withdrawn back up Caim Hill where we were joined by the other section. Later we withdrew two miles and waited for one of our scouts to report back. He informed us that the enemy had retired from the town at the same time as our withdrawal. Volunteer Dan Mahony, rather seriously wounded in the leg, was our only casualty.

On the evening of the 27th, I made my way back to headquarters, where I met Liam Deasy and some others. They had the daily papers announcing the invitation of Lloyd George to President de Valera and to any colleagues he might select to come to London to explore the possibility of a settlement. We paid little heed to this announcement, but when the press of the following day stated that President de Valera had visited Mr Arthur Griffith in Mountjoy Jail, we guessed that serious negotiations were on foot. However, Liam and I had to set out that evening for North Cork, where close by the Paps Mountains, near the Cork–Kerry border, a divisional camp was to open on July 1st and continue for a fortnight. This journey had been arranged some weeks before, when after some discussions with Liam Lynch I had agreed to transfer from the brigade to the 1st Southern Division. My first task on the division was to have taken command of this camp, which was to be attended by the commanders and three senior officers from each of the nine brigades of the division. My opinion of the effectiveness of the division in the immediate future phase of our guerilla fight had not changed, but it was now an established unit of army organisation. The divisional camp would, at least, standardise the policy, tactics, training and organisation of the IRA throughout the counties of Cork, Kerry, Waterford and West Limerick. The officers attending it should gain by becoming acquainted with the responsible officers of the other brigades in whose areas they might have to operate temporarily should the British attempt their area blockade plan. This camp would also give divisional officers an opportunity of studying certain officers who might be required to replace existing commanders. The risk of assembling all those senior divisional and brigade officers in one camp for several weeks was a big one, but it had been accepted. At the end of our first day's journey on the 29th, Deasy and I were stopped by a dispatch from Liam Lynch, informing us that the area around the proposed camp was invested by the British, and that it would be advisable to wait until he would send word that the enemy had withdrawn. On the following day we returned to the West Cork area.

No message arrived from Lynch, and while we waited back in West Cork, the daily press kept us informed of the dramatic developments in Dublin. Arthur Griffith, Robert Barton and Eamonn Duggan, Deputies of Dáil Éireann, were unconditionally released from jail. President de Valera invited and met the leaders of the British loyalists in Ireland – the Earl of Midleton, Sir Robert H. Woods, Sir Maurice Dockrell and Mr Andrew Jameson – on July 4th. Our President, with Griffith, Barton and Duggan, again met those representatives and Sir Nevil Macready, Commander-in-Chief of the British forces in Ireland, on July 8th, and on that evening it was announced that a truce between the Irish and British forces had been agreed on. Dáil Éireann, the elected parliament of the people, being a banned and illegal body, liable to arrest, was unable to be consulted before matters were clinched by de Valera, Griffith, Brugha, Collins, Stack and Cosgrave. No divisional or brigade officer of the IRA knew anything about the negotiations of the Truce except through the reports appearing in the daily press.

This book in not concerned with the aftermath of the Truce, but students of our guerilla days should examine closely the pattern of the negotiations and the terms of the Truce. The letters exchanged between the British Prime Minister, Mr Lloyd George, and President de Valera, and the terms of the Truce were:

From MR LLOYD GEORGE to MR DE VALERA.

June 24th, 1921.

Sir,

The British Government are deeply anxious that, as far as they can assure it, the King's appeal for reconciliation in Ireland shall not have been made in vain. Rather than allow another opportunity of settlement in Ireland to be cast aside, they felt it incumbent upon them to make a final appeal, in the spirit of the King's words, for a Conference between themselves and the representatives of Southern and Northern Ireland.

I write, therefore, to convey the following invitation to you, as the chosen leader of the great majority in Southern Ireland, and to Sir James Craig, the Premier of Northern Ireland:-

(1) That you should attend a conference here in London, in company with Sir James Craig, to explore to the utmost the possibility of a settlement.

(2) That you should bring with you for the purpose any colleagues whom you select. The Government will, of course, give a safe conduct to all who may be chosen to participate in the conference.

(3) We make this invitation with a fervent desire to end the ruinous conflict which has for centuries divided Ireland, and embittered the relations of the peoples of these two islands, who ought to live in neighbourly harmony with each other, and whose co-operation would mean so much, not only to the Empire, but to humanity.

We wish that no endeavour should be lacking on our part to realise the King's prayer, and we ask you to meet us, as we will meet you, in the spirit of conciliation, for which His Majesty appealed.

I am, Sir,
Your obedient servant,
D. LLOYD GEORGE.

Reply from PRESIDENT DE VALERA.

June 28th, 1921.

Sir,

I have received your letter. I am in consultation with such of the principal representatives of our nation as are available. We most earnestly desire to help in bringing about a lasting peace between the peoples of these two islands, but see no avenue by which it can be reached if you deny Ireland's essential unity, and set aside the principle of national self-determination.

Before replying fully to your letter, I am seeking a conference with certain representatives of the political minority in this country.

EAMON DE VALERA.

Mansion House, Dublin.

Further letter from PRESIDENT DE VALERA to MR LLOYD GEORGE, July 8th.

Sir,

The desire you express on the part of the British Government to end the centuries of conflict between the peoples of these two islands, and to establish relations of neighbourly harmony, is the genuine desire of the people of Ireland.

I have consulted with my colleagues and secured the views of the representatives of the minority of our nation in regard to the invitation you have sent me.

In reply, I desire to say that I am ready to meet and discuss with you on what basis such a Conference as that proposed can reasonably hope to achieve the object desired.

I am, Sir,
Faithfully yours,
EAMON DE VALERA.

The terms of the Truce:

On behalf of the British Army is agreed the following:

(1) No incoming troops, R.I.C., and Auxiliary Police and munitions, and no movements for military purposes of troops and munitions, except maintenance drafts.

(2) No provocative display of forces, armed or unarmed.

(3) It is understood that all provisions of the Truce apply to the Martial Law area equally with the rest of Ireland.

(4) No pursuit of Irish officers or men, or war material, or military stores.

(5) No secret agents, noting descriptions or movements and no interference with the movements of Irish persons, military or civil, and no attempt to discover the haunts or habits of Irish officers and men.

NOTE: This supposes the abandonment of curfew restrictions.

(6) No pursuit or observance of lines of communication or connection.

NOTE: There are other details connected with courts-martial, motor permits, and R.O.I.R., to be agreed to later.

On behalf of the Irish Army, it is agreed that:

(a) Attacks on Crown forces and civilians to cease.

(b) No provocative displays of forces, armed or unarmed.

(c) No interference with British Government or private property.

(d) To discountenance and prevent any action likely to cause disturbance of the peace which might necessitate military interference.'

The Truce came into force at noon on Monday July 11th, 1921.

The British Prime Minister's invitation to the Irish leaders to attend a conference to end the war and the terms of the Truce are perhaps the best indication of all as to the success with which the Irish people waged and maintained guerilla war. Those British ministers who had refused so violently and viciously during the preceding years to deal with murderers, criminals and rebels had now somersaulted to approach as equals those very same leaders and to recognise the guerilla forces as the Irish Army. This startling upheaval in British policy was due, and due only, to the British recognition that they had not defeated and could not reasonably hope to defeat in the measurable future, the armed forces of the Irish nation.

Had the enemy felt capable of doing so, different terms would have been offered, terms similar to those at the close of all the many armed efforts of previous generations of Irishmen. Since the Treaty of Limerick in 1691 down to and including 1916 the British terms to the defeated Irish soldiers had always been unconditional surrender followed by a massacre of the Irish leaders. But now they had to deal with an army that was capable, not alone of fighting back but of actually threatening to smash their military power in Ireland in the not far distant future. While the army survived and fought on, nothing under God could have broken the nation's will to victory. Patriotic and brave men might die on the scaffold, on hunger strike or endure in British jails, mass meetings might demand our freedom, electors vote for a Republic, writers and poets cry aloud of British tyranny and of Ireland's sufferings, but none of those would have induced the lords of the conquest to undo their grip or even discuss our liberation. The only language they listened to or could understand was that of the rifle, the revolver, the bomb and the crackling of the flames which cost them so dearly in blood and treasure.

Further proof of the startling success of the Irish Republican Army and the difficulties of the British military position in Ireland immediately before the Truce may be gathered from the diaries of Field Marshal Sir Henry Wilson, GCB, DSO. Wilson, being Chief of the Imperial General Staff from 1918 to 1922, was British supreme commander, and although his diaries seep with hatred of everything Irish, they must, nevertheless, be accepted as an authentic record of his view of the general military situation. In those diaries on the dates recorded he wrote:

May 18th, 1921.

> At 1.30 Curzon rang me. He gave me a long sermon about the state of affairs in Silesia, ending by saying that Prime Minister and he had decided that five battalions should go to Silesia. I

at once attacked. I said that, directly England was safe, every available man should go to Ireland, that even four battalions now on the Rhine ought also to go to Ireland. I said that the troops and the measures taken up to now had been quite inadequate, that I was terrified at the state of that country, and that, in my opinion, unless we crushed out the murder gang this summer, we should lose Ireland and the Empire. I spoke in the strongest manner and I frightened Curzon, who said he must refer it all to the Prime Minister.

May 23rd, 1921.

Then Macready (Commander-in-Chief in Ireland) in, and a long talk, and I brought him into the S. of S. (Secretary of State for War). Macready absolutely backs up my contention that we must knock out, or at least knock under, the Sinn Féiners this summer or we shall lose Ireland, and he told S. of S. so in good round terms, and that it was not wise nor safe to ask the troops now in Ireland to go on as they are now for another winter. As there were no troops with which to relieve them, we must make our effort now, or else, tacitly and in fact, agree that we were beaten. S. of S. is really impressed and frightened.

May 26th, 1921.

Austen (Chamberlain) irritable with me because I said I would pour every man, including Silesia, into Ireland.

June, 1921.

I told him that, unless we had England entirely on our side, I would strongly advise that we should not attempt martial law in all its severity, because I was sure it would not succeed, and failure meant disaster. If the soldiers knew that England was solid behind them they would go on till they won out; if on the

> other hand they found that this was not the case then we should have disaster. I have developed this thesis over and over again to Lloyd George, Bonar (Law), Austen (Chamberlain), Winston (Churchill) and others, and I never made so much impression on anybody as I did to-night on Worthy (Worthington Evans).
>
> July 5th, 1921.
>
> This afternoon, S. of S. (Secretary of State), A. G. (Adjutant-General), Macready and I had a long talk about what we were to do with officers and men who applied not to be sent to Ireland when ordered there. These cases are becoming more and more numerous. I said I thought officers and men should be ordered over to Ireland and treated as on active service, provided that the fathers and mothers of those men (living in Ireland) were brought over to England, if they so wished, and were looked after by England, and their houses and property were insured by the Government.

The Supreme British Military Chief's doubts, so frankly recorded, as to the ability of his troops to destroy the Irish Republican Army, were well founded. Even should the British strip their garrisons from other occupied countries to reinforce Ireland, their task would be a lengthy and costly one. I have already made clear my opinion that at no time in a major and sustained battle up to the Truce was the Irish Republican Army strong enough in armament to defeat the British army of occupation. It is also obvious that our very strength lay in not becoming involved in any such unequal engagement, and that for a long time to come our guerilla tactics would have to be continued.

This policy had prevented British authority from functioning in Ireland, laid its administration in ruins, driven out or under cover the British minions, necessitated a large and costly army of occupation, humiliated British military power, caused the name of Britain to stink in the nostrils of all decent peoples, and inflicted sufficient casualties on their soldiers, Auxiliaries and Black and Tans to seriously disturb a government finding it difficult to supply reinforcements. And in spite of all the British efforts, the Irish Republican Army was a stronger and more effective striking force when the Truce came than at any other period in its history. In West Cork it had twice as many enrolled volunteers, three times as much armament, although the ammunition worry remained, and ten times as many toughened and experienced fighters than it had twelve months previously. Its morale and confidence had grown as that of the enemy slumped, and the brigade had not only survived long summer days of enemy operations, but had increased its pressure and number of attacks in those later months. Never in all my contacts with senior and junior officers had I heard one doubt our ability to force eventually a British evacuation. We had no illusions about our weaknesses or the enemy's strength, and knew well the heavy price that Ireland would have to pay before the dawn of freedom ended the long dark night of terror, devastation and death. Many, many other volunteers would join their dead comrades, but we would go on and on killing those age-old enemies of our race, until they had had enough and departed from the shores of our island.

The sudden ending of hostilities left men dazed at first and uncertain of the future, as no one considered during those early July days that the Truce would continue for more than a month. My own problems were not eased by the arrival of a dispatch on July 9th, from the Adjutant-General, stating that the President had appointed me to an unwelcome and unwanted additional post, subsequently defined as Chief Liaison Officer of the Martial Law Area. But as July 11th approached one slowly began to appreciate what the Truce and all it entailed signified. Gradually it dawned on me that the forcing of the enemy to offer such terms was a signal victory in itself; that days of fear were ended, at least for a time, and that one could return to normal life and thought, away from the hates, the callousness and the ruthless killings of war. The respite might only be brief, but one would not dwell on that. The sun blazed from God's Heavens during those cloudless days of the longest and most brilliant summer in living memory, as if to remind man that the world held brighter things than the darkness of war. At peace and relaxed we rejoiced with our own people, who had been so good to us in the troubled past, until it was time for me to leave for my new liaison post. As noon approached on July 11th, I bade a temporary goodbye to my friends and set out for Cork city; it was the end of a phase, but, alas, not the end of our guerilla days.

# APPENDIX A

# ATTEMPT TO ESCAPE FROM MOUNTJOY

*On Thursday, June 29th, 1922, the second day of the Civil War, Commandant-General Tom Barry of the Republican Army Executive was captured by Free State troops when, in disguise, he attempted to join the besieged Republican garrison in the Four Courts, Dublin. He thus became the first prisoner of the action and was taken to Mountjoy Jail, from which he attempted to escape in July. This is his account of the attempt, as told in a letter to his publisher, March 23rd, 1977.*

Liam Mellows, Rory O'Connor, Joe McKelvey, Dick Barrett, Peadar O'Donnell and I were members of the prisoners' jail council. One of our men under treatment in the prison hospital reported to us that some Free State soldiers were patients also and that he could easily take one of their uniforms if required. He was instructed not to take it until told.

In Free State uniform one of us stood a great chance of getting out of Mountjoy. We discussed who would make the attempt and the others were unanimous that it should be me. I wanted Mellows out as it was my view that the military war was lost already and he could be more useful politically.

Our IO had reported that when soldiers wanted to get out for a jar they went to a wicket-gate between the former women's prison and the one where we were being held. All women civil prisoners were released when the Four Courts was attacked and the men were transferred to the vacated cells to make room for IRA prisoners.

One forenoon late in July a uniform was brought to me and I immediately got into it in my cell, screened from view and otherwise helped by members of the council. Rory gave me a fiver he had kept hidden somehow, and I had the pass of the former owner of the uniform, which was in a pocket.

Rory stepped out of the cell in front of me. I had put on a dust coat and inside it I held the uniform cap under my arm. I followed Rory to an agreed spot where I found that the lower strands of barbed wire had been cut. At the same time Dick Barrett started a mock fight involving four or five of our men. They were slugging it out convincingly inside the exercise ground and a solitary sentry stood gawking at them.

Slipping out of the dust coat I crawled under the barbed wire unseen by the sentry, put on the uniform cap and stood up. I walked towards him and he turned round as if looking for help or advice, which I gladly gave him. He was holding his rifle by the muzzle with the butt trailing on the ground, a major offence for a sentry. 'Shoulder your rifle,' I told him urgently, 'the governor and his staff are coming out – and shout to those fellows to stop fighting.' I walked slowly past him towards the wicket-gate, knocked on it and a slot was drawn back by the lookout warder. 'Open up,' I said, 'I'm going out for a drink.' He shut the slot. I heard the gate bolt being withdrawn and then slammed back. The slot was opened again and the warder stared at me 'You're not a soldier,' he said excitedly, 'You're the prisoner Barry.' With that he closed the slot with finality. I'd swear he was the only warder in the whole prison who knew me.

I made for the main entrance. There were eight soldiers queued up at the first of two iron-barred gates, having their passes glanced at and being allowed through to the main gate in turn. I fell in at the end of the queue and started chatting to the soldiers. One of them gave me an invitation to a hooly, which I readily accepted. I was third from the gate when an officer dashed out of the gatehouse shouting, 'Close the gate. Nobody leaves. A prisoner is loose in uniform.' The other officers came running out also and about a dozen of us were lined up for inspection. We came smartly to attention and all passed muster. Just as I thought we were being allowed away, out came another officer, Seán O'Connell, whom I had met with Michael Collins in May of the previous year. He walked straight up to me, removed my cap and said, 'Hard luck, Tom.' That was that.

O'Connell had put the cap back on my head when out of the administration wing rushed the prison governor, a revolver strapped to each thigh *á la* the Auxiliaries; he was hysterical and kept shouting, 'Where is he, where is he?' I could not resist saying, 'He's gone, gone twenty minutes ago.' Then he recognised me and drew one of his revolvers. 'Where did you get that uniform?' he shouted. The answer he got was no cure for hysterics.

I was escorted into the prison and kept under armed guard outside the governor's office for about an hour. Next, without trial, I was marched away to three weeks' solitary confinement. Down an iron staircase we went to what had been an underground punishment cell that the British had closed in 1876 as not being fit for prisoners. There I served twenty days. Even now, fifty-five years afterwards, I do not like to look back on my treatment below ground. My Free State armed guards, I was told later, were out of Irish regiments in the British Army, disbanded after the Treaty was ratified. They had gone straight to Beggars Bush Barracks and into green uniforms.

In the early hours of my twenty-first morning in punishment, five or six soldiers came to my cell, threw my boots at me and told me to dress at once as I was being taken to another prison. I dressed and then told them that I would not go, that I had done my time in their hell-hole. They threw me on the ground and dragged me legs first up to ground level, my head bumping on the iron steps. Barely conscious, I was pushed into an armoured car and taken to Kilmainham Jail, where the governor, Seán Ó Muirthile, was waiting up although it was well after two o'clock. He demanded to know from the soldiers what they had done to me and he also got me medical attention immediately. Ó Muirthile, also an IRB man and Gaelic Leaguer, was a decent man and a humane prison governor.

*With other Republican prisoners, Commandant-General Barry was removed from Kilmainham and taken to Gormanstown camp, County Louth, in September. In the words of his comrade-in-arms, Peadar O'Donnell: 'He went in the gate, walked sharply across the grounds and out through the wire at the far side before the sentries had come on their beat. It was a chance to be taken in a flash and Barry in such cases is lightning. He got safely away.'* (The Gates Flew Open, *London 1932)*

# APPENDIX B

# CHARLIE HURLEY REMEMBERED

*This tribute to Charlie Hurley, OC Third (West) Cork Brigade, was written in 1935 by Tom Barry, commander of the brigade flying column, 1920–21.*

On March 19th, 1921, an Irish patriot was shot to death by British soldiers at Ballinphellic, Upton, County Cork. His name was Charlie Hurley of Baurleigh, Kilbrittain, and he died alone, pressing the trigger of his half-empty gun, attempting to fight his way through the British. His name is not mentioned in any of the many books written about the Anglo-Irish War; no words of his are handed down to us; no ballads (except a West Cork one) recall his name and his deeds. Yet this Volunteer Commandant of the Irish Republican Army was not less great than any of our greats, for in patriotism, in courage, in effort for his people's freedom, and in his ultimate sacrifice he stands for all time with Clarke, Connolly, Pearse, MacCurtain, MacSwiney and all the others who strove and died for Ireland. Fifty-eight West Cork men died of enemy bullets in the fight for the Republic and it is no easy task to select one of them as the subject for a tribute which may well apply to all of them. All were splendid Irishmen, but I have no doubt that if they could select one of their number as a model of all that was best in the Volunteer movement, Charlie Hurley would be their unanimous choice.

Charlie was born in Baurleigh on March 19th, 1892. At an early age he went to work in a Bandon store and while there he studied and sat a civil service examination. He was successful and was appointed as a boy clerk to Haulbowline, Cork. There he served from 1911 to 1915 when he was promoted to Liverpool. This promotion he refused because its acceptance would entail conscription into the British Army and Charlie was even then a volunteer in the Irish Army. Since his boyhood in Bandon he had also been an active member of Sinn Féin, the Gaelic Athletic Association and the Gaelic League, thus being well grounded in the faith of Irish separatism for which he was to work so hard and eventually to die. He returned to West Cork and started to organise the Irish Volunteers. Early in 1918 he was arrested and charged with being in possession of arms and plans of the British fortifications on Beare Island. Found guilty, he was sentenced to five years' penal servitude, part of which he served in Cork and Maryborough Jails. Towards the end of the year he was released with other hunger-strikers under what was known as the 'Cat and Mouse Act'. Back in West Cork again he was appointed brigade commandant early in 1920, following the arrest and torture of Tom Hales. This post he held until his death nearly twelve months later.

Charlie was the idol of the brigade. He was loved for his patriotism, courage, sincerity, generosity, good humour and unassuming ways. He was a natural leader with an uncommon power of inspiring men in dark and difficult days. There was a stubbornness in him in the issue of Ireland's freedom, which was not based on any material factor but on a mysticism of which one only got a glimpse on rare occasions. That mysticism of the Celt made Charlie's love of country a religion, a faith which allowed him to visualise only two ends: his country's freedom or his own death in attempting to achieve that freedom. Usually gay and of good spirits, he would brood sometimes if matters were not going well. Then one would get a glimpse of the real man. His jaw would set, his eyes shine and his whole face light up as he drove home the doctrine of 'hit back and hit harder'. He had the highest and most noble combination of courage; moral courage and courage in defeat and courage in attack. He was generous to a fault, wholly unambitious and in his unassuming way he continually urged that he should be allowed to relinquish command of the brigade and so be free for whole-time service with the brigade column. He had a premonition of death. Several times he told me he would die alone fighting against the English when none of us was near. He died in just that way.

Charlie was severely wounded during an attack on British military by a group of eight IRA men at Upton railway station on February 15th, 1921. He recovered but sprained an ankle, which was still weak when, about midnight on March 18th, with Seán Buckley, a brigade staff officer, he returned from O'Mahony's of Belrose to his headquarters at Forde's of Ballinphellic, four miles away. He slept in Forde's that night and Seán went about a mile across country to O'Connell's.

Meanwhile the brigade flying column had arrived at Ballyhandle near Crossbarry where they would fight on the following morning. The column was roused at 2 a.m. on the 19th as the brigade column commander had received reports of British forces advancing on them from all directions – Cork city, Ballincollig, Macroom, Bandon and Kinsale. The column assembled at the prearranged point at Crossbarry, and two scouts were sent immediately to bring Charlie and Seán straight to the column as they were in the line of the British advance. The scouts were captured and thus the instruction was not carried out.

About half an hour before dawn on the 19th Charlie was awakened, not by his comrades but by British soldiers battering in the front door of Forde's house with their rifle butts. Thoughtful as ever of others, he told the people of the house to stay upstairs in relative safety and down the stairs he walked, in his shirt and trousers only, his guns in his hands to meet his death like the great Irishman he was. The British were in the kitchen when he walked into view, firing as he rushed them. They fired and broke, leaving one dead and two wounded. Charlie made for the back door. Out the back he rushed and was met by rifle-fire. He fell dead in the farmyard, many bullets through him, mostly through his head. About four miles away at Crossbarry, where we were about to be engaged, we heard the shooting and I remember remarking that Charlie was gone. Somehow one knew that it was his fate to die in such a way and that it had come at last.

Late that evening the British nosed their way back to Crossbarry with reinforcements, to collect their dead. There, too, were our three dead: Jeremiah O'Leary, Leap; Con Daly, Ballinascarthy; and Peter Monahan, Bandon. Charlie's remains were collected also, and the bodies of the four Volunteers were brought into Bandon Military Barracks. Later Charlie's body was thrown into the workhouse morgue, where he lay until the following day (Sunday) when, by subterfuge, he was taken out to the church at Clogagh, his burial place.

Because of the war it was not possible to have the fighting men of West Cork at a public funeral. We had to choose between giving him a public funeral and one where only armed Volunteers would be present. We chose the latter, as we knew he would wish it to be so.

Although weary and tired after the long fight at Crossbarry on Saturday morning, we marched and marched through the nights of Saturday and Sunday. It was two o'clock on Monday morning when we arrived at Clogagh village. Armed sentries were thrown out, the priest was called and a hundred riflemen filed into the church to pray that their comrade would have eternal peace. After a short time, the column formed up outside the church and slow-marched to the graveyard with Charlie's body in their midst. I have experienced many pathetic scenes in a not uneventful life, but the memory of the burial that night remains foremost. Perhaps it may be because Charlie was my staunch comrade and I loved him greatly that the scene was seared into my memory. It is still fresh and clear. The dirge of the war-pipes played by Flor Begley, the slow march of the brigade flying column, the small group of only six other mourners, the rain-soaked earth and the wintry moon that shone through cloud, vanished and shone again, as we bore him to his grave, the present arms, the three volleys and the last post ringing clear in the night. It is all vivid still. The final tribute was given in an oration by the column leader and we turned from the grave and marched away towards the west to cross the main Bandon–Clonakilty road before dawn.

This tribute to Brigadier Charlie Hurley cannot be closed in any more fitting manner than by a verse from a ballad by his friend and comrade Seán Buckley:

*In the lonely Clogagh graveyard he sleeps his last long sleep,*
*But in our homes throughout West Cork his memory we will keep,*
*And teach our youth his love of truth, his scorn of wrong and fear,*
*And teach them, too, to love our land as did our Brigadier.*

## APPENDIX C

# THE GALLANT DEAD OF WEST CORK

*The Third (West) Cork Brigade casualty list prepared by Commandant General Tom Barry in 1935. The list gives date of death, rank, name and address, and place of death.*

Easter Week 1916 – Volunteer John Hurley, Clonakilty; GPO, Dublin (brigade formed January 5th 1919).

August 29th 1920 – Lieutenant Tim Fitzgerald, Gaggin, Bandon; Brinny.

October 1st 1920 – Lieutenant John Connolly, Shannon Street, Bandon; Bandon.

November 28th 1920 – Vice-Commandant Michael McCarthy, East Green, Dunmanway; Kilmichael.

November 28th 1920 – Lieutenant Patrick Deasy, Kilmacsimon Quay, Bandon; Kilmichael.

November 28th 1920 – Lieutenant James O'Sullivan, Knockawaddra, Rossmore; Kilmichael.

December 3rd 1920 – Captain John Galvin, Main Street, Bandon; Bandon.

December 3rd 1920 – Lieutenant Jim O'Donoghue,Shannon Street, Bandon; Bandon.

December 3rd 1920 – Section Commander Joe Begley, Castle Road, Bandon; Bandon.

December 8th 1920 – Lieutenant Michael McLean, Lowertown, Schull; Gaggin, Bandon.

December 14th 1920 – Volunteer Timothy Crowley, Behigullane, Dunmanway; Dunmanway.

December 1920 – Captain Jeremiah O'Mahony, Paddock, Enniskeane; Paddock, Enniskeane.

January 17th 1921 – Volunteer Patrick Donovan, Culnigh, Timoleague; Timoleague.

January 21st 1921 – Volunteer Denis Hegarty, Clashfluck, Timoleague; Courtmacsherry.

January 24th 1921 – Volunteer Daniel O'Reilly, Granassig, Kilbrittain; Bandon.

February 4th 1921 – Lieutenant Patrick Crowley, Kilbrittain; Maryboro', Timoleague.

February 7th 1921 – Section Commander Patrick O'Driscoll, Mohana, Skibereen; Mohana, Skibbereen.

February 14th 1921 – Volunteers Patrick Coffey and James Coffey, Breaghna, Enniskeane; Kilrush, Enniskeane.

February 15th 1921 – Lieutenant John Phelan, late of Liverpool; Upton.

February 15th 1921 – Lieutenant Patrick O'Sullivan, Raheen, Upton; Upton.

February 15th 1921 – Section Commander Batt Falvey, Ballymurphy, Upton; Upton.

February 16th 1921 – Volunteer Cornelius McCarthy, Kilanetig, Ballinadee; Crois na Leanbh, Kilbrittain.

February 16th 1921 – Volunteer John McGrath, Rathclarin, Kilbrittain; Crois na Leanbh.

February 16th 1921 – Volunteer Timothy Connolly, Fearnagark, Kilbrittain; Crois na Leanbh.

February 16th 1921 – Volunteer Jeremiah O'Neill, Knockpogue, Kilbrittain; Crois na Leanbh.

March 19th 1921 – Commandant Charles Hurley, Baurleigh, Kilbrittain; Ballymurphy.

March 19th 1921 – Volunteer Peter Monahan, Bandon; Crossbarry.

March 19th 1921 – Volunteer Jeremiah O'Leary, Corrin, Leap; Crossbarry.

March 19th 1921 – Volunteer Con Daly, Carrig, Ballinascarthy; Crossbarry.

March 22nd 1921 – Volunteer Timothy Whooley, Carrycrowley, Ballineen; Shannonvale.

May 9th 1921 – Captain Frank Hurley, Laragh, Bandon; Bandon.

May 9th 1921 – Volunteer Geoffrey Canty, Scrahan, Newcestown; Morragh.

May 11th 1921 – Lieutenant Con Murphy, Clashfluck, Timoleague; Cloundreen, Kilbrittain.

June 7th 1921 – Volunteer Daniel Crowley, Behigullane, Dunmanway; Behigullane.

June 10th 1921 – Volunteer Matthew Donovan, Quarries Cross, Bandon; Quarries Cross.

June 22nd 1921 – Volunteer John Murphy, Cloghane, Bandon; Cloghane.

April 29th 1922 – Commandant Michael O'Neill, Maryboro', Kilbrittain; Ballygroman.

August 1922 – Section Commander Patrick McCarthy, Monahin, Kilcoe, Ballydehob; Skibbereen.

August 30th 1922 – Commandant Gibbs Ross, Glandart, Bantry; Bantry.

August 30th 1922 – Captain Patrick Cooney, Bridge Street, Skibbereen; Bantry.

August 30th 1922 – Lieutenant Donal McCarthy, Carrigbawn, Drinagh; Bantry.

August 30th 1922 – Lieutenant Michael Crowley, Reenogreena, Glandore; Bantry.

October 4th 1922 – Volunteer Patrick Pearse, Kinsale; Upton.

October 4th 1922 – Volunteer Daniel Sullivan, Kinsale; Upton.

October 4th 1922 – Volunteer Michael Hayes, Shannon Street, Bandon; Upton.

October 4th 1922 – Volunteer Daniel Donovan, Clogagh; Timoleague.

November 4th 1922 – Section Commander Tadhg O'Leary, South Square, Macroom; Ballineen.

November 4th 1922 – Volunteer John Howel, Clonakilty (formerly of Doneraile); Enniskeane.

November 17th 1922 – Volunteer Patrick Duggan, Kilbrogan, Bandon; Glengarriff.

December 8th 1922 – Assistant QMG Richard Barrett, Hollyhill, Ballineen; murdered in Mountjoy Jail.

December 8th 1922 – Volunteer George Dease, Castlehaven; Kealkil.

December 8th 1922 – Volunteer J. Dwyer, Castletownbere; Kealkil.

December 11th 1922 – Captain Timothy Kennefick, Fairhill, Cork; Coachford.

February 15th 1923 – Captain Laurence Cunningham, Clonakilty; Lyre.

March 7th 1923 – Volunteer John O'Connor, Innishannon; murdered at Ballyseedy, Tralee.

April 17th 1923 – Lieutenant Denis Kelly, Scart Road, Bantry; Kealkil.

November 1923 – Volunteer Michael Tobin, Ballineen; Grattan Street, Cork.

# Index

## D



## E



## F

## P



## R



## S



## T



## W

CPSIA information can be obtained
at www.ICGtesting.com
Printed in the USA
LVHW040347120723
752251LV00004B/30

9 781781 171714